THE JUNIOR CLASSICS

VOLUME 5

By

WILLIAM PATTEN

The Junior Classics
Volume 5

by **William Patten**

Copyright © 2024

ISBN: 978-93-58011-10-4

Published by

DOUBLE 9 BOOKS

2/13-B, Ansari Road, Daryaganj
New Delhi – 110002
info@double9books.com
www.double9books.com
Tel. 011-40042856

ABOUT THE AUTHOR

William Patten served in government during the reigns of King Edward VI and Queen Elizabeth I as an author, scholar, and government officer. William Patten, the son of clothworker Richard Patten and John Baskerville's daughter Grace, was born in London. William Waynflete, Bishop of Winchester, was a brother of his grandpa, Richard Patten of Boslow, Derbyshire. His sister, Alice, was married to Armagil Waad, whom Patten referred to as a "friend" during his expedition into Scotland, and his mother, Grace, is supposed to have predeceased her husband. Patten was a student at Gonville Hall in Cambridge as well as the parish clerk and minor chaplain at St. Mary-at-Hill in Billingsgate, London. In Billingsgate, Patten's first wife, whose identity is unknown, passed away in 1549. Afterwards, he married Anne, who was a Johnson heiress's daughter from Boston, Lincolnshire. In The Calendar of Scripture, he defines

CONTENTS

PREFACE

Consciously or unconsciously we are influenced by the characters we admire. A book that exerts a deep as well as a wide influence must produce changes in the reader's way of thinking, and excite him to activity; the world for him can never be quite the same that it was before. Such books have an important part in moulding the character of a people.

It is because the books represented in this volume have been doing just that for many years that they have become so prized. In the characters of Crusoe, Gulliver and Christian, to mention only three, English-speaking people recognize pictures of the independent, self-reliant men, often self-educated (at least in many important particulars), adventurous and daring by nature, dependent upon themselves and the use of their faculties for happiness, who made England great among nations, and wrote the Constitution of the United States.

With the passage of time the books have lost nothing of the charm and fascination which they have ever possessed for young and old. "Was there ever yet anything written by mere man," said Dr. Samuel Johnson, "that was wished longer by its readers, excepting Robinson Crusoe, Pilgrim's Progress
, and Don Quixote?"

At this time, when the subject of vocational training is receiving so much attention, and public school instruction is being criticized because, its critics say, it does not prepare boys and girls to meet the demands which life makes upon them, it is interesting to read what was said almost a hundred years ago by a man whose influence on education has been both deep and lasting in character.

They have just been celebrating in France the centenary of Jean Jacques Rousseau. In the early chapters of "Emile" we read: "Since we must have books, there is one which, to my mind, furnishes the finest treatise on Education according to nature. My Emile shall read this book before any other. It shall for a long time be his entire library. It shall be a test for all we meet during our progress toward a ripened judgment, and so long as our taste is unspoiled we shall enjoy reading it. What wonderful book is this? Aristotle? Pliny? Buffon? No; it is Robinson Crusoe."

There is no more useful talent than the ability to think and speak (or write) clearly and simply, no matter what our vocation in life. None know better how difficult it is to find writers with a good narrative style than those editors whose training and experience have made them realize its value and importance. If we examine the experience of those who, in comparatively recent days, have stirred men with the force and directness of their simple speech, as Lincoln, for example, we find that as boys they were great readers of the Bible, and Robinson Crusoe, Gulliver's Travels, Shakespeare, Bunyan, and Scott. As examples of English these books stand preeminent.

Lord Brougham relates that one of his friends, a professor in a university, consulted one of the ablest historians of his time as to what would be the best discipline for acquiring a good narrative style, as a prelude to writing a book of travels through Asia. The advice given him was to read Robinson Crusoe carefully. When the professor expressed astonishment, supposing it to be a jest, the historian said he was quite serious, but that if Robinson Crusoe would not help him, for any reason, he recommended Gulliver's Travels. The late Donald G. Mitchell once said: "If you should ever have any story of your own to tell, and want to tell it well, I advise you to take Robinson Crusoe for a model!"

Parents and teachers who do not read aloud to young children, or who do not practise telling stories to children, probably do not realize what simple but extraordinarily valuable opportunities for self-education they are ignoring, to say nothing of the help they can be to children. In order to be successful we have to try and put ourselves in the child's place.

The average reader does not concentrate sufficiently to get the thought clearly from the text, and does not imagine himself to be actually in the midst of the scene he is describing. The consequence is that his voice and actions are not, except perhaps in a slight degree, affected by the emotions he is supposed to be experiencing. Dramatic rendering of dramatic passages is worth striving for, and should be encouraged on the part of children.

The story-teller who roars with the lion and bleats with the lamb is sure to be rewarded with shouts of enthusiastic delight from the audience.

THE ARABIAN NIGHTS

All nations have their fairy tales, but India seems to have been the country from which they all started, carried on their travels by the professional story-tellers who kept the tales alive throughout Asia. In Bagdad and Cairo to-day, that cafe never lacks customers where the blind storyteller relates to the spell-bound Arabs some chapter from the immortal Arabian Nights, the King of all Wonder Books.

No one knows where the tales were written, except that they came out of the Far East, India, Arabia and Persia. Haroun Al Raschid, who was called The Just, was a real Eastern monarch who lived in Bagdad over eleven hundred years ago, about the same time that Charlemagne was King of France. We can believe that the tales are very old, but the most we know is that they were translated from Arabic into French in 1704-17 by a Frenchman named Galland, and that the manuscript of his translation is preserved in the French National Library. American boys first had the chance to read the notes in English about the time President Monroe was elected._

ALI BABA AND THE FORTY THIEVES

There once lived in a town of Persia two brothers, one named Cassim, and the other Ali Baba. Their father divided a small inheritance equally between them. Cassim married a very rich wife, and became a wealthy merchant. Ali Baba married a woman as poor as himself, and lived by cutting wood, and bringing it upon three asses into the town to sell.

One day, when Ali Baba was in the forest, and had just cut wood enough to load his asses, he saw at a distance a great cloud of dust, which seemed to approach him. He observed it with attention, and distinguished soon after a body of horsemen, whom he suspected might be robbers. He determined to leave his asses to save himself. He climbed up a large tree, planted on a high rock, whose branches were thick enough to conceal him, and yet enabled him to see all that passed without being discovered.

The troop, who were to the number of forty, all well mounted and armed, came to the foot of the rock on which the tree stood, and there dismounted. Every man unbridled his horse, tied him to some shrub, and hung about his neck a bag of corn which they brought behind them. Then each of them took off his saddle-bag, which seemed to Ali Baba to be full of gold and silver from its weight. One, whom he took to be their captain, came under the tree in which Ali Baba was concealed; and, making his way through some shrubs, pronounced these words—"Open, Sesame!" As soon as the captain of the robbers had thus spoken, a door opened in the rock; and after he had made all his troop enter before him, he followed them, when the door shut again of itself.

The robbers stayed some time within the rock, during which Ali Baba, fearful of being caught, remained in the tree.

At last the door opened again, and as the captain went in last, so he came out first, and stood to see them all pass by him; when Ali Baba heard him make the door close by pronouncing these words, "Shut, Sesame!" Every man at once went and bridled his horse, fastened his wallet, and mounted again. When the captain saw them all ready, he put himself at their head, and they returned the way they had come.

Ali Baba followed them with his eyes as far as he could see them, and afterward stayed a considerable time before he descended. Remembering the words the captain of the robbers used to cause the door to open and shut, he had the curiosity to try if his pronouncing them would have the same effect. Accordingly, he went among the shrubs, and perceiving the door concealed behind them, stood before it and said, "Open, Sesame!" The door instantly flew wide open.

Ali Baba, who expected a dark, dismal cavern, was surprised to see a well-lighted and spacious chamber, which received the light from an opening at the top of the rock, and in which were all sorts of provisions, rich bales of silk, stuff, brocade, and valuable carpeting, piled upon one another, gold and silver ingots in great heaps, and money in bags. The sight of all these riches made him suppose that this cave must have been occupied for ages by robbers, who had succeeded one another.

Ali Baba went boldly into the cave, and collected as much of the gold coin, which was in bags, as he thought his three asses could carry. When he had loaded them with the bags, he laid wood over them in such a manner that they could not be seen. When he had passed in and out as often as he wished, he stood before the door, and pronouncing the words, "Shut, Sesame!" the door closed of itself. He then made the best of his way to town.

When Ali Baba got home, he drove his asses into a little yard, shut the gates very carefully, threw off the wood that covered the panniers, carried the bags into the house, and ranged them in order before his wife. He then emptied the bags, which raised such a great heap of gold as dazzled his wife's eyes, and then he told her the whole adventure from beginning to end, and, above all, recommended her to keep it secret.

The wife rejoiced greatly at their good-fortune, and would count all the gold piece by piece. "Wife," replied Ali Baba, "you do not know what you undertake, when you pretend to count the money; you will never have done. I will dig a hole and bury it. There is no time to be lost." "You are in the right, husband," replied she; "but let us know, as nigh as possible, how much we have. I will borrow a small measure, and measure it while you dig the hole."

Away the wife ran to her brother-in-law Cassim, who lived just by, and, addressing herself to his wife, desired her to lend her a measure for a little while. Her sister-in-law asked her whether she would have a great or a small one. The other asked for a small one. She bade her stay a little, and she would readily fetch one.

The sister-in-law did so, but as she knew Ali Baba's poverty, she was curious to know what sort of grain his wife wanted to measure, and, artfully putting some suet at the bottom of the measure, brought it to her, with the excuse that she was sorry that she had made her stay so long, but that she could not find it sooner.

Ali Baba's wife went home, set the measure upon the heap of gold, filled it, and emptied it often upon the sofa, till she had done, when she was very well satisfied to find the number of measures amounted to so many as they did, and went to tell her husband, who had almost finished digging the hole. While Ali Baba was burying the gold, his wife, to show her exactness and diligence to her sister-in-law, carried the measure back again, but without taking notice that a piece of gold had stuck to the bottom. "Sister," said she, giving it to her again, "you see that I have not kept your measure long. I am obliged to you for it, and return it with thanks."

As soon as Ali Baba's wife was gone, Cassim's wife looked at the bottom of the measure, and was in inexpressible surprise to find a piece of gold sticking to it. Envy immediately possessed her breast. "What!" said she, "has Ali Baba gold so plentiful as to measure it? Whence has he all this wealth?"

Cassim, her husband, was at his counting-house. When he came home his wife said to him, "Cassim, I know you think yourself rich, but Ali Baba is infinitely richer than you. He does not count his money, but measures it." Cassim desired her to explain the riddle, which she did by telling him the stratagem she had used to make the discovery, and showed him the piece of money, which was so old that they could not tell in what prince's reign it was coined.

Cassim, after he had married the rich widow, had never treated Ali Baba as a brother, but neglected him; and now, instead of being pleased, he conceived a base envy at his brother's prosperity. He could not sleep all that night, and went to him in the morning before sunrise. "Ali Baba," said he, "I am surprised at you! you pretend to be miserably poor, and yet you measure gold. My wife found this at the bottom of the measure you borrowed yesterday."

By this discourse, Ali Baba perceived that Cassim and his wife, through his own wife's folly, knew what they had so much reason to conceal; but what was done could not be undone. Therefore, without showing the least surprise or trouble, he confessed all, and offered his brother part of his treasure to keep the secret.

"I expect as much," replied Cassim haughtily; "but I must know exactly where this treasure is, and how I may visit it myself when I choose; otherwise, I will go and inform against you, and then you will not only get no more, but will lose all you have, and I shall have a share for my information."

Ali Baba told him all he desired, even to the very words he was to use to gain admission into the cave.

Cassim rose the next morning long before the sun, and set out for the forest with ten mules bearing great chests, which he designed to fill, and followed the road which Ali Baba had pointed out to him. It was not long before he reached the rock, and found out the place, by the tree and other marks which his brother had given him. When he reached the entrance of the cavern, he pronounced the words, "Open, Sesame!" The door immediately opened, and when he was in, closed upon him. On examining the cave, he was in great admiration to find much more riches than he had expected from Ali Baba's relation. He quickly laid as many bags of gold as he could carry at the door of the cavern; but his thoughts were so full of the great riches he should possess, that he could not think of the necessary word to make it open, and instead of "Sesame" said, "Open, Barley!" and was much amazed to find that the door remained fast shut. He named several sorts of grain, but still the door would not open.

Cassim had never expected such an incident, and was so alarmed at the danger he was in, that the more he endeavored to remember the word "Sesame," the more his memory was confounded, and he had as much forgotten it as if he had never heard it mentioned, He threw down the bags he had loaded himself with, and walked distractedly up and down the cave, without having the least regard to the riches that were round him.

About noon the robbers visited their cave. At some distance they saw Cassim's mules straggling about the rock, with great chests on their backs. Alarmed at this, they galloped full speed to the cave. They drove away the mules, who strayed through the forest so far that they were soon out of sight, and went directly, with their naked sabres in their hands, to the door, which, on their captain pronouncing the proper words, immediately opened.

Cassim, who heard the noise of the horses' feet, at once guessed the arrival of the robbers, and resolved to make one effort for his life. He rushed to the door, and no sooner saw the door open, than he ran out and threw the leader down, but could not escape the other robbers, who with their cimeters soon deprived him of life.

The first care of the robbers after this was to examine the cave. They found all the bags which Cassim had brought to the door, to be ready to load his mules, and carried them again to their places, but they did not miss what Ali Baba had taken away before. Then holding a council, and deliberating upon this occurrence, they guessed that Cassim, when he was in, could not get out again, but could not imagine how he had learned the secret words by which alone he could enter. They could not deny the fact of his being there; and to terrify any person or accomplice who should attempt the same thing, they agreed to cut Cassim's body into four quarters — to hang two on one side, and two on the other, within the door of the cave. They had no sooner taken this resolution than they put it in execution; and when they had nothing more to detain them, left the place of their hoards well closed. They mounted their horses, went to beat the roads again, and to attack the caravans they might meet.

In the meantime, Cassim's wife was very uneasy when night came, and her husband was not returned. She ran to Ali Baba in great alarm, and said: "I believe, brother-in-law, that you know Cassim is gone to the forest, and upon what account; it is now night, and he has not returned; I am afraid some misfortune has happened to him." Ali Baba told her that she need not frighten herself, for that certainly Cassim would not think it proper to come into the town till the night should be pretty far advanced.

Cassim's wife, considering how much it concerned her husband to keep the business secret, was the more easily persuaded to believe her brother-in-law. She went home again, and waited patiently till midnight. Then her fear redoubled, and her grief was the more sensible because she was forced to keep it to herself. She repented of her foolish curiosity, and cursed her desire of prying into the affairs of her brother and sister-in-law. She spent all the night in weeping; and, as soon as it was day, went to them, telling them, by her tears, the cause of her coming.

Ali Baba did not wait for his sister-in-law to desire him to go to see what was become of Cassim, but departed immediately with his three asses, begging of her first to moderate her affliction. He went to the forest, and when he came near the rock, having seen neither his brother nor the mules in his way, was seriously alarmed at finding some blood spilled near the door, which he took for an ill omen; but when he had pronounced the word, and the door had opened, he was struck with horror at the dismal sight of his brother's body. He was not long in determining how he should pay the last dues to his brother; but without adverting to the little fraternal affection he had shown for him, went into the cave to find something to enshroud his remains; and having loaded one of his asses with them, covered them over with wood. The other two asses he loaded with bags of gold, covering them with wood also as before; and then bidding the door shut, came away; but was so cautious as to stop some time at the end of the forest, that he might not go into the town before night. When he came home, he drove the two asses loaded with gold into his little yard, and left the care of unloading them to his wife, while he led the other to his sister-in-law's house.

Ali Baba knocked at the door, which was opened by Morgiana, a clever, intelligent slave, who was fruitful in inventions to meet the most difficult circumstances. When he came into the court, he unloaded the ass, and taking

Morgiana aside, said to her: "You must observe an inviolable secrecy. Your master's body is contained in these two panniers. We must bury him as if he had died a natural death. Go now and tell your mistress. I leave the matter to your wit and skilful devices."

Ali Baba helped to place the body in Cassim's house, again recommended to Morgiana to act her part well, and then returned with his ass.

Morgiana went out, early the next morning to a druggist, and asked for a sort of lozenge which was considered efficacious in the most dangerous disorders. The apothecary inquired who was ill. She replied, with a sigh, Her good master, Cassim himself, and that he could neither eat nor speak. In the evening Morgiana went to the same druggist's again, and with tears in her eyes, asked for an essence which they used to give to sick people only when at the last extremity. "Alas!" said she, taking it from the apothecary, "I am afraid that this remedy will have no better effect than the lozenges; and that I shall lose my good master."

On the other hand, as Ali Baba and his wife were often seen to go between Cassim's and their own house all that day, and to seem melancholy, nobody was surprised in the evening to hear the lamentable shrieks and cries of Cassim's wife and Morgiana, who gave out everywhere that her master was dead. The next morning at daybreak, Morgiana went to an old cobbler whom she knew to be always early at his stall, and bidding him good-morrow, put a piece of gold into his hand, saying, "Baba Mustapha, you must bring with you your sewing tackle, and come with me; but I must tell you, I shall blindfold you when you come to such a place."

Baba Mustapha seemed to hesitate a little at these words. "Oh! oh!" replied he, "you must have me do something against my conscience, or against my honor?" "God forbid," said Morgiana, putting another piece of gold into his hand, "that I should ask anything that is contrary to your honor! only come along with me and fear nothing."

Baba Mustapha went with Morgiana, who, after she had bound his eyes with a handkerchief at the place she had mentioned, conveyed him to her deceased master's house, and never unloosed his eyes till he had entered the room where she had put the corpse together.

"Baba Mustapha," said she, "you must make haste and sew the parts of this body together; and when you have done, I will give you another piece of gold."

After Baba Mustapha had finished his task, she blindfolded him again, gave him the third piece of gold as she had promised, and recommending secrecy to him, carried him back to the place where she first bound his eyes, pulled off the bandage, and let him go home, but watched him that he returned toward his stall, till he was quite out of sight, for fear he should have the curiosity to return and dodge her; she then went home. Morgiana, on her return, warmed some water to wash the body, and at the same time Ali Baba perfumed it with incense, and wrapped it in the burying clothes with the accustomed ceremonies. Not long after, the proper officer brought the bier, and when the attendants of the mosque, whose business it was to wash the dead, offered to perform their duty, she told them that it was done already. Shortly after this the imaun and the other ministers of the mosque arrived. Four neighbors carried the corpse to the burying ground, following the imaun, who recited some prayers. Ali Baba came after with some neighbors, who often relieved the others in carrying the bier to the burying ground. Morgiana, a slave to the deceased, followed in the procession, weeping, beating her breast, and tearing her hair. Cassim's wife stayed at home mourning, uttering lamentable cries with the women of the neighborhood, who came, according to custom, during the funeral, and, joining their lamentations with hers, filled the quarter far and near with sounds of sorrow.

In this manner Cassim's melancholy death was concealed, and hushed up between Ali Baba, his widow, and Morgiana, his slave, with so much contrivance that nobody in the city had the least knowledge or suspicion of the cause of it. Three or four days after the funeral, Ali Baba removed his few goods openly to his sister-in- law's house, in which it was agreed that he should in future live; but the money he had taken from the robbers he conveyed thither by night. As for Cassim's warehouse, he intrusted it entirely to the management of his eldest son.

While these things were being done, the forty robbers again visited their retreat in the forest. Great, then, was their surprise to find Cassim's body taken away, with some of their bags of gold. "We are certainly discovered," said the captain. "The removal of the body and the loss of some of our money plainly show that the man whom we killed had an accomplice; and for our own lives' sake we must try and find him. What say you, my lads?"

All the robbers unanimously approved of the captain's proposal.

"Well," said the captain, "one of you, the boldest and most skilful among you, must go into the town, disguised as a traveller and a stranger, to try if he can hear any talk of the man whom we have killed, and endeavor to find out who he was, and where he lived. This is a matter of the first importance, and for fear of any treachery, I propose that whoever undertakes this business without success, even though the failure arises only from an error of judgment, shall suffer death."

Without waiting for the sentiments of his companions, one of the robbers started up, and said, "I submit to this condition, and think it an honor to expose my life to serve the troop."

After this robber had received great commendations from the captain and his comrades, he disguised himself so that nobody would take him for what he was; and taking his leave of the troop that night, went into the town just at daybreak, and walked up and down, till accidentally he came to Baba Mustapha's stall, which was always open before any of the shops.

Baba Mustapha was seated with an awl in his hand, just going to work.

The robber saluted him, bidding him good-morrow; and, perceiving that he was old, said, "Honest man, you begin to work very early: is it possible that one of your age can see so well? I question, even if it were somewhat lighter, whether you could see to stitch."

"You do not know me," replied Baba Mustapha; "for old as I am, I have extraordinary good eyes; and you will not doubt it when I tell you that I sewed the body of a dead man together in a place where I had not so much light as I have now."

"A dead body!" exclaimed the robber, with affected amazement. "Yes, yes," answered Baba Mustapha; "I see you want to have me speak out, but you shall know no more."

The robber felt sure that he had discovered what he sought. He pulled out a piece of gold, and putting it into Baba Mustapha's hand, said to him, "I do not want to learn your secret, though I can assume you you might safely trust me with it. The only thing I desire of you is to show me the house where you stitched up the dead body."

"If I were disposed to do you that favor," replied Baba Mustapha, "I assure you I cannot. I was taken to a certain place, whence I was led blindfold to the house, and afterward brought back again in the same manner; you see, therefore, the impossibility of my doing what you desire."

"Well," replied the robber, "you may, however, remember a little of the way that you were led blindfold. Come, let me blind your eyes at the same place. We will walk together; perhaps you may recognize some part; and as everybody ought to be paid for their trouble, there is another piece of gold for you; gratify me in what I ask you." So saying, he put another piece of gold into his hand.

The two pieces of gold were great temptations to Baba Mustapha. He looked at them a long time in his hand without saying a word, but at last he pulled out his purse and put them in. "I cannot promise," said he to the robber, "that I can remember the way exactly; but since you desire, I will try what I can do." At these words Baba Mustapha rose up, to the great joy of the robber, and led him to the place where Morgiana had bound his eyes. "It was here," said Baba Mustapha, "I was blindfolded; and I turned this way." The robber tied his handkerchief over his eyes, and walked by him till they stopped directly at Cassim's house, where Ali Baba then lived. The thief, before he pulled off the band, marked the door with a piece of chalk, which he had ready in his hand, and then asked him if he knew whose house that was; to which Baba Mustapha replied, that as he did not live in that neighborhood he could not tell.

The robber, finding he could discover no more from Baba Mustapha, thanked him for the trouble he had taken, and left him to go back to his stall, while he returned to the forest, persuaded that he should be very well received.

A little after the robber and Baba Mustapha had parted, Morgiana went out of Ali Baba's house upon some errand, and upon her return, seeing the mark the robber had made, stopped to observe it. "What can be the meaning of this mark?" said she to herself; "somebody intends my master no good: however, with whatever intention it was done, it is advisable to guard against the worst." Accordingly, she fetched a piece of chalk, and marked two or three doors on each side, in the same manner, without saying a word to her master or mistress.

In the meantime, the robber rejoined his troop in the forest, and recounted to them his success, expatiating upon his good fortune in meeting so soon with the only person who could inform him of what he wanted to know. All the robbers listened to him with the utmost satisfaction; when the captain, after commending his diligence, addressing himself to them all, said, "Comrades, we have no time to lose: let us set off well armed, without its appearing who we are; but that we may not excite any suspicion, let only one or two go into the town together, and join at our rendezvous, which shall be the great square. In the meantime, our comrade who brought us the good news and I will go and find out the house, that we may consult what had best be done."

This speech and plan were approved of by all, and they were soon ready. They filed off in parties of two each, after some interval of time, and got into the town without being in the least suspected. The captain, and he who had visited the town in the morning as spy, came in the last. He led the captain into the street where he had marked Ali Baba's residence; and when they came to the first of the houses which Morgiana had marked, he pointed it out. But the captain observed that the next door was chalked in the same manner, and in the same place; and showing it to his guide, asked him which house it was, that, or the first. The guide was so confounded that he knew not what answer to make, but still more puzzled when he and the captain saw five or six houses similarly marked. He assured the captain, with an oath, that he had marked but one, and could not tell who had chalked the rest, so that he could not distinguish the house which the cobbler had stopped at.

The captain, finding that their design had proved abortive, went directly to the place of rendezvous, and told his troop that they had lost their labor, and must return to their cave. He himself set them the example, and they all returned as they had come.

When the troop was all got together, the captain told them the reason of their returning; and presently the conductor was declared by all worthy of death. He condemned himself, acknowledging that he ought to have taken better precaution, and prepared to receive the stroke from him who was appointed to cut off his head. But as the safety of the troop required the discovery of the second intruder into the cave, another of the gang, who promised himself that he should succeed better, presented himself, and his offer being accepted, he went and corrupted Baba Mustapha, as the other had done; and, being shown the house, marked it in a place more remote from sight with red chalk.

Not long after, Morgiana, whose eyes nothing could escape, went out, and seeing the red chalk, and arguing with herself as she had done before, marked the other neighbors' houses in the same place and manner.

The robber, at his return to his company, valued himself much on the precaution he had taken, which he looked upon as an infallible way of distinguishing Ali Baba's house from the others; and the captain and all of them thought it must succeed. They conveyed themselves into the town with the same precaution as before; but when the robber and his captain came to the street they found the same difficulty; at which the captain was enraged, and the robber in as great confusion as his predecessor.

Thus the captain and his troop were forced to retire a second time, and much more dissatisfied; while the robber, who had been the author of the mistake, underwent the same punishment, which he willingly submitted to.

The captain, having lost two brave fellows of his troop, was afraid of diminishing it too much by pursuing this plan to get information of the residence of their plunderer. He found by their example that their heads were not so good as their hands on such occasions, and therefore resolved to take upon himself the important commission.

Accordingly, he went and addressed himself to Baba Mustapha, who did him the same service he had done to the other robbers. He did not set any particular mark on the house, but examined and observed it so carefully, by passing often by it, that it was impossible for him to mistake it.

The captain, well satisfied with his attempt, and informed of what he wanted to know, returned to the forest; and when he came into the cave, where the troop waited for him, said, "Now, comrades, nothing can prevent our full revenge, as I am certain of the house; and in my way hither I have thought how to put it into execution, but if any one can form a better expedient, let him communicate it." He then told them his contrivance; and as they approved of it, ordered them to go into the villages about, and buy nineteen mules, with thirty-eight large leather jars, one full of oil, and the others empty.

In two or three days' time the robbers had purchased the mules and jars, and as the mouths of the jars were rather too narrow for his purpose, the captain caused them to be widened; and after having put one of his men into each, with the weapons which he thought fit, leaving open the seam which had been undone to leave them room to breathe, he rubbed the jars on the outside with oil from the full vessel.

Things being thus prepared, when the nineteen mules were loaded with thirty-seven robbers in jars, and the jar of oil, the captain, as their driver, set out with them, and reached the town by the dusk of the evening, as he had intended. He led them through the streets till he came to Ali Baba's, at whose door he designed to have knocked; but was prevented by his sitting there after supper to take a little fresh air. He stopped his mules, addressed himself to him, and said, "I have brought some oil a great way to sell at to-morrow's market; and it is now so late that I do not know where to lodge. If I should not be troublesome to you, do me the favor to let me pass the night with you, and I shall be very much obliged by your hospitality."

Though Ali Baba had seen the captain of the robbers in the forest, and had heard him speak, it was impossible to know him in the disguise of an oil merchant. He told him he should be welcome, and immediately opened his gates for the mules to go into the yard. At the same time he called to a slave, and ordered him, when the mules were unloaded, to put them into the stable, and to feed them; and then went to Morgiana to bid her to get a good supper for his guest. After they had finished supper, Ali Baba, charging Morgiana afresh to take care of his guest, said to her, "To-morrow morning I design to go to the bath before day; take care my bathing linen be ready, give them to Abdalla (which was the slave's name) and make me some good broth against I return." After this he went to bed.

In the meantime the captain of the robbers went into the yard, took off the lid of each jar, and gave his people orders what to do. Beginning at the first jar, and so on to the last, he said to each man: "As soon as I throw some stones out of the chamber window where I lie, do not fail to come out, and I will immediately join you." After this he returned into the house, when Morgiana, taking up a light, conducted him to his chamber, where she left him; and he, to avoid any suspicion, put the light out soon after, and laid himself down in his clothes, that he might be the more ready to rise.

Morgiana, remembering Ali Baba's orders, got his bathing linen ready, and ordered Abdalla to set on the pot for the broth; but while she was preparing it the lamp went out, and there was no more oil in the house, nor any candles. What to do she did not know, for the broth must be made. Abdalla, seeing her very uneasy, said, "Do not fret and tease yourself, but go into the yard, and take some oil out of one of the jars."

Morgiana thanked Abdalla for his advice, took the oil-pot, and went into the yard; when, as she came nigh the first jar, the robber within said softly, "Is it time?"

Though naturally much surprised at finding a man in the jar instead of the oil she wanted, she immediately felt the importance of keeping silence, as Ali Baba, his family, and herself were in great danger; and, collecting herself, without showing the least emotion, she answered, "Not yet, but presently." She went quietly in this manner to all the jars, giving the same answer, till she came to the jar of oil.

By this means Morgiana found that her master Ali Baba had admitted thirty-eight robbers into his house, and that this pretended oil merchant was their captain. She made what haste she could to fill her oil-pot, and returned into the kitchen, where, as soon as she had lighted her lamp, she took a great kettle, went again to the oil-jar, filled the kettle, set it on a large wood fire, and as soon as it boiled, went and poured enough into every jar to stifle and destroy the robber within.

When this action, worthy of the courage of Morgiana, was executed without any noise, as she had projected, she returned into the kitchen with the empty kettle; and having put out the great fire, she had made to boil the oil, and leaving just enough to make the broth, put out the lamp also, and remained silent, resolving not to go to rest till she had observed what might follow through a window of the kitchen, which opened into the yard.

She had not waited long before the captain of the robbers got up, opened the window, and finding no light, and hearing no noise, or any one stirring in the house, gave the appointed signal by throwing little stones, several of which hit the jars, as he doubted not by the sound they gave. He then listened, but not hearing or perceiving anything whereby he could judge that his companions stirred, he began to grow very uneasy, threw stones a second and also a third time, and could not comprehend the reason that none of them should answer his signal. Much alarmed, he went softly down into the yard, and going to the first jar, while asking the robber, whom he thought alive, if he was in readiness, smelled the hot boiled oil, which sent forth a steam out of the jar. Hence he suspected that his plot to murder Ali Baba, and plunder his house, was discovered. Examining all the jars, one after another, he found that all his gang were dead; and, enraged to despair at having failed in his design, he forced the lock of a door that led from the yard to the garden, and, climbing over the walls, made his escape.

When Morgiana saw him depart, she went to bed, satisfied and pleased to have succeeded so well in saving her master and family.

Ali Baba rose before day, and, followed by his slave, went to the baths, entirely ignorant of the important event which had happened at home.

When he returned from the baths, he was very much surprised to see the oil jars, and that the merchant was not gone with the mules. He asked Morgiana, who opened the door, the reason of it. "My good master," answered she, "God preserve you and all your family. You will be better informed of what you wish to know when you have seen what I have to show you, if you will follow me."

As soon as Morgiana had shut the door, Ali Baba followed her, when she requested him to look into the first jar, and see if there was any oil. Ali Baba did so, and seeing a man, started back in alarm, and cried out. "Do not be afraid," said Morgiana, "the man you see there can neither do you nor anybody else any harm. He is dead." "Ah, Morgiana," said Ali Baba, "what is it you show me? Explain yourself." "I will," replied Morgiana. "Moderate your astonishment, and do not excite the curiosity of your neighbors; for it is of great importance to keep this affair secret. Look into all the other jars."

Ali Baba examined all the other jars, one after another; and when he came to that which had the oil in, found it prodigiously sunk, and stood for some time motionless, sometimes looking at the jars, and sometimes at Morgiana, without saying a word, so great was his surprise.

At last, when he had recovered himself, he said, "And what is become of the merchant?"

"Merchant!" answered she; "he is as much one as I am. I will tell you who he is, and what is become of him; but you had better hear the story in your own chamber; for it is time for your health that you had your broth after your bathing."

Morgiana then told him all she had done, from the first observing the mark upon the house, to the destruction of the robbers, and the flight of their captain.

On hearing of these brave deeds from the lips of Morgiana, Ali Baba said to her, "God, by your means, has delivered me from the snares these robbers laid for my destruction. I owe, therefore, my life to you; and, for the first token of my acknowledgment, give you your liberty from this moment, till I can complete your recompense, as I intend."

Ali Baba's garden was very long, and shaded at the further end by a great number of large trees. Near these he and the slave Abdalla dug a trench, long and wide enough to hold the bodies of the robbers; and as the earth was light, they were not long in doing it. When this was done, Ali Baba hid the jars and weapons; and as he had no occasion for the mules, he sent them at different times to be sold in the market by his slave.

While Ali Baba took these measures, the captain of the forty robbers returned to the forest with inconceivable mortification. He did not stay long: the loneliness of the gloomy cavern became frightful to him. He determined, however, to avenge the fate of his companions, and to accomplish the death of Ali Baba. For this purpose he returned to the town and took a lodging in a khan, and disguised himself as a merchant in silks. Under this assumed character, he gradually conveyed a great many sorts of rich stuffs and fine linen to his lodging from the cavern, but with all the necessary precautions to conceal the place whence he brought them. In order to dispose of the merchandise, when he had thus amassed them together, he took a warehouse, which happened to be opposite to Cassim's, which Ali Baba's son had occupied since the death of his uncle.

He took the name of Cogia Houssain, and, as a newcomer, was, according to custom, extremely civil and complaisant to all the merchants his neighbors. Ali Baba's son was, from his vicinity, one of the first to converse with Cogia Houssain, who strove to cultivate his friendship more particularly. Two or three days after he was settled, Ali Baba came to see his son, and the captain of the robbers recognized him at once, and soon learned from his son who he was. After this he increased his assiduities, caressed him in the most engaging manner, made him some small presents, and often asked him to dine and sup with him, when he treated him very handsomely.

Ali Baba's son did not choose to lie under such obligation to Cogia Houssain; but was so much straitened for want of room in his house that he could not entertain him. He therefore acquainted his father, Ali Baba, with his wish to invite him in return.

Ali Baba with great pleasure took the treat upon himself. "Son," said he, "to-morrow being Friday, which is a day that the shops of such great merchants as Cogia Houssain and yourself are shut, get him to accompany you, and as you pass by my door, call in. I will go and order Morgiana to provide a supper."

The next day Ali Baba's son and Cogia Houssain met by appointment, took their walk, and as they returned, Ali Baba's son led Cogia Houssain through the street where his father lived, and when they came to the house, stopped and knocked at the door. "This, sir," said he, "is my father's house, who, from the account I have given him of your friendship, charged me to procure him the honor of your acquaintance; and I desire you to add this pleasure to those for which I am already indebted to you."

Though it was the sole aim of Cogia Houssain to introduce himself into Ali Baba's house that he might kill him, without hazarding his own life or making any noise, yet he excused himself and offered to take his leave; but a slave having opened the door, Ali Baba's son took him obligingly by the hand, and, in a manner, forced him in.

Ali Baba received Cogia Houssain with a smiling countenance, and in the most obliging manner he could wish. He thanked him for all the favors he had done his son; adding withal, the obligation was the greater as he was a young man, not much acquainted with the world, and that he might contribute to his information.

Cogia Houssain returned the compliment by assuring Ali Baba that though his son might not have acquired the experience of older men, he had good sense equal to the experience of many others. After a little more conversation on different subjects, he offered again to take his leave, when Ali Baba, stopping him, said, "Where are you going, sir, in so much haste? I beg you would do me the honor to sup with me, though my entertainment may not be worthy of your acceptance; such as it is, I heartily offer it." "Sir," replied Cogia Houssain, "I am thoroughly persuaded of your good-will; but the truth is, I can eat no victuals that have any salt in them; therefore judge how I should feel at your table." "If that is the only reason," said Ali Baba, "it ought not to deprive me of the honor of your company; for, in the first place, there is no salt ever put into my bread, and as to the meat we shall have to-night, I promise you there shall be none in that. Therefore you must do me the favor to stay. I will return immediately."

Ali Baba went into the kitchen, and ordered Morgiana to put no salt in the meat that was to be dressed that night; and to make quickly two or three ragouts besides what he had ordered, but be sure to put no salt in them.

Morgiana, who was always ready to obey her master, could not help being surprised at his strange order. "Who is this strange man," said she, "who eats no salt with his meat? Your supper will be spoiled if I keep it back so long." "Do not be angry, Morgiana," replied Ali Baba; "he is an honest man, therefore do as I bid you."

Morgiana obeyed, though with no little reluctance, and had a curiosity to see this man who ate no salt. To this end, when she had finished what she had to do in the kitchen, she helped Abdalla to carry up the dishes; and looking at Cogia Houssain, knew him at first sight, notwithstanding his disguise, to be the captain of the robbers, and examining him very carefully, perceived that he had a dagger under his garment. "I am not in the least amazed," said she to herself, "that this wicked man, who is my master's greatest enemy, would eat no salt with him, since he intends to assassinate him; but I will prevent him."

Morgiana, while they were at supper, determined in her own mind to execute one of the boldest acts ever meditated.

When Abdalla came for the dessert or fruit, and had put it with the wine and glasses before Ali Baba, Morgiana retired, dressed herself neatly, with a suitable head-dress like a dancer, girded her waist with a silver-gilt girdle, to which there hung a poniard with a hilt and guard of the same metal, and put a handsome mask on her face.

When she had thus disguised herself, she said to Abdalla, "Take your tabor, and let us go and divert our master and his son's friend, as we do sometimes when he is alone."

Abdalla took his tabor and played all the way into the hall before Morgiana, who, when she came to the door, made a low obeisance by way of asking leave to exhibit her skill, while Abdalla left off playing. "Come in, Morgiana," said Ali Baba, "and let Cogia Houssain see what you can do, that he may tell us what he thinks of your performance."

Cogia Houssain, who did not expect this diversion after supper, began to fear he should not be able to take advantage of the opportunity he thought he had found; but hoped, if he now missed his aim to secure it another time, by keeping up a friendly correspondence with the father and son; therefore, though he could have wished Ali Baba would have declined the dance, he pretended to be obliged to him for it, and had the complaisance to express his satisfaction at what he saw, which pleased his host.

As soon as Abdalla saw that Ali Baba and Cogia Houssain had done talking, he began to play on the tabor, and accompanied it with an air, to which Morgiana, who was an excellent performer, danced in such a manner as would have created admiration in any company.

After she had danced several dances with much grace, she drew the poniard, and holding it in her hand, began a dance, in which she outdid herself, by the many different figures, light movements, and the surprising leaps and wonderful exertions with which she accompanied it. Sometimes she presented the poniard to one breast, sometimes to another, and oftentimes seemed to strike her own. At last she snatched the tabor from Abdalla with her left hand, and holding the dagger in her right, presented the other side of the tabor, after the manner of those who get a livelihood by dancing, and solicit the liberality of the spectators.

Ali Baba put a piece of gold into the tabor, as did also his son; and Cogia Houssain, seeing that she was coming to him, had pulled his purse out of his bosom to make her a present; but while he was putting his hand into it, Morgiana, with a courage and resolution worthy of herself, plunged the poniard into his heart.

Ali Baba and his son, shocked at this action, cried out aloud. "Unhappy woman!" exclaimed Ali Baba, "what have you done, to ruin me and my family?" "It was to preserve, not to ruin you," answered Morgiana; "for see here," continued she, opening the pretended Cogia Houssain's garment, and showing the dagger, "what an enemy you had entertained! Look well at him, and you will find him to be both the fictitious oil merchant, and the captain of the gang of forty robbers. Remember, too, that he would eat no salt with you; and what would you have more to persuade you of his wicked design? Before I saw him, I suspected him as soon as you told me you had such a guest. I knew him, and you now find that my suspicion was not groundless."

Ali Baba, who immediately felt the new obligation he had to Morgiana for saving his life a second time, embraced her: "Morgiana," said he, "I gave you your liberty, and then promised you that my gratitude should not stop there, but that I would soon give you higher proofs of its sincerity, which I now do by making you my daughter-in-law." Then addressing himself to his son, he said: "I believe you, son, to be so dutiful a child, that you will not refuse Morgiana for your wife. You see that Cogia Houssain sought your friendship with a treacherous design to take away my life; and if he had succeeded, there is no doubt but he would have sacrificed you also to his revenge. Consider, that by marrying Morgiana you marry the preserver of my family and your own."

The son, far from showing any dislike, readily consented to the marriage; not only because he would not disobey his father, but also because it was agreeable to his inclination. After this they thought of burying the captain of the robbers with his comrades, and did it so privately that nobody discovered their bones till many years after, when no one had any concern in the publication of this remarkable history. A few days afterward Ali Baba celebrated the nuptials of his son and Morgiana with great solemnity, a sumptuous feast, and the usual dancing and spectacles; and had the satisfaction to see that his friends and neighbors, whom he invited, had no knowledge of the true motives of the marriage; but that those who were not unacquainted with Morgiana's good qualities, commended his generosity and goodness of heart. Ali Baba did not visit the robbers' cave for a whole year, as he supposed the other two might be alive.

At the year's end, when he found they had not made any attempt to disturb him, he had the curiosity to make another journey. He mounted his horse, and when he came to the cave he alighted, tied his horse to a tree, then approaching the entrance, and pronouncing the words, "Open, Sesame!" the door opened. He entered the cavern and by the condition he found things in, judged that nobody had been there since the captain had fetched the goods for his shop. From this time he believed he was the only person in the world who had the secret of opening the cave, and that all the treasure was at his sole disposal. He put as much gold into his saddle-bag as his horse could carry, and returned to town. Some years later he carried his son to the cave and taught him the secret, which descended to his posterity, who, using their good- fortune with moderation, lived in honor and splendor.

THE STORY OF ALADDIN; OR THE WONDERFUL LAMP

There once lived, in one of the large and rich cities of China, a tailor, named Mustapha. He was very poor. He could hardly, by his daily labor, maintain himself and his family, which consisted only of his wife and a son.

His son, who was called Aladdin, was a very careless and idle fellow. He was disobedient to his father and mother, and would go out early in the morning and stay out all day, playing in the streets and public places with idle children of his own age.

When he was old enough to learn a trade, his father took him into his own shop, and taught him how to use his needle; but all his father's endeavors to keep him to his work were vain, for no sooner was his back turned than he was gone for that day. Mustapha chastised him; but Aladdin was incorrigible, and his father, to his great grief, was forced to abandon him to his idleness, and was so much troubled about him that he fell sick and died in a few months.

Aladdin, who was now no longer restrained by the fear of a father, gave himself entirely over to his idle habits, and was never out of the streets from his companions. This course he followed till he was fifteen years old, without giving his mind to any useful pursuit, or the least reflection on what would become of him. As he was one day playing, according to custom, in the street with his evil associates, a stranger passing by stood to observe him.

This stranger was a sorcerer, known as the African magician, as he had been but two days arrived from Africa, his native country.

The African magician, observing in Aladdin's countenance something which assured him that he was a fit boy for his purpose, inquired his name and history of some of his companions; and when he had learned all he desired to know, went up to him, and taking him aside from his comrades, said, "Child, was not your father called Mustapha the tailor?" "Yes, sir," answered the boy; "but he has been dead a long time."

At these words the African magician threw his arms about Aladdin's neck, and kissed him several times, with tears in his eyes, and said, "I am your uncle. Your worthy father was my own brother. I knew you at first sight; you are so like him." Then he gave Aladdin a handful of small money, saying, "Go, my son, to your mother, give my love to her, and tell her that I will visit her to-morrow, that I may see where my good brother lived so long, and ended his days."

Aladdin ran to his mother, overjoyed at the money his uncle had given him. "Mother," said he, "have I an uncle?" "No, child," replied his mother, "you have no uncle by your father's side or mine." "I am just now come," said Aladdin, "from a man who says he is my uncle and my father's brother. He cried and kissed me when I told him my father was dead, and gave me money, sending his love to you, and promising to come and pay you a visit, that he may see the house my father lived and died in." "Indeed, child," replied the mother, "your father had no brother, nor have you an uncle."

The next day the magician found Aladdin playing in another part of the town, and embracing him as before, put two pieces of gold into his hand, and said to him, "Carry this, child, to your mother. Tell her that I will come and see her to-night, and bid her get us something for supper; but first show me the house where you live."

Aladdin showed the African magician the house, and carried the two pieces of gold to his mother, who went out and bought provisions; and, considering she wanted various utensils, borrowed them of her neighbors. She spent the whole day in preparing the supper; and at night, when it was ready, said to her son, "Perhaps the stranger knows not how to find our house; go and bring him, if you meet with him."

Aladdin was just ready to go, when the magician knocked at the door, and came in loaded with wine and all sorts of fruits, which he brought for a dessert. After he had given what he brought into Aladdin's hands, he saluted his mother, and desired her to show him the place where his brother Mustapha used to sit on the sofa; and when she had done so, he fell down and kissed it several times, crying out, with tears in his eyes, "My poor brother! how unhappy am I, not to have come soon enough to give you one last embrace!" Aladdin's mother desired him to sit down in the same place, but he declined.

"No," said he, "I shall not do that; but give me leave to sit opposite to it, that, although I see not the master of a family so dear to me, I may at least behold the place where he used to sit."

When the magician had made choice of a place, and sat down, he began to enter into discourse with Aladdin's mother. "My good sister," said he, "do not be surprised at your never having seen me all the time you have been married to my brother Mustapha of happy memory. I have been forty years absent from this country, which is my native place, as well as my late brother's; and during that time have travelled into the Indies, Persia, Arabia, Syria, and Egypt, and afterward crossed over into Africa, where I took up my abode. At last, as it is natural for a man, I was desirous to see my native country again, and to embrace my dear brother; and finding I had strength enough to undertake so long a journey, I made the necessary preparations, and set out. Nothing ever afflicted me so much as hearing of my brother's death. But God be praised for all things! It is a comfort for me to find, as it were, my brother in a son who has his most remarkable features."

The African magician, perceiving that the widow wept at the remembrance of her husband, changed the conversation, and turning toward her son, asked him, "What business do you follow? Are you of any trade?"

At this question the youth hung down his head, and was not a little abashed when his mother answered, "Aladdin is an idle fellow. His father, when alive, strove all he could to teach him his trade, but could not succeed; and since his death, notwithstanding all I can say to him, he does nothing but idle away his time in the streets, as you saw him, without considering he is no longer a child; and if you do not make him ashamed of it, I despair of his ever coming to any good. For my part, I am resolved, one of these days, to turn him out of doors, and let him provide for himself."

After these words Aladdin's mother burst into tears; and the magician said, "This is not well, nephew; you must think of helping yourself, and getting your livelihood. There are many sorts of trades. Perhaps you do not like your father's, and would prefer another; I will endeavor to help you. If you have no mind to learn any handicraft, I will take a shop for you, furnish it with all sorts of fine stuffs and linens, and then with the money you make of them you can lay in fresh goods, and live in an honorable way. Tell me freely what you think of my proposal; you shall always find me ready to keep my word."

This plan just suited Aladdin, who hated work. He told the magician he had a greater inclination to that business than to any other, and that he should be much obliged to him for his kindness. "Well, then," said the African magician, "I will carry you with me to-morrow, clothe you as handsomely as the best merchants in the city, and afterward we will open a shop as I mentioned."

The widow, after his promises of kindness to her son, no longer doubted that the magician was her husband's brother. She thanked him for his good intentions; and after having exhorted Aladdin to render himself worthy of his uncle's favor, served up supper, at which they talked of several indifferent matters; and then the magician took his leave and retired.

He came again the next day, as he had promised, and took Aladdin with him to a merchant, who sold all sorts of clothes for different ages and ranks ready made, and a variety of fine stuffs, and bade Aladdin choose those he preferred, which he paid for.

When Aladdin found himself so handsomely equipped, he returned his uncle thanks, who thus addressed him: "As you are soon to be a merchant, it is proper you should frequent these shops, and be acquainted with them." He then showed him the largest and finest mosques, carried him to the khans or inns where the merchants and travellers lodged, and afterward to the sultan's palace, where he had free access; and at last brought him to his own khan, where, meeting with some merchants he had become acquainted with since his arrival, he gave them a treat, to make them and his pretended nephew acquainted.

This entertainment lasted till night, when Aladdin would have taken leave of his uncle to go home; the magician would not let him go by himself, but conducted him to his mother, who, as soon as she saw him so well dressed, was transported with joy, and bestowed a thousand blessings upon the magician.

Early the next morning, the magician called again for Aladdin, and said he would take him to spend that day in the country, and on the next he would purchase the shop. He then led him out at one of the gates of the city, to some magnificent palaces, to each of which belonged beautiful gardens, into which anybody might enter. At every building he came to, he asked Aladdin if he did not think it fine; and the youth was ready to answer, when any one presented itself, crying out, "Here is a finer house, uncle, than any we have yet seen." By this artifice the cunning magician led Aladdin some way into the country; and as, he meant to carry him further, to execute his design, he took an opportunity to sit down in one of the gardens, on the brink of a fountain of clear water, which discharged itself by a lion's mouth of bronze into a basin, pretending to be tired. "Come, nephew," said he, "you must be weary, as well as I; let us rest ourselves, and we shall be better able to pursue our walk."

The magician next pulled from his girdle a handkerchief with cakes and fruit, and during this short repast he exhorted his nephew to leave off bad company, and to seek that of wise and prudent men, to improve by their conversation; "for," said he, "you will soon be at man's estate, and you cannot too early begin to imitate their example." When they had eaten as much as they liked, they got up, and pursued their walk through gardens separated from one another only by small ditches, which marked out the limits without interrupting the communication, so great was the confidence the inhabitants reposed in each other. By this means the African magician drew Aladdin insensibly beyond the gardens, and crossed the country till they nearly reached the mountains.

At last they arrived between two mountains of moderate height, and equal size, divided by a narrow valley, which was the place where the magician intended to execute the design that had brought him from Africa to China. "We will go no further now," said he to Aladdin; "I will show you here some extraordinary things, which, when you have seen, you will thank me for; but while I strike a light, gather up all the loose dry sticks you can see, to kindle a fire with."

Aladdin found so many dried sticks that he soon collected a great heap. The magician presently set them on fire; and when they were in a blaze, threw in some incense, pronouncing several magical words which Aladdin did not understand.

He had scarcely done so when the earth opened just before the magician, and discovered a stone with a brass ring fixed in it. Aladdin was so frightened that he would have run away, but the magician caught hold of him, and gave him such a box on the ear that he knocked him down. Aladdin got up trembling, and, with tears in his eyes, said to the magician: "What have I done, uncle, to be treated in this severe manner?" "I am your uncle," answered the magician; "I supply the place of your father, and you ought to make no reply. But child," added he, softening, "do not be afraid; for I shall not ask anything of you, but that you obey me punctually, if you would reap the advantages which I intend you. Know, then, that under this stone there is hidden a treasure, destined to be yours, and which will make you richer than the greatest monarch in the world. No person but yourself is permitted to lift this stone, or enter the cave; so you must punctually execute what I may command, for it is a matter of great consequence both to you and me."

Aladdin, amazed at all he saw and heard, forgot what was past, and, rising, said: "Well, uncle, what is to be done? Command me, I am ready to obey." "I am overjoyed, child," said the African magician, embracing him. "Take hold of the ring, and lift up that stone." "Indeed, uncle," replied Aladdin, "I am not strong enough; you must help me." "You have no occasion for my assistance," answered the magician; "if I help you, we shall be able to do nothing. Take hold of the ring and lift it up; you will find it will come easily." Aladdin did as the magician bade him, raised the stone with ease, and laid it on one side.

When the stone was pulled up, there appeared a staircase about three or four feet deep, leading to a door. "Descend, my son," said the African magician, "those steps, and open that door. It will lead you into a palace, divided into three great halls. In each of these you will see four large brass cisterns placed on each side, full of gold and silver; but take care you do not meddle with them. Before you enter the first hall, be sure to tuck up your robe, wrap it about you, and then pass through the second into the third without stopping. Above all things, have a care that you do not touch the walls, so much as with your clothes; for if you do, you will die instantly. At the end of the third hall, you will find a door which opens into a garden, planted with fine trees loaded with fruit. Walk directly across the garden to a terrace, where you will see a niche before you, and in that niche a lighted lamp. Take the lamp down, and put it out. When you have thrown away the wick and poured out the liquor, put it in your waistband and bring it to me. Do not be afraid that the liquor will spoil your clothes, for it is not oil, and the lamp will be dry as soon as it is thrown out."

After these words the magician drew a ring off his finger, and put it on one of Aladdin's, saying: "It is a talisman against all evil, so long as you obey me. Go, therefore, boldly, and we shall both be rich all our lives."

Aladdin descended the steps, and, opening the door, found the three halls just as the African magician had described. He went through them with all the precaution the fear of death could inspire, crossed the garden without stopping, took down the lamp from the niche, threw out the wick and the liquor, and, as the magician had desired, put it in his waistband. But as he came down from the terrace, seeing it was perfectly dry, he stopped in the garden to observe the trees, which were loaded with extraordinary fruit, of different colors on each tree. Some bore fruit entirely white, and some clear and transparent as crystal; some pale red, and others deeper; some green, blue, and purple, and others yellow; in short, there was fruit of all colors. The white were pearls; the clear and transparent, diamonds; the deep red, rubies; the paler, balas rubies; the green, emeralds; the blue, turquoises; the purple, amethysts; and the yellow, topazes. Aladdin, ignorant of their value, would have preferred figs, or grapes, or pomegranates; but as he had his uncle's permission, he resolved to gather some of every sort. Having filled the two new purses his uncle had bought for him with his clothes, he wrapped some up in the skirts of his vest, and crammed his bosom as full as it could hold.

Aladdin, having thus loaded himself with riches of which he knew not the value, returned through the three halls with the utmost precaution, and soon arrived at the mouth of the cave, where the African magician awaited him with the utmost impatience. As soon as Aladdin saw him, he cried out, "Pray, uncle, lend me your hand, to help me out." "Give me the lamp first," replied the magician; "it will be troublesome to you." "Indeed, uncle," answered Aladdin, "I cannot now, but I will as soon as I am up." The African magician was determined that he would have the lamp before he would help him up; and Aladdin, who had encumbered himself so much with his fruit that he could not well get at it, refused to give it him till he was out of the cave. The African magician, provoked at this obstinate refusal, flew into a passion, threw a little of his incense into the fire, and pronounced two magical words, when the stone which had closed the mouth of the staircase moved into its place, with the earth over it in the same manner as it lay at the arrival of the magician and Aladdin.

This action of the magician plainly revealed to Aladdin that he was no uncle of his, but one who designed him evil. The truth was that he had learned from his magic books the secret and the value of this wonderful lamp, the owner of which would be made richer than any earthly ruler, and hence his journey to China. His art had also told him that he was not permitted to take it himself, but must receive it as a voluntary gift from the hands of another person. Hence he employed young Aladdin, and hoped by a mixture of kindness and authority to make him obedient to his word and will. When he found that his attempt had failed, he set out to return to Africa, but avoided the town, lest any person who had seen him leave in company with Aladdin should make inquiries after the youth. Aladdin being suddenly enveloped in darkness, cried, and called out to his uncle to tell him he was ready to give him the lamp; but in vain, since his cries could not be heard. He descended to the bottom of the steps, with a design to get into the palace, but the door, which was opened before by enchantment, was now shut by the same means. He then redoubled his cries and tears, sat down on the steps without any hopes of ever seeing light again, and in an expectation of passing from the present darkness to a speedy death. In this great emergency he said, "There is no strength or power but in the great and high God"; and in joining his hands to pray he rubbed the ring which the magician had put on his finger. Immediately a genie of frightful aspect appeared, and said, "What wouldst thou have? I am ready to obey thee. I serve him who possesses the ring on thy finger; I and the other slaves of that ring." At another time Aladdin would have been frightened at the sight of so extraordinary a figure, but the danger he was in made him answer without hesitation, "Whoever thou art, deliver me from this place."

He had no sooner spoken these words than he found himself on the very spot where the magician had last left him, and no sign of cave or opening, nor disturbance of the earth. Returning God thanks to find himself once more in the world, he made the best of his way home. When he got within his mother's door, the joy to see her and his weakness for want of sustenance made him so faint that he remained for a long time as dead. As soon as he recovered he related to his mother all that had happened to him, and they were both very vehement in their complaints of the cruel magician. Aladdin slept very soundly till late the next morning, when the first thing he said to his mother was that he wanted something to eat, and wished she would give him his breakfast.

"Alas! child," said she, "I have not a bit of bread to give you: you ate up all the provisions I had in the house yesterday; but I have a little cotton, which I have spun; I will go and sell it, and buy bread and something for our dinner."

"Mother," replied Aladdin, "keep your cotton for another time, and give me the lamp I brought home with me yesterday; I will go and sell it, and the money I shall get for it will serve both for breakfast and dinner, and perhaps supper too."

Aladdin's mother took the lamp, and said to her son, "Here it is, but it is very dirty; if it was a little cleaner I believe it would bring something more." She took some fine sand and water to clean it; but had no sooner begun to rub it than in an instant a hideous genie of gigantic size appeared before her, and said to her in a voice of thunder, "What wouldst thou have? I am ready to obey thee as thy slave, and the slave of all those who have that lamp in their hands; I and the other slaves of the lamp."

Aladdin's mother, terrified at the sight of the genie, fainted; when Aladdin, who had seen such a phantom in the cavern, snatched the lamp out of his mother's hand, and said to the genie boldly, "I am hungry; bring me something to eat." The genie disappeared immediately, and in an instant returned with a large silver tray, holding twelve covered dishes of the same metal, which contained the most delicious viands; six large white bread cakes on two plates, two flagons of wine, and two silver cups. All these he placed upon a carpet, and disappeared; this was done before Aladdin's mother recovered from her swoon.

Aladdin had fetched some water, and sprinkled it in her face to recover her. Whether that or the smell of the meat effected her cure, it was not long before she came to herself. "Mother" said Aladdin, "be not afraid; get up and eat; here is what will put you in heart, and at the same time satisfy my extreme hunger."

His mother was much surprised to see the great tray, twelve dishes, six loaves, the two flagons and cups, and to smell the savory odor which exhaled from the dishes. "Child," said she, "to whom are we obliged for this great plenty and liberality? Has the sultan been made acquainted with our poverty, and had compassion on us?" "It is no matter, mother," said Aladdin, "let us sit down and eat; for you have almost as much need of a good breakfast as myself; when we have done, I will tell you."

Accordingly, both mother and son sat down, and ate with the better relish as the table was so well furnished. But all the time Aladdin's mother could not forbear looking at and admiring the tray and dishes, though she could not judge whether they were silver or any other metal, and the novelty more than the value attracted her attention.

The mother and son sat at breakfast till it was dinner time, and then they thought it would be best to put the two meals together; yet after this they found they should have enough left for supper, and two meals for the next day.

When Aladdin's mother had taken away and set by what was left, she went and sat down by her son on the sofa, saying, "I expect now that you should satisfy my impatience, and tell me exactly what passed between the genie and you while I was in a swoon"; which he readily complied with.

She was in as great amazement at what her son told her as at the appearance of the genie; and said to him, "But, son, what have we to do with genies? I never heard that any of my acquaintance had ever seen one. How came that vile genie to address himself to me, and not to you, to whom he had appeared before in the cave?" "Mother," answered Aladdin, "the genie you saw is not the one who appeared to me. If you remember, he that I first saw called himself the slave of the ring on my finger; and this you saw called himself the slave of the lamp you had in your hand; but I believe you did not hear him, for I think you fainted as soon as he began to speak."

"What!" cried the mother, "was your lamp, then, the occasion of that cursed genie's addressing himself rather to me than to you? Ah! my son, take it out of my sight, and put it where you please. I had rather you would sell it than run the hazard of being frightened to death again by touching it; and if you would take my advice you would part also with the ring, and not have anything to do with genies, who, as our prophet has told us, are only devils."

"With your leave, mother," replied Aladdin, "I shall now take care how I sell a lamp which may be so serviceable both to you and me. That false and wicked magician would not have undertaken so long a journey to secure this wonderful lamp if he had not known its value to exceed that of gold and silver. And since we have honestly come by it, let us make a profitable use of it, without making any great show, and exciting the envy and jealousy of our neighbors. However, since the genies frighten you so much I will take it out of your sight, and put it where I may find it when I want it. The ring I cannot resolve to part with; for without that you had never seen me again; and though I am alive now, perhaps, if it were gone, I might not be so some moments hence; therefore, I hope you will give me leave to keep it, and to wear it always on my finger."

Aladdin's mother replied that he might do what he pleased; for her part she would have nothing to do with genies, and never say anything more about them.

By the next night they had eaten all the provisions the genie had brought; and the next day Aladdin, who could not bear the thought of hunger, putting one of the silver dishes under his vest, went out early to sell it, and addressing himself to a Jew whom he met in the streets, took him aside, and pulling out the plate, asked him if he would buy it. The cunning Jew took the dish, examined it, and as soon as he found that it was good silver asked Aladdin at how much he valued it. Aladdin, who had never been used to such traffic, told him he would trust to his judgment and honor. The Jew was somewhat confounded at this plain dealing; and doubting whether Aladdin understood the material or the full value of what he offered to sell, took a piece of gold out of his purse and gave it him, though it was but the sixtieth part of the worth of the plate. Aladdin, taking the money very eagerly, retired with so much haste that the Jew, not content with the exorbitancy of his profit, was vexed he had not penetrated into his ignorance, and was going to run after him, to endeavor to get some change out of the piece of gold; but he ran so fast, and had got so far, that it would have been impossible for him to overtake him.

Before Aladdin went home he called at a baker's, bought some cakes of bread, changed his money, and on his return gave the rest to his mother, who went and purchased provisions enough to last them some time. After this manner they lived, till Aladdin had sold the twelve dishes singly, as necessity pressed, to the Jew, for the same money; who, after the first time, durst not offer him less for fear of losing so good a bargain. When he had sold the last dish he had recourse to the tray, which weighed ten times as much as the dishes, and would have carried it to his old purchaser, but that it was too large and cumbersome; therefore he was obliged to bring him home with him to his mother's, where, after the Jew had examined the weight of the tray, he laid down ten pieces of gold, with which Aladdin was very well satisfied.

When all the money was spent, Aladdin had recourse again to the lamp. He took it in his hand, looked for that part where his mother had rubbed it with the sand, rubbed it also, when the genie immediately appeared, and said, "What wouldst thou have? I am ready to obey thee as thy slave, and the slave of all those who have that lamp in their hands; I and the other slaves of the lamp." "I am hungry," said Aladdin; "bring me something to eat." The genie disappeared, and presently returned with a tray, the same number of covered dishes as before, set them down, and vanished.

As soon as Aladdin found that their provisions were again expended, he took one of the dishes, and went to look for his Jew chapman; but passing by a goldsmith's shop, the goldsmith perceiving him called to him and said, "My lad, I imagine that you have something to sell to the Jew, whom I often see you visit; but perhaps you do not know that he is the greatest rogue even among the Jews.

I will give you the full worth of what you have to sell, or I will direct you to other merchants who will not cheat you."

This offer induced Aladdin to pull his plate from under his vest and show it to the goldsmith, who at first sight saw that it was made of the finest silver, and asked him if he had sold such as that to the Jew; when Aladdin told him that he had sold him twelve such, for a piece of gold each. "What a villain!" cried the goldsmith. "But," added he, "my son, what is past cannot be recalled. By showing you the value of this plate, which is of the finest silver we use in our shops, I will let you see how much the Jew has cheated you."

The goldsmith took a pair of scales, weighed the dish, and assured him that his plate would fetch by weight sixty pieces of gold, which he offered to pay down immediately.

Aladdin thanked him for his fair dealing, and never after went to any other person.

Though Aladdin and his mother had an inexhaustible treasure in their lamp, and might have had whatever they wished for, yet they lived with the same frugality as before, and it may easily be supposed that the money for which Aladdin had sold the dishes and tray was sufficient to maintain them some time.

During this interval, Aladdin frequented the shops of the principal merchants, where they sold cloth of gold and silver, linens, silk stuffs, and jewelry, and oftentimes joining in their conversation, acquired a knowledge of the world and a desire to improve himself. By his acquaintance among the jewellers he came to know that the fruits which he had gathered when he took the lamp were, instead of colored glass, stones of inestimable value; but he had the prudence not to mention this to anyone, not even to his mother.

One day as Aladdin was walking about the town he heard an order proclaimed commanding the people to shut up their shops and houses, and keep within doors while the Princess Buddir al Buddoor, the sultan's daughter, went to the bath and returned.

This proclamation inspired Aladdin with an eager desire to see the princess's face, which he determined to gratify by placing himself behind the door of the bath, so that he could not fail to see her face.

Aladdin had not long concealed himself before the princess came. She was attended by a great crowd of ladies, slaves, and mutes, who walked on each side and behind her. When she came within three or four paces of the door of the bath, she took off her veil, and gave Aladdin an opportunity of a full view of her face.

The princess was a noted beauty: her eyes were large, lively, and sparkling; her smile bewitching; her nose faultless; her mouth small; her lips vermilion. It is not therefore surprising that Aladdin, who had never before seen such a blaze of charms, was dazzled and enchanted.

After the princess had passed by, and entered the bath, Aladdin quitted his hiding-place and went home. His mother perceived him to be more thoughtful and melancholy than usual, and asked what had happened to make him so, or if he was ill. He then told his mother all his adventure, and concluded by declaring, "I love the princess more than I can express, and am resolved that I will ask her in marriage of the sultan."

Aladdin's mother listened with surprise to what her son told her; but when he talked of asking the princess in marriage, she laughed aloud. "Alas! child," said she, "what are you thinking of? You must be mad to talk thus."

"I assure you, mother," replied Aladdin, "that I am not mad, but in my right senses. I foresaw that you would reproach me with folly and extravagance; but I must tell you once more that I am resolved to demand the princess of the sultan in marriage, nor do I despair of success. I have the slaves of the Lamp and of the Ring to help me, and you know how powerful their aid is. And I have another secret to tell you: those pieces of glass, which I got from the trees in the garden of the subterranean palace, are jewels of inestimable value, and fit for the greatest monarchs. All the precious stones the jewellers have in Bagdad are not to be compared to mine for size or beauty; and I am sure that the offer of them will secure the favor of the sultan. You have a large porcelain dish fit to hold them; fetch it, and let us see how they will look, when we have arranged them according to their different colors."

Aladdin's mother brought the china dish, when he took the jewels out of the two purses in which he had kept them, and placed them in order according to his fancy. But the brightness and lustre they emitted in the daytime, and the variety of the colors, so dazzled the eyes both of mother and son that they were astonished beyond measure. Aladdin's mother, emboldened by the sight of these rich jewels, and fearful lest her son should be guilty of greater extravagance, complied with his request, and promised to go early in the next morning to the palace of the sultan. Aladdin rose before daybreak, awakened his mother, pressing her to go to the sultan's palace, and to get admittance, if possible, before the grand vizier, the other viziers, and the great officers of state went in to take their seats in the divan, where the sultan always attended in person.

Aladdin's mother took the china dish, in which they had put the jewels the day before, wrapped it in two fine napkins, and set forward for the sultan's palace. When she came to the gates, the grand vizier, the other viziers, and most distinguished lords of the court were just gone in; but notwithstanding the crowd of people was great, she got into the divan, a spacious hall, the entrance into which was very magnificent. She placed herself just before the sultan, grand vizier, and the great lords, who sat in council on his right and left hand. Several causes were called, according to their order, pleaded and adjudged, until the time the divan generally broke up, when the sultan, rising, returned to his apartment, attended by the grand vizier; the other viziers and ministers of state then retired, as also did all those whose business had called them thither.

Aladdin's mother, seeing the sultan retire, and all the people depart, judged rightly that he would not sit again that day, and resolved to go home; and on her arrival said, with much simplicity, "Son, I have seen the sultan, and am very well persuaded he has seen me too, for I placed myself just before him; but he was so much taken up with those who attended on all sides of him, that I pitied him and wondered at his patience. At last I believe he was heartily tired, for he rose up suddenly, and would not hear a great many who were ready prepared to speak to him, but went away, at which I was well pleased, for indeed I began to lose all patience, and was extremely fatigued with staying so long. But there is no harm done: I will go again tomorrow; perhaps the sultan may not be so busy."

The next morning she repaired to the sultan's palace with the present, as early as the day before; but when she came there she found the gates of the divan shut. She went six times afterward on the days appointed, placed herself always directly before the sultan, but with as little success as the first morning.

On the sixth day, however, after the divan was broken up, when the sultan returned to his own apartment, he said to his grand vizier, "I have for some time observed a certain woman, who attends constantly every day that I give audience, with something wrapped up in a napkin; she always stands up from the beginning to the breaking up of the audience, and affects to place herself just before me. If this woman comes to our next audience, do not fail to call her, that I may hear what she has to say." The grand vizier made answer by lowering his hand, and then lifting it up above his head, signifying his willingness to lose it if he failed.

On the next audience day, when Aladdin's mother went to the divan, and placed herself in front of the sultan as usual, the grand vizier immediately called the chief of the mace-bearers, and, pointing to her, bade him bring her before the sultan. The old woman at once followed the mace-bearer, and when she reached the sultan, bowed her head down to the carpet which covered the platform of the throne, and remained in that posture till he bade her rise, which she had no sooner done than he said to her, "Good woman, I have observed you to stand many days, from the beginning to the rising of the divan; what business brings you here?"

After these words, Aladdin's mother prostrated herself a second time, and, when she arose, said, "Monarch of monarchs I beg of you to pardon the boldness of my petition, and to assure me of your pardon and forgiveness." "Well,". replied the sultan, "I will forgive you, be it what it may, and no hurt shall come to you. Speak boldly."

When Aladdin's mother had taken all these precautions for fear of the sultan's anger, she told him faithfully the errand on which her son had sent her, and the event which led to his making so bold a request in spite of all her remonstrances.

The sultan hearkened to this discourse without showing the least anger; but, before he gave her any answer, asked her what she had brought tied up in the napkin. She took the china dish, which she had set down at the foot of the throne, untied it, and presented it to the sultan.

The sultan's amazement and surprise were inexpressible when he saw so many large, beautiful, and valuable jewels collected in the dish. He remained for some time lost in admiration. At last, when he had recovered himself, he received the present from Aladdin's mother's hand, saying, "How rich! how beautiful!" After he had admired and handled all the jewels one after another, he turned to his grand vizier, and, showing him the dish, said, "Behold! admire! wonder! and confess that your eyes never beheld jewels so rich and beautiful before!" The vizier was charmed. "Well," continued the sultan, "what sayest thou to such a present? Is it not worthy of the princess my daughter? And ought I not to bestow her on one who values her at so great a price?" "I cannot but own," replied the grand vizier, "that the present is worthy of the princess; but I beg of your majesty to grant me three months before you come to a final resolution. I hope before that time my son, whom you have regarded with your favor, will be able to make a nobler present than this Aladdin, who is an entire stranger to your majesty."

The sultan granted his request, and he said to the old woman, "Good woman, go home, and tell your son that I agree to the proposal you have made me; but I cannot marry the princess my daughter for three months. At the expiration of that time come again."

Aladdin's mother returned home much more gratified than she had expected, and told her son with much joy the condescending answer she had received from the sultan's own mouth; and that she was to come to the divan again that day three months.

Aladdin thought himself the most happy of all men at hearing this news, and thanked his mother for the pains she had taken in the affair, the good success of which was of so great importance to his peace that he counted every day, week, and even hour as it passed. When two of the three months were passed, his mother one evening, having no oil in the house, went out to buy some, and found a general rejoicing—the houses dressed with foliage, silks, and carpeting, and every one striving to show their joy according to their ability. The streets were crowded with officers in habits of ceremony, mounted on horses richly caparisoned, each attended by a great many footmen. Aladdin's mother asked the oil merchant what was the meaning of all this preparation of public festivity. "Whence came you, good woman," said he, "that you don't know that the grand vizier's son is to marry the princess Buddir al Buddoor, the sultan's daughter, to-night? She will presently return from the bath; and these officers whom you see are to assist at the cavalcade to the palace, where the ceremony is to be solemnized."

Aladdin's mother on hearing this news ran home very quickly. "Child," cried she, "you are undone; the sultan's fine promise will come to naught! This night the grand vizier's son is to marry the Princess Buddir al Buddoor."

At this account Aladdin was thunderstruck, and he bethought himself of the lamp, and of the genie who had promised to obey him; and without indulging in idle words against the sultan, the vizier, or his son, he determined, if possible, to prevent the marriage.

When Aladdin had got into his chamber, he took the lamp, rubbed it in the same place as before, when immediately the genie appeared, and said to him, "What wouldst thou have? I am ready to obey thee as thy slave; I and the other slaves of the lamp." "Hear me," said Aladdin. "Thou hast hitherto obeyed me; but now I am about to impose on thee a harder task. The sultan's daughter, who was promised me as my bride, is this night married to the son of the grand vizier. Bring them both hither to me immediately they retire to their bedchamber."

"Master," replied the genie, "I obey you."

Aladdin supped with his mother as was their wont, and then went to his own apartment, and sat up to await the return of the genie, according to his commands.

In the meantime, the festivities in honor of the princess's marriage were conducted in the sultan's palace with great magnificence. The ceremonies were at last brought to a conclusion, and the princess and the son of the vizier retired to the bedchamber prepared for them. No sooner had they entered it and dismissed their attendants, than the genie, the faithful slave of the lamp, to the great amazement and alarm of the bride and bridegroom, took up the bed, and, by an agency invisible to them, transported it in an instant into Aladdin's chamber, where he set it down. "Remove the bridegroom," said Aladdin to the genie, "and keep him a prisoner till to-morrow dawn, and then return with him here." On Aladdin being left alone with the princess, he endeavored to assuage her fears, and explained to her the treachery practised upon him by the sultan her father. He then laid himself down beside her, putting a drawn scimitar between them, to show that he was determined to secure her safety, and to treat her with the utmost possible respect. At break of day the genie appeared at the appointed hour, bringing back the bridegroom, whom, by breathing upon, he had left motionless and entranced at the door of Aladdin's chamber during the night; and, at Aladdin's command, transported the couch with the bride and bridegroom on it, by the same invisible agency, into the palace of the sultan.

At the instant that the genie had set down the couch with the bride and bridegroom in their own chamber, the sultan came to the door to offer his good wishes to his daughter.

The grand vizier's son, who was almost perished with cold by standing in his thin under-garment all night, no sooner heard the knocking at the door than he got out of bed and ran into the robing chamber, where he had undressed himself the night before.

The sultan, having opened the door, went to the bedside, kissed the princess on the forehead, but was extremely surprised to see her look so melancholy. She only cast at him a sorrowful look, expressive of great affliction. He suspected there was something extraordinary in this silence, and thereupon went immediately to the sultaness's apartment, told her in what a state he found the princess, and how she had received him. "Sire," said the sultaness, "I will go and see her; she will not receive me in the same manner."

The princess received her mother with sighs and tears, and signs of deep dejection. At last, upon her pressing on her the duty of telling her all her thoughts, she gave to the sultaness a precise description of all that happened to her during the night; on which the sultaness enjoined on her the necessity of silence and discretion, as no one would give credence to so strange a tale. The grand vizier's son, elated with the honor of being the sultan's son-in-law, kept silence on his part, and the events of the night were not allowed to cast the least gloom on the festivities on the following day, in continued celebration of the royal marriage.

When night came the bride and bridegroom were again attended to their chamber with the same ceremonies as on the preceding evening. Aladdin, knowing that this would be so, had already given his commands to the genie of the lamp; and no sooner were they alone than their bed was removed in the same mysterious manner as on the preceding evening; and having passed the night in the same unpleasant way, they were in the morning conveyed to the palace of the sultan. Scarcely had they been replaced in their apartment than the sultan came to make his compliments to his daughter, when the princess could no longer conceal from him the unhappy treatment she had been subjected to, and told him all that had happened, as she had already related it to her mother. The sultan, on hearing these strange tidings, consulted with the grand vizier; and finding from him that his son had been subjected to even worse treatment by an invisible agency, he determined to declare the marriage to be cancelled, and all the festivities, which were yet to last for several days, to be countermanded and terminated.

This sudden change in the mind of the sultan gave rise to various speculations and reports. Nobody but Aladdin knew the secret, and he kept it with the most scrupulous silence; and neither the sultan nor the grand vizier, who had forgotten Aladdin and his request, had the least thought that he had any hand in the strange adventures that befel the bride and bridegroom.

On the very day that the three months contained in the sultan's promise expired, the mother of Aladdin again went to the palace, and stood in the same place in the divan. The sultan knew her again, and directed his vizier to have her brought before him.

After having prostrated herself she made answer, in reply to the sultan: "Sire, I come at the end of three months to ask of you the fulfilment of the promise you made to my son." The sultan little thought the request of Aladdin's mother was made to him in earnest, or that he would hear any more of the matter. He therefore took counsel with his vizier, who suggested that the sultan should attach such conditions to the marriage that no one in the humble condition of Aladdin could possibly fulfil.

In accordance with this suggestion of the vizier, the sultan replied to the mother of Aladdin: "Good woman, it is true sultans ought to abide by their word, and I am ready to keep mine, by making your son happy in marriage with the princess my daughter. But as I cannot marry her without some further proof of your son being able to support her in royal state, you may tell him I will fulfil my promise as soon as he shall send me forty trays of massy gold, full of the same sort of jewels you have already made me a present of, and carried by the like number of black slaves, who shall be led by as many young and handsome white slaves, all dressed magnificently. On these conditions I am ready to bestow the princess my daughter upon him; therefore, good woman, go and tell him so, and I will wait till you bring me his answer."

Aladdin's mother prostrated herself a second time before the sultan's throne, and retired. On her way home she laughed within herself at her son's foolish imagination. "Where," said she, "can he get so many large gold trays, and such precious stones to fill them? It is altogether out of his power, and I believe he will not be much pleased with my embassy this time." When she came home, full of these thoughts, she told Aladdin all the circumstances of her interview with the sultan, and the conditions on which he consented to the marriage. "The sultan expects your answer immediately," said she; and then added, laughing, "I believe he may wait long enough!"

"Not so long, mother, as you imagine," replied Aladdin. "This demand is a mere trifle, and will prove no bar to my marriage with the princess. I will prepare at once to satisfy his request."

Aladdin retired to his own apartment and summoned the genie of the lamp, and required him to immediately prepare and present the gift, before the sultan closed his morning audience, according to the terms in which it had been prescribed. The genie professed his obedience to the owner of the lamp, and disappeared. Within a very short time, a train of forty black slaves, led by the same number of white slaves, appeared opposite the house in which Aladdin lived. Each black slave carried on his head a basin of massy gold, full of pearls, diamonds, rubies, and emeralds. Aladdin then addressed his mother; "Madam, pray lose no time; before the sultan and the divan rise, I would have you return to the palace with this present as the dowry demanded for the princess, that he may judge by my diligence and exactness of the ardent and sincere desire I have to procure myself the honor of this alliance."

As soon as this magnificent procession, with Aladdin's mother at its head, had begun to march from Aladdin's house, the whole city was filled with the crowds of people desirous to see so grand a sight. The graceful bearing, elegant form, and wonderful likeness of each slave; their grave walk at an equal distance from each other; the lustre of their jewelled girdles, and the brilliancy of the aigrettes of precious stones in their turbans, excited the greatest admiration in the spectators. As they had to pass through several streets to the palace, the whole length of the way was lined with files of spectators. Nothing, indeed, was ever seen so beautiful and brilliant in the sultan's palace, and the richest robes of the emirs of his court were not to be compared to the costly dresses of these slaves, whom they supposed to be kings.

As the sultan, who had been informed of their approach, had given orders for them to be admitted, they met with no obstacle, but went into the divan in regular order, one part turning to the right, and the other to the left. After they were all entered, and had formed a semi-circle before the sultan's throne, the black slaves laid the golden trays on the carpet, prostrated themselves, touching the carpet with their foreheads, and at the same time the white slaves did the same. When they rose, the black slaves uncovered the trays, and then all stood with their arms crossed over their breasts.

In the meantime, Aladdin's mother advanced to the foot of the throne, and having prostrated herself, said to the sultan, "Sire, my son knows this present is much below the notice of Princess Buddir al Buddoor; but hopes, nevertheless, that your majesty will accept of it, and make it agreeable to the princess, and with the greater confidence since he has endeavored to conform to the conditions you were pleased to impose."

The sultan, overpowered at the sight of such more than royal magnificence, replied without hesitation to the words of Aladdin's mother: "Go and tell your son that I wait with open arms to embrace him; and the more haste he makes to come and receive the princess my daughter from my hands, the greater pleasure he will do me." As soon as Aladdin's mother had retired, the sultan put an end to the audience; and rising from his throne, ordered that the princess's attendants should come and carry the trays into their mistress's apartment, whither he went himself to examine them with her at his leisure. The fourscore slaves were conducted into the palace; and the sultan, telling the princess of their magnificent apparel, ordered them to be brought before her apartment, that she might see through the lattices he had not exaggerated in his account of them.

In the meantime Aladdin's mother reached home, and showed in her air and countenance the good news she brought her son. "My son," said she, "you may rejoice you are arrived at the height of your desires. The sultan has declared that you shall marry the Princess Buddir al Buddoor. He waits for you with impatience."

Aladdin, enraptured with this news, made his mother very little reply, but retired to his chamber. There he rubbed his lamp, and the obedient genie appeared. "Genie," said Aladdin, "convey me at once to a bath, and supply me with the richest and most magnificent robe ever worn by a monarch."

No sooner were the words out of his mouth than the genie rendered him, as well as himself, invisible, and transported him into a hummum of the finest marble of all sorts of colors, where he was undressed, without seeing by whom, in a magnificent and spacious hall. He was then well rubbed and washed with various scented waters. After he had passed through several degrees of heat, he came out quite a different man from what he was before. His skin was clear as that of a child, his body lightsome and free; and when he returned into the hall, he found, instead of his own poor raiment, a robe the magnificence of which astonished him. The genie helped him to dress, and when he had done, transported him back to his own chamber, where he asked him if he had any other commands. "Yes," answered Aladdin; "bring me a charger that surpasses in beauty and goodness the best in the sultan's stables, with a saddle, bridle, and other caparisons to correspond with his value. Furnish also twenty slaves, as richly clothed as those who carried the present to the sultan, to walk by my side and follow me, and twenty more to go before me in two ranks. Besides these, bring my mother six women slaves to attend her, as richly dressed at least as any of the Princess Buddir al Buddoor's, each carrying a complete dress fit for any sultaness. I want also ten thousand pieces of gold in ten purses; go, and make haste,"

As soon as Aladdin had given these orders, the genie disappeared, but presently returned with the horse, the forty slaves, ten of whom carried each a purse containing ten thousand pieces of gold, and six women slaves, each carrying on her head a different dress for Aladdin's mother, wrapped up in a piece of silver tissue, and presented them all to Aladdin.

He presented the six women slaves to his mother, telling her they were her slaves, and that the dresses they had brought were for her use. Cf the ten purses Aladdin took four, which he gave to his mother, telling her those were to supply her with necessaries; the other six he left in the hands of the slaves who brought them, with an order to throw them by handfuls among the people as they went to the sultan's palace. The six slaves who carried the purses he ordered likewise to march before him, three on the right hand and three on the left.

When Aladdin had thus prepared himself for his first interview with the sultan, he dismissed the genie, and immediately mounting his charger, began his march, and though he never was on horseback before, appeared with a grace the most experienced horseman might envy. The innumerable concourse of people through whom he passed made the air echo with their acclamations, especially every time the six slaves who carried the purses threw handfuls of gold among the populace.

On Aladdin's arrival at the palace, the sultan was surprised to find him more richly and magnificently robed than he had ever been himself, and was impressed with his good looks and dignity of manner, which were so different from what he expected in the son of one so humble as Aladdin's mother. He embraced him with all the demonstrations of joy, and when he would have fallen at his feet, held him by the hand, and made him sit near his throne. He shortly after led him, amid the sounds of trumpets, hautboys, and all kinds of music, to a magnificent entertainment, at which the sultan and Aladdin ate by themselves, and the great lords of the court, according to their rank and dignity, sat at different tables. After the feast the sultan sent for the chief cadi, and commanded him to draw up a contract of marriage between the Princess Buddir al Buddoor and Aladdin. When the contract had been drawn, the sultan asked Aladdin if he would stay in the palace and complete the ceremonies of the marriage that day.

"Sire," said Aladdin, "though great is my impatience to enter on the honor granted me by your majesty, yet I beg you to permit me first to build a palace worthy to receive the princess your daughter. I pray you to grant me sufficient ground near your palace, and I will have it completed with the utmost expedition."

The sultan granted Aladdin his request, and again embraced him. After which he took his leave with as much politeness as if he had been bred up and had always lived at court.

Aladdin returned home in the order he had come, amid the acclamations of the people, who wished him all happiness and prosperity. As soon as he dismounted, he retired to his own chamber, took the lamp, and summoned the genie as usual, who professed his allegiance.

"Genie," said Aladdin, "build me a palace fit to receive the Princess Buddir al Buddoor. Let its materials be made of nothing less than porphyry, jasper, agate, lapis-lazuli, and the finest marble. Let its walls be massive gold and silver bricks laid alternately. Let each front contain six windows, and let the lattices of these (except one, which must be left unfinished) be enriched with diamonds, rubies, and emeralds, so that they shall exceed everything of the kind ever seen in the world. Let there be an inner and outer court in front of the palace, and a spacious garden; but, above all things, provide a safe treasure-house, and fill it with gold and silver. Let there be also kitchens and storehouses, stables full of the finest horses, with their equerries and grooms, and hunting equipage, officers, attendants, and slaves, both men and women, to form a retinue for the princess and myself. Go and execute my wishes."

When Aladdin gave these commands to the genie the sun was set. The next morning at daybreak the genie presented himself, and having obtained Aladdin's consent, transported him in a moment to the palace he had made. The genie led him through all the apartments, where he found officers and slaves, habited according to their rank and the services to which they were appointed. The genie then showed him the treasury, which was opened by a treasurer, where Aladdin saw large vases of different sizes, piled up to the top with money, ranged all round the chamber. The genie thence led him to the stables, where were some of the finest horses in the world, and the grooms busy in dressing them; from thence they went to the storehouses, which were filled with all things necessary, both for food and ornament.

When Aladdin had examined every portion of the palace, and particularly the hall with the four-and-twenty windows, and found it to far exceed his fondest expectations, he said, "Genie, there is one thing wanting—a fine carpet for the princess to walk upon from the sultan's palace to mine. Lay one down immediately."

The genie disappeared, and Aladdin saw what he desired executed in an instant. The genie then returned and carried him to his own home.

When the sultan's porters came to open the gates they were amazed to find what had been an unoccupied garden filled up with a magnificent palace, and a splendid carpet extending to it all the way from the sultan's palace. They told the strange tidings to the grand vizier, who informed the sultan, who exclaimed, "It must be Aladdin's palace, which I gave him leave to build for my daughter. He has wished to surprise us, and let us see what wonders can be done in only one night."

Aladdin, on his being conveyed by the genie to his own home, requested his mother to go to the Princess Buddir al Buddoor, and tell her that the palace would be ready for her reception in the evening. She went, attended by her women slaves, in the same order as on the preceding day. Shortly after her arrival at the princess's apartment, the sultan himself came in, and was surprised to find her, whom he knew as his suppliant at his divan in such humble guise, to be now more richly and sumptuously attired than his own daughter. This gave him a higher opinion of Aladdin, who took such care of his mother, and made her share his wealth and honors. Shortly after her departure Aladdin, mounting his horse, and attended by his retinue of magnificent attendants, left his paternal home forever, and went to the palace in the same pomp as on the day before. Nor did he forget to take with him the wonderful lamp, to which he owed all his good-fortune, nor to wear the ring which was given him as a talisman. The sultan entertained Aladdin with the utmost magnificence, and at night, on the conclusion of the marriage ceremonies, the princess took leave of the sultan her father. Bands of music led the procession, followed by a hundred state ushers, and the like number of black mutes, in two files, with their officers at their head. Four hundred of the sultan's young pages carried flambeaux on each side, which, together with the illuminations of the sultan's and Aladdin's palaces, made it as light as day. In this order the princess, conveyed in her litter, and accompanied also by Aladdin's mother, carried in a superb litter and attended by her women slaves, proceeded on the carpet which was spread from the sultan's palace to that of Aladdin. On her arrival Aladdin was ready to receive her at the entrance, and led her into a large hall, illuminated with an infinite number of wax candles, where a noble feast was served up. The dishes were of massy gold, and contained the most delicate viands. The vases, basins, and goblets were gold also, and of exquisite workmanship, and all the other ornaments and embellishments of the hall were answerable to this display. The princess, dazzled to see so much riches collected in one place, said to Aladdin: "I thought, prince, that nothing in the world was so beautiful as the sultan my father's palace, but the sight of this hall alone is sufficient to show I was deceived."

When the supper was ended, there entered a company of female dancers, who performed, according to the custom of the country, singing at the same time verses in praise of the bride and bridegroom.

About midnight Aladdin's mother conducted the bride to the nuptial apartment, and he soon after retired.

The next morning the attendants of Aladdin presented themselves to dress him, and brought him another habit, as rich and magnificent as that worn the day before. He then ordered one of the horses to be got ready, mounted him, and went in the midst of a large troop of slaves to the sultan's palace, to entreat him to take a repast in the princess's palace, attended by his grand vizier and all the lords of his court. The sultan consented with pleasure, rose up immediately, and, preceded by the principal officers of his palace, and followed by all the great lords of his court, accompanied Aladdin.

The nearer the sultan approached Aladdin's palace the more he was struck with its beauty; but when he entered it, came into the hall, and saw the windows enriched with diamonds, rubies, emeralds, all large, perfect stones, he was completely surprised, and said to his son-in-law: "This palace is one of the wonders of the world; for where in all the world besides shall we find walls built of massy gold and silver, and diamonds, rubies, and emeralds composing the windows? But what most surprises me is that a hall of this magnificence should be left with one of its windows incomplete and unfinished." "Sire," answered Aladdin, "the omission was by design, since I wished that you should have the glory of finishing this hall." "I take your intention kindly," said the sultan, "and will give orders about it immediately."

After the sultan had finished this magnificent entertainment provided for him and for his court by Aladdin, he was informed that the jewellers and goldsmiths attended; upon which he returned to the hall, and showed them the window which was unfinished. "I sent for you," said he, "to fit up this window in as great perfection as the rest. Examine them well, and make all the despatch you can."

The jewellers and goldsmiths examined the three-and-twenty windows with great attention, and after they had consulted together, to know what each could furnish, they returned, and presented themselves before the sultan, whose principal jeweller, undertaking to speak for the rest, said: "Sire, we are all willing to exert our utmost care and industry to obey you; but among us all we cannot furnish jewels enough for so great a work." "I have more than are necessary," said the sultan; "come to my palace, and you shall choose what may answer your purpose."

When the sultan returned to his palace, he ordered his jewels to be brought out, and the jewellers took a great quantity, particularly those Aladdin had made him a present of, which they soon used, without making any great advance in their work. They came again several times for more, and in a month's time had not finished half their work. In short, they used all the jewels the sultan had, and borrowed of the vizier, but yet the work was not half done.

Aladdin, who knew that all the sultan's endeavors to make this window like the rest were in vain, sent for the jewellers and goldsmiths, and not only commanded them to desist from their work, but ordered them to undo what they had begun, and to carry all their jewels back to the sultan and to the vizier. They undid in a few hours what they had been six weeks about, and retired, leaving Aladdin alone in the hall. He took the lamp, which he carried about him, rubbed it, and presently the genie appeared. "Genie," said Aladdin, "I ordered thee to leave one of the four- and-twenty windows of this hall imperfect, and thou hast executed my commands punctually; now I would have thee make it like the rest." The genie immediately disappeared. Aladdin went out of the hall, and returning soon after, found the window, as he wished it to be, like the others.

In the meantime, the jewellers and goldsmiths repaired to the palace, and were introduced into the sultan's presence, where the chief jeweller presented the precious stones which he had brought back. The sultan asked them if Aladdin had given them any reason for so doing, and they answering that he had given them none, he ordered a horse to be brought, which he mounted, and rode to his son-in-law's palace, with some few attendants on foot, to inquire why he had ordered the completion of the window to be stopped. Aladdin met him at the gate, and without giving any reply to his inquiries conducted him to the grand saloon, where the sultan, to his great surprise, found the window which was left imperfect to correspond exactly with the others. He fancied at first that he was mistaken, and examined the two windows on each side, and afterward all the four and twenty; but when he was convinced that the window which several workmen had been so long about was finished in so short a time, he embraced Aladdin and kissed him between his eyes. "My son," said he, "what a man you are to do such surprising things always in the twinkling of an eye! There is not your fellow in the world; the more I know, the more I admire you."

The sultan returned to the palace, and after this went frequently to the window to contemplate and admire the wonderful palace of his son-in-law.

Aladdin did not confine himself in his palace, but went with much state, sometimes to one mosque, and sometimes to another, to prayers, or to visit the grand vizier, or the principal lords of the court. Every time he went out, he caused two slaves, who walked by the side of his horse, to throw handfuls of money among the people as he passed through the streets and squares. This generosity gained him the love and blessings of the people, and it was common for them to swear by his head. Thus Aladdin, while he paid all respect to the sultan, won by his affable behavior and liberality the affections of the people.

Aladdin had conducted himself in this manner several years, when the African magician, who had for some years dismissed him from his recollection, determined to inform himself with certainty whether he perished, as he supposed, in the subterranean cave or not. After he had resorted to a long course of magic ceremonies, and had formed a horoscope by which to ascertain Aladdin's fate, what was his surprise to find the appearances to declare that Aladdin, instead of dying in the cave, had made his escape, and was living in royal splendor, by the aid of the genie of the wonderful lamp!

On the very next day, the magician set out and travelled with the utmost haste to the capital of China, where, on his arrival, he took up his lodging in a khan.

He then quickly learned about the wealth, charities, happiness, and splendid palace of Prince Aladdin. Directly he saw the wonderful fabric, he knew that none but the genies, the slaves of the lamp, could have performed such wonders; and piqued to the quick at Aladdin's high estate, he returned to the khan.

On his return he had recourse to an operation of geomancy to find out where the lamp was—whether Aladdin carried it about with him, or where he left it. The result of his consultation informed him, to his great joy, that the lamp was in the palace. "Well," said he, rubbing his hands in glee, "I shall have the lamp, and I shall make Aladdin return to his original mean condition."

The next day the magician learned, from the chief superintendent of the khan where he lodged, that Aladdin had gone on a hunting expedition, which was to last for eight days, of which only three had expired. The magician wanted to know no more. He resolved at once on his plans. He went to a coppersmith, and asked for a dozen copper lamps: the master of the shop told him he had not so many by him, but if he would have patience till the next day, he would have them ready. The magician appointed his time, and desired him to take care that they should be handsome and well polished.

The next day the magician called for the twelve lamps, paid the man his full price, put them into a basket hanging on his arm, and went directly to Aladdin's palace. As he approached, he began crying, "Who will change old lamps for new ones?" As he went along, a crowd of children collected, who hooted, and thought him, as did all who chanced to be passing by, a madman or a fool, to offer to change new lamps for old ones.

The African magician regarded not their scoffs, hootings, or all they could say to him, but still continued crying, "Who will change old lamps for new ones?" He repeated this so often, walking backward and forward in front of the palace, that the princess, who was then in the hall with the four-and-twenty windows, hearing a man cry something, and seeing a great mob crowding about him, sent one of her women slaves to know what he cried.

The slave returned laughing so heartily that the princess rebuked her. "Madam," answered the slave, laughing still, "who can forbear laughing, to see an old man with a basket on his arm, full of fine new lamps, asking to change them for old ones? The children and mob crowding about him so that he can hardly stir, make all the noise they can in derision of him."

Another female slave, hearing this, said: "Now you speak of lamps, I know not whether the princess may have observed it, but there is an old one upon a shelf of the Prince Aladdin's robing-room, and whoever owns it will not be sorry to find a new one in its stead. If the princess chooses, she may have the pleasure of trying if this old man is so silly as to give a new lamp for an old one, without taking anything for the exchange."

The princess, who knew not the value of this lamp, and the interest that Aladdin had to keep it safe, entered into the pleasantry, and commanded a slave to take it and make the exchange. The slave obeyed, went out of the hall, and no sooner got to the palace gates than he saw the African magician, called to him, and, showing him the old lamp, said, "Give me a new lamp for this."

The magician never doubted but this was the lamp he wanted. There could be no other such in this palace, where every utensil was gold or silver. He snatched it eagerly out of the slave's hand, and, thrusting it as far as he could into his breast, offered him his basket, and bade him choose which he liked best. The slave picked out one, and carried it to the princess; but the change was no sooner made than the place rung with the shouts of the children, deriding the magician's folly.

The African magician stayed no longer near the palace, nor cried any more, "New lamps for old ones!" but made the best of his way to his khan.

His end was answered; and by his silence he got rid of the children and the mob.

As soon as he was out of sight of the two palaces, he hastened down the least frequented streets; and, having no more occasion for his lamps or basket, set all down in a spot where nobody saw him. Then going down another street or two, he walked till he came to one of the city gates, and pursuing his way through the suburbs, which were very extensive, at length reached a lonely spot, where he stopped till the darkness of the night, as the most suitable time for the design he had in contemplation. When it became quite dark, he pulled the lamp out of his breast and rubbed it. At that summons the genie appeared, and said, "What wouldst thou have? I am ready to obey thee as thy slave, and the slave of all those who have that lamp in their hands; both I and the other slaves of the lamp." "I command thee," replied the magician, "to transport me immediately, and the palace which thou and the other slaves of the lamp have built in this dity, with all the people in it, to Africa." The genie made no reply, but, with the assistance of the other genies, the slaves of the lamp, immediately transported him and the palace entire to the spot whither he had been desired to convey it.

Early the next morning when the sultan, according to custom, went to contemplate and admire Aladdin's palace, his amazement was unbounded to find that it could nowhere be seen. He could not comprehend how so large a palace, which he had seen plainly every day for some years, should vanish so soon and not leave the least remains behind. In his perplexity he ordered the grand vizier to be sent for with expedition.

The grand vizier, who in secret bore no goodwill to Aladdin, intimated his suspicion that the palace was built by magic, and that Aladdin had made his hunting excursion an excuse for the removal of his palace with the same suddenness with which it had been erected. He induced the sultan to send a detachment of his guards and to have Aladdin seized as a prisoner of state. On his son-in-law being brought before him, he would not hear a word from him, but ordered him to be put to death. The decree caused so much discontent among the people, whose affection Aladdin had secured by his largesses and charities, that the sultan, fearful of an insurrection, was obliged to grant him his life. When Aladdin found himself at liberty, he again addressed the sultan: "Sire, I pray you to let me know the crime by which I have thus lost the favor of thy countenance." "Your crime," answered the sultan, "wretched man! do you not know it? Follow me, and I will show you." The sultan then took Aladdin into the apartment from whence he was wont to look at and admire his palace, and said, "You ought to know where your palace stood. Look! mind, and tell me what has become of it." Aladdin did so, and, being utterly amazed at the loss of his palace, was speechless. At last, recovering himself, he said: "It is true, I do not see the palace. It is vanished; but I had no concern in its removal. I beg you to give me forty days, and if in that time I cannot restore it, I will offer my head to be disposed of at your pleasure." "I give you the time you ask, but at the end of the forty days forget not to present yourself before me."

Aladdin went out of the sultan's palace in a condition of exceeding humiliation. The lords who had courted him in the days of his splendor now declined to have any communication with him. For three days he wandered about the city, exciting the wonder and compassion of the multitude, by asking everybody he met if they had seen his palace, or could tell him anything of it. On the third day he wandered into the country, and, as he was approaching a river, he fell down the bank with so much violence that he rubbed the ring which the magician had given him, so hard, by holding on the rock to save himself, that immediately the same genie appeared whom he had seen in the cave where the magician had left him. "What wouldst thou have?" said the genie. "I am ready to obey thee as thy slave, and the slave of all those that have that ring on their finger; both I and the other slaves of the ring."

Aladdin, agreeably surprised at an offer of help so little expected, replied, "Genie, show me where the palace I caused to be built now stands, or transport it back where it first stood." "Your command," answered the genie, "is not wholly in my power; I am only the slave of the ring, and not of the lamp." "I command thee, then," replied Aladdin, "by the power of the ring, to transport me to the spot where my palace stands, in what part of the world soever it may be." These words were no sooner out of his mouth, than the genie transported him into Africa, to the midst of a large plain, where his palace stood, at no great distance from a city, and, placing him exactly under the window of the princess's apartment, left him.

Now it so happened that shortly after Aladdin had been transported by the slave of the ring to the neighborhood of his palace, one of the Attendants of the Princess Buddir al Buddoor, looking through the window, perceived him, and instantly told her mistress. The princess, who could not believe the joyful tidings, hastened herself to the window, and, seeing Aladdin, immediately opened it. The noise of opening the window made Aladdin turn his head that way, and perceiving the princess, he saluted her with an air that expressed his joy.

"To lose no time," said she to him, "I have sent to have the private door opened for you. Enter, and come up."

The private door, which was just under the princess's apartment, was soon opened, and Aladdin conducted up into the chamber. It is impossible to express the joy of both at seeing each other after so cruel a separation. After embracing, and shedding tears of joy, they sat down, and Aladdin said, "I beg of you, princess, to tell me what is become of an old lamp which stood upon a shelf in my robing chamber?"

"Alas!" answered the princess, "I was afraid our misfortune might be owing to that lamp; and What grieves me" most is, that I have been the cause of it. I was foolish enough to change the old lamp for a new one, and the next morning I found myself in this unknown country, which I am told is Africa."

"Princess," said Aladdin, interrupting her, "you have explained all by telling me we are in Africa. I desire you only to tell me if you know where the old lamp now is." "The African magician carries it carefully wrapt up in his bosom," said the princess; "and this I can assure you, because he pulled it out before me, and showed it to me in triumph."

"Princess," said Aladdin, "I think I have found the means to deliver you and to regain possession of the lamp, on which all my prosperity depends. To execute this design it is necessary for me to go to the town. I shall return by noon, and will then tell you what must be done by you to insure success. In the meantime I shall disguise myself; and I beg that the private door may be opened at the first knock."

When Aladdin was out of the palace, he looked around him on all sides, and perceiving a peasant going into the country, hastened after him; and when he had overtaken him, made a proposal to him to change clothes, which the man agreed to. When they had made the exchange, the countryman went about his business, and Aladdin entered the neighboring city. After traversing several streets, he came to that part of the town where the merchants and artisans had their particular streets according to their trades. He went into that of the druggists, and entering one of the largest and best furnished shops, asked the druggist if he had a certain powder, which he named.

The druggist, judging Aladdin by his habit to be very poor, told him he had it, but that it was very dear. Upon which Aladdin, penetrating his thoughts, pulled out his purse, and, showing him some gold, asked for half a dram of the powder, which the druggist weighed and gave him, telling him the price was a piece of gold. Aladdin put the money into his hand, and hastened to the palace, which he entered at once by the private door. When he came into the princess's apartment, he said to her, "Princess, you must take your part in the scheme which I propose for our deliverance. You must overcome your aversion to the magician, and assume a most friendly manner toward him, and ask him to oblige you by partaking of an entertainment in your apartments. Before he leaves ask him to exchange cups with you, which he, gratified at the honor you do him, will gladly do, when you must give him the cup containing this powder. On drinking it he will instantly fall asleep, and we will obtain the lamp, whose slaves will do all our bidding, and restore us and the palace to the capital of China."

The princess obeyed to the utmost her husband's instructions. She assumed a look of pleasure on the next visit of the magician, and asked him to an entertainment, which he most willingly accepted. At the close of the evening, during which the princess had tried all she could to please him, she asked him to exchange cups with her, and, giving the signal, had the drugged cup brought to her, which she gave to the magician. He drank it out of compliment to the princess to the very last drop, when he fell backward lifeless on the sofa.

The princess, in anticipation of the success of her scheme, had so placed her women from the great hall to the foot of the staircase, that the word was no sooner given that the African magician was fallen backward, than the door was opened and Aladdin admitted to the hall. The princess rose from her seat, and ran overjoyed to embrace him; but he stopped her, and said, "Princess, retire to your apartment, and let me be left alone, while I endeavor to transport you back to China as speedily as you were brought from thence."

When the princess, her women, and slaves were gone out of the hall, Aladdin shut the door, and going directly to the dead body of the magician, opened his vest, took out the lamp, which was carefully wrapped up, and rubbing it, the genie immediately appeared. "Genie," said Aladdin, "I command thee to transport this palace instantly to the place from whence it was brought hither." The genie bowed his head in token of obedience, and disappeared. Immediately the palace was transported into China, and its removal was only felt by two little shocks, the one when it was lifted up, the other when it was set down, and both in a very short interval of time.

On the morning after the restoration of Aladdin's palace, the sultan was looking out of his window, and mourning over the fate of his daughter, when he thought that he saw the vacancy created by the disappearance of the palace to be again filled up. On looking more attentively he was convinced beyond the power of doubt that it was his son-in-law's palace. Joy and gladness succeeded to sorrow and grief. He at once ordered a horse to be saddled, which he mounted that instant, thinking he could not make haste enough to the place.

Aladdin rose that morning by daybreak, put on one of the most magnificent habits his wardrobe afforded, and went up into the hall of twenty-four windows, from whence he perceived the sultan approaching, and received him at the foot of the great staircase, helping him to dismount.

He led the sultan into the princess's apartment. The happy father embraced her with tears of joy; and the princess, on her side, afforded similar testimonies of her extreme pleasure. After a short interval devoted to mutual explanations of all that had happened, the sultan restored Aladdin to his favor, and expressed his regret for the apparent harshness with which he had treated him. "My son," said he, "be not displeased at my proceedings against you; they arose from my paternal love, and therefore you ought to forgive the excesses to which it hurried me." "Sire," replied Aladdin, "I have not the least reason to complain of your conduct, since you did nothing but what your duty required. This infamous magician, the basest of men, was the sole cause of my misfortune."

The African magician, who was thus twice foiled in his endeavor to ruin Aladdin, had a younger brother, who was as skilful a magician as himself, and exceeded him in wickedness and hatred of mankind. By mutual agreement they communicated with each other once a year, however widely separate might be their place of residence from each other. The younger brother, not having received as usual his annual communication, prepared to take a horoscope and ascertain his brother's proceedings. He, as well as his brother, always carried a geomantic square instrument about him; he prepared the sand, cast the points, and drew the figures. On examining the planetary crystal, he found that his brother was no longer living, but had been poisoned; and by another observation, that he was in the capital of the kingdom of China; also that the person who had poisoned him was of mean birth, though married to a princess, a sultan's daughter.

When the magician had informed himself of his brother's fate, he resolved immediately to avenge his death, and at once departed for China; where, after crossing plains, rivers, mountains, deserts, and a long tract of country without delay, he arrived after incredible fatigues. When he came to the capital of China, he took a lodging at a khan. His magic art soon revealed to him that Aladdin was the person who had been the cause of the death of his brother. He had heard, too, all the persons of repute in the city talking of a woman called Fatima, who was retired from the world, and of the miracles she wrought. As he fancied that this woman might be serviceable to him in the project he had conceived, he made more minute inquiries, and requested to be informed more particularly who that holy woman was, and what sort of miracles she performed.

"What!" said the person whom he addressed, "have you never seen or heard of her? She is the admiration of the whole town, for her fasting, her austerities, and her exemplary life. Except Mondays and Fridays, she never stirs out of her little cell; and on those days on which she comes into the town she does an infinite deal of good; for there is not a person who is diseased but she puts her hand on them and cures them."

Having ascertained the place where the hermitage of the holy woman was, the magician went at night, and, plunging a poniard into her heart—killed this good woman. In the morning he dyed his face of the same hue as hers, and arraying himself in her garb, taking her veil, the large necklace she wore round her waist, and her stick, went straight to the palace of Aladdin.

As soon as the people saw the holy woman, as they imagined him to be, they presently gathered about him in a great crowd. Some begged his blessing, some kissed his hand, and others, more reserved, only the hem of his garment; while others, suffering from disease, stooped for him to lay his hands upon them, which he did, muttering some words in form of prayer, and, in short, counterfeiting so well that everybody took him for the holy woman. He came at last to the square before Aladdin's palace. The crowd and the noise was so great that the princess, who was in the hall of four-and-twenty windows, heard it, and asked what was the matter. One of her women told her it was a great crowd of people collected about the holy woman to be cured of diseases by the imposition of her hands.

The princess, who had long heard of this holy woman, but had never seen her, was very desirous to have some conversation with her; which the chief officer perceiving, told her it was an easy matter to bring her to her, if she desired and commanded it; and the princess, expressing her wishes, he immediately sent four slaves for the pretended holy woman.

As soon as the crowd saw the attendants from the palace, they made way; and the magician, perceiving also that they were coming for him, advanced to meet them, overjoyed to find his plot succeed so well. "Holy woman," said one of the slaves, "the princess wants to see you, and has sent us for you." "The princess does me too great an honor," replied the false Fatima; "I am ready to obey her command," and at the same time followed the slaves to the palace.

When the pretended Fatima had made her obeisance, the princess said, "My good mother, I have one thing to request, which you must not refuse me: it is, to stay with me, that you may edify me with your way of living, and that I may learn from your good example." "Princess," said the counterfeit Fatima, "I beg of you not to ask what I cannot consent to without neglecting my prayers and devotion." "That shall be no hindrance to you," answered the princess; "I have a great many apartments unoccupied; you shall choose which you like best, and have as much liberty to perform your devotions as if you were in your own cell."

The magician, who really desired nothing more than to introduce himself into the palace, where it would be a much easier matter for him to execute his designs, did not long excuse himself from accepting the obliging offer which the princess made him. "Princess," said he, "whatever resolution a poor wretched woman as I am may have made to renounce the pomp and grandeur of this world, I dare not presume to oppose the will and commands of so pious and charitable a princess."

Upon this the princess, rising up, said, "Come with me; I will show you what vacant apartments I have, that you may make choice of that you like best." The magician followed the princess, and of all the apartments she showed him made choice of that which was the worst, saying that it was too good for him, and that he only accepted it to please her.

Afterward, the princess would have brought him back again into the great hall to make him dine with her; but he, considering that he should then be obliged to show his face, which he had always taken care to conceal with Fatima's veil, and fearing that the princess should find out that he was not Fatima, begged of her earnestly to excuse him, telling her that he never ate anything but bread and dried fruits, and desiring to eat that slight repast in his own apartment. The princess granted his request, saying, "You may be as free here, good mother, as if you were in your own cell: I will order you a dinner, but remember I expect you as soon as you have finished your repast."

After the princess had dined, and the false Fatima had been sent for by one of the attendants, he again waited upon her.

"My good mother," said the princess, "I am overjoyed to see so holy a woman as yourself, who will confer a blessing upon this palace. But now I am speaking of the palace, pray how do you like it? And before I show it all to you, tell me first what you think of this hall."

Upon this question the counterfeit Fatima surveyed the hall from one end to the other. When he had examined it well, he said to the princess, "As far as such a solitary being as I am, who am unacquainted with what the world calls beautiful, can judge, this hall is truly admirable; there wants but one thing." "What is that, good mother?" demanded the princess; "tell me, I conjure you. For my part, I always believed, and have heard say, it wanted nothing; but if it does, it shall be supplied."

"Princess," said the false Fatima, with great dissimulation, "forgive me the liberty I have taken; but my opinion is, if it can be of any importance, that if a roc's egg were hung up in the middle of the dome, this hall would have no parallel in the four quarters of the world, and your palace would be the wonder of the universe."

"My good mother," said the princess, "what is a roc, and where may one get an egg?" "Princess," replied the pretended Fatima, "it is a bird of prodigious size, which inhabits the summit of Mount Caucasus; the architect who built your palace can get you one."

After the princess had thanked the false Fatima for what she believed her good advice, she conversed with her upon other matters; but could not forget the roc's egg, which she resolved to request of Aladdin when next he should visit her apartments. He did so in the course of that evening, and shortly after he entered, the princess thus addressed him: "I always believed that our palace was the most superb, magnificent, and complete in the world: but I will tell you now what it wants, and that is a roc's egg hung up in the midst of the dome." "Princess," replied Aladdin, "it is enough that you think it wants such an ornament; you shall see by the diligence which I use in obtaining it, that there is nothing which I would not do for your sake."

Aladdin left the Princess Buddir al Buddoor that moment, and went up into the hall of four-and-twenty windows, where, pulling out of his bosom the lamp, which after the danger he had been exposed to he always carried about him, he rubbed it; upon which the genie immediately appeared. "Genie," said Aladdin, "I command thee in the name of this lamp, bring a roc's egg to be hung up in the middle of the dome of the hall of the palace."

Aladdin had no sooner pronounced these words than the hall shook as if ready to fall; and the genie said in a loud and terrible voice, "Is it not enough that I and the other slaves of the lamp have done everything for you, but you, by an unheard of ingratitude, must command me to bring my master, and hang him up in the midst of this dome? This attempt deserves that you, the princess, and the palace, should be immediately reduced to ashes; but you are spared because this request does not come from yourself. Its true author is the brother of the African magician, your enemy, whom you have destroyed. He is now in your palace, disguised in the habit of the holy woman Fatima, whom he has murdered; at his suggestion your wife makes this pernicious demand. His design is to kill you, therefore take care of yourself." After these words the genie disappeared.

Aladdin resolved at once what to do. He returned to the princess's apartment, and, without mentioning a word of what had happened, sat down, and complained of a great pain which had suddenly seized his head. On hearing this the princess told him how she had invited the holy Fatima to stay with her, and that she was now in the palace; and at the request of the prince, ordered her to be summoned to her at once.

When the pretended Fatima came, Aladdin said, "Come hither, good mother; I am glad to see you here at so fortunate a time. I am tormented with a violent pain in my head, and request your assistance, and hope you will not refuse me that cure which you impart to afflicted persons."

So saying, he rose, but held down his head. The counterfeit Fatima advanced toward him, with his hand all the time on a dagger concealed in his girdle under his gown; which Aladdin observing, he snatched the weapon from his hand, pierced him to the heart with his own dagger, and then pushed him down on the floor.

"My dear prince, what have you done?" cried the princess in surprise. "You have killed the holy woman!" "No, my princess," answered Aladdin with emotion, "I have not killed Fatima, but a villain, who would have assassinated me if I had not prevented him. This wicked man," added he, uncovering his face, "is the brother of the magician who attempted our ruin. He has strangled the true Fatima, and disguised himself in her clothes with intent to murder me."

Aladdin then informed her how the genie had told him these facts, and how narrowly she and the palace had escaped destruction through his treacherous suggestion which had led to her request.

Thus was Aladdin delivered from the persecution of the two brothers, who were magicians. Within a few years afterward the sultan died in a good old age, and as he left no male children, the Princess Buddir al Buddoor succeeded him, and she and Aladdin reigned together many years, and left a numerous and illustrious posterity.

SINDBAD THE SAILOR

In the reign of the same caliph, Haroun-al-Raschid, of whom we have already heard, there lived at Bagdad a poor porter called Hindbad. One day, when the weather was excessively hot, he was employed to carry a heavy burden from one end of the town to the other. Being much fatigued, he took off his load, and sat upon it, near a large mansion.

He was much pleased that he stopped at this place; for the agreeable smell of wood of aloes and of pastils that came from the house, mixing with the scent of the rose-water, completely perfumed and embalmed the air. Besides, he heard from within a concert of instrumental music, accompanied with the harmonious notes of nightingales and other birds. This charming melody, and the smell of several sorts of savory dishes, made the porter conclude there was a feast with great rejoicings within. He went to some of the servants, whom he saw standing at the gate in magnificent apparel, and asked the name of the proprietor. "How," replied one of them, "do you live in Bagdad, and know not that this is the house of Sindbad the Sailor, that famous voyager who has sailed round the world?" The porter lifted up his eyes to heaven, and said, loud enough to be heard, "Almighty Creator of all things, consider the difference between Sindbad and me! I am every day exposed to fatigues and calamities, and can scarcely get coarse barley-bread for myself and my family, while happy Sindbad expends immense riches, and leads a life of continual pleasure. What has he done to obtain from Thee a lot so agreeable? And what have I done to deserve one so wretched?"

While the porter was thus indulging his melancholy, a servant came out of the house, and taking him by the arm, bade him follow him, for Sindbad, his master, wanted to speak to him. The servants brought him into a great hall, where a number of people sat round a table, covered with all sorts of savory dishes. At the upper end sat a comely, venerable gentleman, with a long white beard, and behind him stood a number of officers and domestics, all ready to attend his pleasure. This person was Sindbad. Hindbad, whose fear was increased at the sight of so many people, and of a banquet so sumptuous, saluted the company trembling. Sindbad bade him draw near, and seating him at his right hand, served him himself, and gave him excellent wine, of which there was abundance upon the sideboard.

Now, Sindbad had heard the porter complain through the window, and this it was that induced him to have him brought in. When the repast was over, Sindbad addressed his conversation to Hindbad, and inquired his name and employment, and said: "I wish to hear from your own mouth what it was you lately said in the street."

At this request Hindbad hung down his head in confusion, and replied: "My lord, I confess that my fatigue put me out of humor, and occasioned me to utter some indiscreet words, which I beg you to pardon." "Do not think I am so unjust," resumed Sindbad, "as to resent such a complaint. But I must correct your error concerning myself. You think, no doubt, that I have acquired without labor and trouble the ease and indulgence which I now enjoy. But do not mistake; I did not attain to this happy condition without enduring for several years more trouble of body and mind than can well be imagined. Yes, gentlemen," he added, speaking to the whole company, "I assure you that my sufferings have been of a nature so extraordinary as would deprive the greatest miser of his love of riches; and as an opportunity now offers, I will, with your leave, relate the dangers I have encountered, which I think will not be uninteresting to you."

THE FIRST VOYAGE

My father was a rich merchant. He bequeathed me a large estate, which I wasted in riotous living. I quickly, perceived that I was misspending my time, which is of all things the most valuable. I remembered the saying of the great Solomon, which I had frequently heard from my father, "A good name is better than precious ointment"; and again, "Wisdom is good with an inheritance." I resolved to walk in my father's ways, and I entered into a contract with some merchants, and embarked with them on board a ship we had fitted out in partnership.

We set sail, and steered our course toward the Indies, through the Persian Gulf. At first I was troubled with sea-sickness, but speedily recovered my health. In our voyage we touched at several islands, where we sold or exchanged our goods. One day we were becalmed near a small island, but little elevated above the level of the water, and resembling a green meadow. The captain ordered his sails to be furled, and permitted such persons as were so inclined to land. While we were enjoying ourselves eating and drinking, and recovering from the fatigue of the sea, the island of a sudden trembled and shook us terribly.

The trembling of the island was noticed on board ship, and we were called upon to re-embark speedily, lest we should all be lost; for what we took for an island proved to be the back of a sea monster.

The nimblest got into the sloop, others betook themselves to swimming; but as for myself, I was still upon the island when it disappeared into the sea, and I had only time to catch hold of a piece of wood that we had brought out of the ship to make a fire. Meanwhile, the captain, having received on board those who were in the sloop, and taken up some of those that swam, resolved to take advantage of the favorable gale that had just risen, and, hoisting his sails, pursued his voyage.

Thus was I exposed to the mercy of the waves the rest of that day and the following night. By this time I found my strength gone, and despaired of saving my life, when happily a wave threw me on an island. The bank was high and rugged, so that I could scarcely have got up had it not been for some roots of trees which I found within reach. When the sun arose I was very feeble. I found some herbs fit to eat, and had the good luck to discover a spring of excellent water. After this I advanced further into the island, and at last reached a fine plain, where I perceived some horses feeding. On my way toward them I heard the voice of a man, who asked me who I was. I related to him my adventure, after which, taking me by the hand, he led me into a cave, where there were several other people, no less amazed to see me than I was to see them.

I partook of some provisions which they offered me, and asked them what they did in such a desert place; to which they answered that they were grooms belonging to the sovereign of the island, and that every year they brought thither the king's horses for pasturage. They were to return home on the morrow, and had I been one day later I must have perished, because the inhabited part of the island was a great distance off, and it would have been impossible for me to have reached it without a guide.

Next morning they returned to the capital of the island, took me with them, and presented me to their king. He asked me who I was, and by what adventure I had come into his dominions. After I had satisfied him, he ordered that I should want for nothing.

Being a merchant, I frequented men of my own profession, and particularly inquired for those who were strangers, that perchance I might hear news from Bagdad, or find an opportunity to return. For the Maharaja's capital is situated on the sea-coast, and has a fine harbor, where ships arrive daily from the different quarters of the world. I frequented also the society of the learned Indians, and took delight to hear them converse; but withal, I took care to make my court regularly to the Maharaja, and conversed with the governors and petty kings, his tributaries, that were about him. They put a thousand questions respecting my country; and I, being willing to inform myself as to their laws and customs, asked them concerning everything which I thought worth knowing.

There belongs to this king an island named Cassel.

They assured me that every night a noise of drums was heard there, whence the mariners fancied that it was the residence of Degial. I determined to visit this wonderful place, and in my way thither saw fishes of 100 and 200 cubits long that occasion more fear than hurt; for they are so timorous that they will fly upon the rattling of two sticks or boards. I saw likewise other fish about a cubit in length, that had heads like owls.

As I was one day at the port after my return, the ship arrived in which I had embarked at Bussorah. I at once knew the captain, and I went and asked him for my bales. "I am Sindbad," said I, "and those bales marked with his name are mine."

When the captain heard me speak thus, "Heavens!" he exclaimed, "whom can we trust in these times? I saw Sindbad perish with my own eyes, as did also the passengers on board, and yet you tell me you are that Sindbad. What impudence is this! and what a false tale to tell, in order to possess yourself of what does not belong to you!" "Have patience," replied I; "do me the favor to hear what I have to say." The captain was at length persuaded that I was no cheat; for there came people from his ship who knew me, paid me great compliments, and expressed much joy at seeing me alive. At last he recollected me himself, and embracing me, "Heaven be praised," said he, "for your happy escape! I cannot express the joy it affords me. There are your goods; take and do with them as you please."

I took out what was most valuable in my bales, and presented them to the Maharaja, who, knowing my misfortune, asked me how I came by such rarities. I acquainted him with the circumstance of their recovery. He was pleased at my good luck, accepted my present, and in return gave me one much more considerable. Upon this I took leave of him, and went aboard the same ship, after I had exchanged my goods for the commodities of that country. I carried with me wood of aloes, sandals, camphire, nutmegs, cloves, pepper, and ginger. We passed by several islands, and at last arrived at Bussorah, from whence I came to this city, with the value of 100,000 sequins.

Sindbad stopped here, and ordered the musicians to proceed with their concert, which the story had interrupted. When it was evening, Sindbad sent for a purse of 100 sequins, and giving it to the porter, said, "Take this, Hindbad, return to your home, and come back to-morrow to hear more of my adventures." The porter went away, astonished at the honor done him and the present made him. The account of this adventure proved very agreeable to his wife and children, who did not fail to return thanks for what Providence had sent them by the hand of Sindbad.

Hindbad put on his best robe next day, and returned to the bountiful traveller, who received him with a pleasant air, and welcomed him heartily. When all the guests had arrived, dinner was served, and continued a long time. When it was ended, Sindbad, addressing himself to the company, said, "Gentlemen, be pleased to listen to the adventures of my second voyage. They deserve your attention even more than those of the first." Upon which every one held his peace, and Sindbad proceeded.

THE SECOND VOYAGE

I designed, after my first voyage, to spend the rest of my days at Bagdad, but it was not long ere I grew weary of an indolent life, and I put to sea a second time, with merchants of known probity. We embarked on board a good ship, and, after recommending ourselves to God, set sail. We traded from island to island, and exchanged commodities with great profit. One day we landed on an island covered with several sorts of fruit-trees, but we could see neither man nor animal We walked in the meadows, along the streams that watered them. While some diverted themselves with gathering flowers, and others fruits, I took my wine and provisions, and sat down near a stream between two high trees, which formed a thick shade. I made a good meal, and afterward fell asleep. I cannot tell how long I slept, but when I awoke the ship was gone.

In this sad condition, I was ready to die with grief.

I cried out in agony, beat my head and breast, and threw myself upon the ground, where I lay some time in despair. I upbraided myself a hundred times for not being content with the produce of my first voyage, that might have sufficed me all my life. But all this was in vain, and my repentance came too late. At last I resigned myself to the will of God. Not knowing what to do, I climbed up to the top of a lofty tree, from which I looked about on all sides, to see if I could discover anything that could give me hopes. When I gazed toward the sea I could see nothing but sky and water; but looking over the land I beheld something white; and coming down, I took what provision I had left, and went toward it, the distance being so great that I could not distinguish what it was.

As I approached, I thought it to be a white dome, of a prodigious height and extent; and when I came up to it, I touched it, and found it to be very smooth. I went round to see if it was open on any side, but saw it was not, and that there was no climbing up to the top, as it was so smooth. It was at least fifty paces round.

By this time the sun was about to set, and all of a sudden the sky became as dark as if it had been covered with a thick cloud. I was much astonished at this sudden darkness, but much more when I found it occasioned by a bird of a monstrous size, that came flying toward me. I remembered that I had often heard mariners speak of a miraculous bird called the roc, and conceived that the great dome which I so much admired must be its egg. In short, the bird alighted, and sat over the egg. As I perceived her coming, I crept close to the egg, so that I had before me one of the legs of the bird, which was as big as the trunk of a tree. I tied myself strongly to it with my turban, in hopes that the roc next morning would carry me with her out of this desert island. After having passed the night in this condition, the bird flew away as soon as it was daylight, and carried me so high that I could not discern the earth; she afterward descended with so much rapidity that I lost my senses. But when I found myself on the ground, I speedily untied the knot, and had scarcely done so, when the roc, having taken up a serpent of monstrous length in her bill, flew away.

The spot where it left me was encompassed on all sides by mountains, that seemed to reach above the clouds, and so steep that there was no possibility of getting out of the valley. This was a new perplexity; so that when I compared this place with the desert island from which the roc had brought me, I found that I had gained nothing by the change.

As I walked through this valley, I perceived it was strewn with diamonds, some of which were of a surprising bigness. I took pleasure in looking upon them; but shortly saw at a distance such objects as greatly diminished my satisfaction, and which I could not view without terror, namely, a great number of serpents, so monstrous that the least of them was capable of swallowing an elephant. They retired in the daytime to their dens, where they hid themselves from the roc, their enemy, and came out only in the night.

I spent the day in walking about in the valley, resting myself at times in such places as I thought most convenient. When night came on I went into a cave, where I thought I might repose in safety. I secured the entrance, which was low and narrow, with a great stone, to preserve me from the serpents, but not so far as to exclude the light. I supped on part of my provisions, but the serpents, which began hissing round me, put me into such extreme fear that I did not sleep. When day appeared the serpents retired, and I came out of the cave trembling. I can justly say that I walked upon diamonds, without feeling any inclination to touch them. At last I sat down, and notwithstanding my apprehensions, not having closed my eyes during the night, fell asleep, after having eaten a little more of my provisions. But I had scarcely shut my eyes when something that fell by me with a great noise awaked me. This was a large piece of raw meat; and at the same time I saw several others fall down from the rocks in different places. I had always regarded as fabulous what I had heard sailors and others relate of the valley of diamonds, and of the stratagems employed by merchants to obtain jewels from thence; but now I found that they had stated nothing but the truth. For the fact is, that the merchants come to the neighborhood of this valley, when the eagles have young ones, and throwing great joints of meat into the valley, the diamonds, upon whose points they fall, stick to them; the eagles, which are stronger in this country than anywhere else, pounce with great force upon those pieces of meat and carry them to their nests on the precipices of the rocks to feed their young: the merchants at this time run to their nests, disturb and drive off the eagles by their shouts, and take away the diamonds that stick to the meat.

I perceived in this device the means of my deliverance.

Having collected together the largest diamonds I could find, and put them into the leather bag in which I used to carry my provisions, I took the largest of the pieces of meat, tied it close round me with the cloth of my turban, and then laid myself upon the ground, with my face downward, the bag of diamonds being made fast to my girdle.

I had scarcely placed myself in this posture when one of the eagles, having taken me up with the piece of meat to which I was fastened, carried me to his nest on the top of the mountain. The merchants immediately began their shouting to frighten the eagles; and when they had obliged them to quit their prey, one of them came to the nest where I was. He was much alarmed when he saw me; but recovering himself, instead of inquiring how I came thither, began to quarrel with me, and asked why I stole his goods. "You will treat me," replied I, "with more civility, when you know me better. Do not be uneasy; I have diamonds enough for you and myself, more than all the other merchants together. Whatever they have they owe to chance; but I selected for myself, in the bottom of the valley, those which you see in this bag." I had scarcely done speaking, when the other merchants came crowding about us, much astonished to see me; but they were much more surprised when I told them my story.

They conducted me to their encampment; and there, having opened my bag, they were surprised at the largeness of my diamonds, and confessed that they had never seen any of such size and perfection. I prayed the merchant who owned the nest to which I had been carried (for every merchant had his own), to take as many for his share as he pleased. He contented himself with one, and that, too, the least of them; and when I pressed him to take more, without fear of doing me any injury, "No," said he, "I am very well satisfied with this, which is valuable enough to save me the trouble of making any more voyages, and will raise as great a fortune as I desire."

I spent the night with the merchants, to whom I related my story a second time, for the satisfaction of those who had not heard it. I could not moderate my joy when I found myself delivered from the danger I have mentioned. I thought myself in a dream, and could scarcely believe myself out of danger.

The merchants had thrown their pieces of meat into the valley for several days; and each of them being satisfied with the diamonds that had fallen to his lot, we left the place the next morning, and travelled near high mountains, where there were serpents of a prodigious length, which we had the good-fortune to escape. We took shipping at the first port we reached, and touched at the isle of Roha, where the trees grow that yield camphire. This tree is so large, and its branches so thick, that one hundred men may easily sit under its shade. The juice of which the camphire is made exudes from a hole bored in the upper part of the tree, is received in a vessel, where it thickens to a consistency, and becomes what we call camphire. After the juice is thus drawn out the tree withers and dies.

In this island is also found the rhinoceros, an animal less than the elephant, but larger than the buffalo.

It has a horn upon its nose, about a cubit in length; this horn is solid, and cleft through the middle. The rhinoceros fights with the elephant, runs his horn into his belly, and carries him off upon his head; but the blood and the fat of the elephant running into his eyes and making him blind, he falls to the ground; and then, strange to relate, the roc comes and carries them both away in her claws for food for her young ones.

I pass over many other things peculiar to this island, lest I should weary you. Here I exchanged some of my diamonds for merchandise.

From hence we went to other islands, and at last, having touched at several trading towns of the continent, we landed at Bussorah, from whence I proceeded to Bagdad. There I immediately gave large presents to the poor, and lived honorably upon the vast riches I had bought and gained with so much fatigue.

Thus Sindbad ended the relation of the second voyage, gave Hindbad another hundred sequins, and invited him to come the next day to hear the account of the third.

THE THIRD VOYAGE

I soon again grew weary of living a life of idleness, and hardening myself against the thought of any danger, I embarked with some merchants on another long voyage. We touched at several ports, where we traded. One day we were overtaken by a dreadful tempest, which drove us from our course.

The storm continued several days, and brought us before the port of an island, which the captain was very unwilling to enter; but we were obliged to cast anchor. When we had furled our sails, the captain told us that this and some other neighboring islands were inhabited by hairy savages, who would speedily attack us; and though they were but dwarfs, yet that we must make no resistance, for they were more in number than the locusts; and if we happened to kill one, they would all fall upon us and destroy us.

We soon found that what the captain had told us was but too true. An innumerable multitude of frightful savages, about two feet high, covered all over with red hair, came swimming toward us and encompassed our ship. They chattered as they came near, but we understood not their language. They climbed up the sides of the ship with such agility as surprised us. They took down our sails, cut the cable, and, hauling to the shore, made us all get out, and afterward carried the ship into another island, whence they had come. As we advanced, we perceived at a distance a vast pile of building, and made toward it. We found it to be a palace, elegantly built, and very lofty, with a gate of ebony of two leaves, which we opened. We saw before us a large apartment, with a porch, having on one side a heap of human bones, and on the other a vast number of roasting-spits. We trembled at this spectacle, and were seized with deadly apprehension, when suddenly the gate of the apartment opened with a loud crash, and there came out the horrible figure of a black man, as tall as a lofty palm- tree. He had but one eye, and that in the middle of his forehead, where it blazed bright as a burning coal. His fore teeth were very long and sharp, and stood out of his mouth, which was as deep as that of a horse. His upper lip hung down upon his breast. His ears resembled those of an elephant, and covered his shoulders; and his nails were as long and crooked as the talons of the greatest birds.

At the sight of so frightful a genie, we became insensible, and lay like dead men.

At last we came to ourselves, and saw him sitting in the porch looking at us. When he had considered us well, he advanced toward us, and laying his hand upon me, took me up by the nape of my neck, and turned me round, as a butcher would do a sheep's head. After having examined me, and perceiving me to be so lean that I had nothing but skin and bone, he let me go. He took up all the rest one by one, and viewed them in the same manner. The captain being the fattest, he held him with one hand, as I would do a sparrow, and thrust a spit through him; he then kindled a great fire, roasted, and ate him in his apartment for his supper. Having finished his repast, he returned to his porch, where he lay and fell asleep, snoring louder than thunder. He slept thus till morning. As to ourselves, it was not possible for us to enjoy any rest, so that we passed the night in the most painful apprehension that can be imagined. When day appeared the giant awoke, got up, went out, and left us in the palace.

The next night we determined to revenge ourselves on the brutish giant, and did so in the following manner. After he had again finished his inhuman supper on another of our seamen, he lay down on his back, and fell asleep. As soon as we heard him snore according to his custom, nine of the boldest among us, and myself, took each of us a spit, and putting the points of them into his fire till they were burning hot, we thrust them into his eye all at once, and blinded him. The pain made him break out into a frightful yell: he started up, and stretched out his hands, in order to sacrifice I some of us to his rage; but we ran to such places as he could not reach; and after having sought for us in vain, he groped for the gate, and went out, howling in agony.

We immediately left the palace, and came to the shore, where we made some rafts, each large enough to carry three men, with some timber that lay about in great quantities. We waited till day in order to get upon them, for we hoped if the giant did not appear by sunrising, and give over his howling, which we still heard, that he would prove to be dead; and if that happened to be the case, we resolved to stay in that island, and not to risk our lives upon the rafts. But day had scarcely appeared when we perceived our cruel enemy, accompanied by two others, almost of the same size, leading him; and a great number more coming before him at a quick pace.

We did not hesitate to take to our rafts, and put to sea with all the speed we could. The giants, who perceived this, took up great stones, and, running to the shore, entered the water up to the middle, and threw so exactly that they sunk all the rafts but that I was upon; and all my companions except the two with me, were drowned. We rowed with all our might, and got out of the reach of the giants. But when we got out to sea, we were exposed to the mercy of the waves and winds, and spent that day and the following night under the most painful uncertainty as to our fate; but next morning we had the good fortune to be thrown upon an island, where we landed with much joy. We found excellent fruit, which afforded us great relief, and recruited our strength.

At night we went to sleep on the sea-shore; but were awakened by the noise of a serpent of surprising length and thickness, whose scales made a rustling noise as he wound himself along. It swallowed up one of my comrades, notwithstanding his loud cries, and the efforts he made to extricate himself from it; dashing him several times against the ground, it crushed him, and we could hear it gnaw and tear the poor fellow's bones, though we had fled to a considerable distance. The following day, to our great terror, we saw the serpent again, when I exclaimed, "O Heaven, to what dangers are we exposed! We rejoiced yesterday at having escaped from the cruelty of a giant and the rage of the waves, now are we fallen into another danger equally dreadful."

As we walked about we saw a large, tall tree, upon which we designed to pass the following night for our security; and having satisfied our hunger with fruit, we mounted it accordingly. Shortly after the serpent came hissing to the foot of the tree; raised itself up against the trunk of it, and meeting with my comrade, who sat lower than I, swallowed him at once, and went off.

I remained upon the tree till it was day, and then came down, more like a dead man than one alive, expecting the same fate with my two companions. This filled me with horror, and I advanced some steps to throw myself into the sea; but I withstood this dictate of despair, and submitted myself to the will of God, who disposes of our lives at His pleasure.

In the meantime I collected together a great quantity of small wood, brambles, and dry thorns, and making them up into fagots, made a wide circle with them round the tree, and also tied some of them to the branches over my head. Having done this, when the evening came, I shut myself up within this circle, with the melancholy satisfaction that I had neglected nothing which could preserve me from the cruel destiny with which I was threatened. The serpent failed not to come at the usual hour, and went round the tree seeking for an opportunity to devour me, but was prevented by the rampart I had made; so that he lay till day, like a cat watching in vain for a mouse that has fortunately reached a place of safety.

When day appeared he retired, but I dared not leave my fort until the sun arose.

God took compassion on my hopeless state; for just as I was going, in a fit of desperation, to throw myself into the sea, I perceived a ship in the distance. I called as loud as I could, and, unfolding the linen of my turban, displayed it that they might observe me. This had the desired effect; the crew perceived me, and the captain sent his boat for me. As soon as I came on board, the merchants and seamen flocked about me to know how I came into that desert island; and after I had related to them all that had befallen me, the oldest among them said they had several times heard of the giants that dwelt in that island, that they were cannibals; and as to the serpents, they added that there were abundance in the island; that they hid themselves by day and came abroad by night. After having testified their joy at my escaping so many dangers, they brought me the best of their provisions; and took me before the captain, who, seeing that I was in rags, gave me one of his own suits. Looking steadfastly upon him, I knew him to be the person who, in my second voyage, had left me in the island where I fell asleep, and sailed without me, or sending to seek for me.

I was not surprised that he, believing me to be dead, did not recognize me.

"Captain," said I, "look at me, and you may know that I am Sindbad, whom you left in that desert island."

The captain having considered me attentively recognized me.

"God be praised!" said he, embracing me; "I rejoice that fortune has rectified my fault. There are your goods, which I always took care to preserve."

I took them from him, and made him my acknowledgments for his care of them.

We continued at sea for some time, touched at several islands, and at last landed at that of Salabat, where sandal-wood is obtained, which is much used in medicine.

From the isle of Salabat we went to another, where I furnished myself with cloves, cinnamon, and other spices. As we sailed from this island we saw a tortoise twenty cubits in length and breadth. We observed also an amphibious animal like a cow, which gave milk; its skin is so hard that they usually make bucklers of it. I saw another, which had the shape and color of a camel.

In short, after a long voyage, I arrived at Bussorah, and thence returned to Bagdad with so much wealth that I knew not its extent. I gave a great deal to the poor, and bought another considerable estate in addition to what I had already.

Thus Sindbad finished the story of his third voyage. He gave another hundred sequins to Hindbad, and invited him to dinner again the next day to hear.

THE FOURTH VOYAGE

After I had rested from the dangers of my third voyage, my passion for trade and my love of novelty soon again prevailed. I therefore settled my affairs, and provided a stock of goods fit for the traffic I designed to engage in. I took the route of Persia, travelled over several provinces, and then arrived at a port, where I embarked. On putting out to sea, we were overtaken by such a sudden gust of wind as obliged the captain to lower his yards and take all other necessary precautions to prevent the danger that threatened us. But all was in vain; our endeavors had no effect; the sails were split into a thousand pieces, and the ship was stranded; several of the merchants and seamen were drowned, and the cargo was lost.

I had the good fortune, with several of the merchants and mariners, to get upon some planks, and we were carried by the current to an island which lay before us. There we found fruit and spring water, which preserved our lives. We stayed all night near the place where we had been cast ashore.

Next morning, as soon as the sun was up, we explored the island, and saw some houses, which we approached. As soon as we drew near, we were encompassed by a great number of negroes, who seized us, shared us among them, and carried us to their respective habitations.

I and five of my comrades were carried to one place; here they made us sit down, and gave us a certain herb, which they made signs to us to eat. My comrades not taking notice that the blacks ate none of it themselves, thought only of satisfying their hunger, and ate with greediness. But I, suspecting some trick, would not so much as taste it, which happened well for me; for in a little time after I perceived my companions had lost their senses, and that when they spoke to me they knew not what they said.

The negroes fed us afterward with rice, prepared with oil of cocoanuts; and my comrades, who had lost their reason, ate of it greedily. I also partook of it, but very sparingly. They gave us that herb at first on purpose to deprive us of our senses, that we might not be aware of the sad destiny prepared for us; and they supplied us with rice to fatten us; for, being cannibals, their design was to eat us as soon as we grew fat. This accordingly happened, for they devoured my comrades, who were not sensible of their condition; but my senses being entire, you may easily guess that instead of growing fat, as the rest did, I grew leaner every day. The fear of death under which I labored turned all my food into poison. I fell into a languishing distemper, which proved my safety; for the negroes, having killed and eaten my companions, seeing me to be withered, lean and sick, deferred my death.

Meanwhile I had much liberty, so that scarcely any notice was taken of what I did, and this gave me an opportunity one day to get at a distance from the houses and to make my escape. An old man who saw me, and suspected my design, called to me as loud as he could to return; but instead of obeying him I redoubled my speed, and quickly got out of sight. At that time there was none but the old man about the houses, the rest being abroad, and not to return till night, which was usual with them. Therefore, being sure that they could not arrive in time to pursue me, I went on till night, when I stopped to rest a little, and to eat some of the provisions I had secured; but I speedily set forward again, and travelled seven days, avoiding those places which seemed to be inhabited, and lived for the most part upon cocoanuts, which served me both for meat and drink. On the eighth day I came near the sea, and saw some white people like myself gathering pepper, of which there was great plenty in that place. This I took to be a good omen, and went to them without any scruple.

The people who gathered pepper came to meet me as soon as they saw me, and asked me in Arabic who I was, and whence I came. I was overjoyed to hear them speak in my own language, and satisfied their curiosity by giving them an account of my shipwreck, and how I fell into the hands of the negroes. "Those negroes," replied they, "eat men; and by what miracle did you escape their cruelty?" I related to them the circumstances I have just mentioned, at which they were wonderfully surprised.

I stayed with them till they had gathered their quantity of pepper, and then sailed with them to the island from whence they had come. They presented me to their king, who was a good prince. He had the patience to hear the relation of my adventures, which surprised him, and he afterward gave me clothes, and commanded care to be taken of me.

The island was very well peopled, plentiful in everything, and the capital a place of great trade. This agreeable retreat was very comfortable to me after my misfortunes, and the kindness of this generous prince completed my satisfaction. In a word, there was not a person more in favor with him than myself, and consequently every man in court and city sought to oblige me, so that in a very little time I was looked upon rather as a native than a stranger.

I observed one thing, which to me appeared very extraordinary. All the people, the king himself not excepted, rode their horses without bridle or stirrups. I went one day to a workman, and gave him a model for making the stock of a saddle. When that was done, I covered it myself with velvet and leather, and embroidered it with gold. I afterward went to a smith, who made me a bit, according to the pattern I showed him, and also some stirrups. When I had all things completed, I presented them to the king, and put them upon one of his horses. His majesty mounted immediately, and was so pleased with them that he testified his satisfaction by large presents.

I made several others for the ministers and principal officers of his household, which gained me great reputation and regard.

As I paid my court very constantly to the king, he said to me one day, "Sindbad, I love thee, I have one thing to demand of thee, which thou must grant. I have a mind thou shouldst marry, that so thou mayst stay in my dominions, and think no more of thy own country." I durst not resist the prince's will, and he gave me one of the ladies of his court, noble, beautiful, and rich. The ceremonies of marriage being over, I went and dwelt with my wife and for some time we lived together in perfect harmony. I was not, however, satisfied with my banishment; therefore designed to make my escape the first opportunity, and to return to Bagdad, which my present settlement, how advantageous soever, could not make me forget.

At this time the wife of one of my neighbors, with whom I had contracted a very strict friendship, fell sick and died. I went to see and comfort him in his affliction, and, finding him absorbed in sorrow, I said to him as soon as I saw him, "God preserve you and grant you a long life." "Alas!" replied he, "how do you think I should obtain the favor you wish me? I have not above an hour to live, for I must be buried this day with my wife. This is a law in this island. The living husband is interred with the dead wife, and the living wife with the dead husband."

While he was giving an account of this barbarous custom, the very relation of which chilled my blood, his kindred, friends, and neighbors came to assist at the funeral. They dressed the corpse of the woman in her richest apparel and all her jewels as if it had been her wedding day; then they placed her on an open bier, and began their march to the place of burial. The husband walked first, next to the dead body. They proceeded to a high mountain, and when they had reached the place of their destination, they took up a large stone which formed the mouth of a deep pit, and let down the body with all its apparel and jewels. Then the husband, embracing his kindred and friends, suffered himself to be placed on another bier without resistance, with a pot of water and seven small loaves, and was let down in the same manner. The ceremony being over, the mouth of the pit was again covered with the stone, and the company returned.

I mention this ceremony the more particularly, because I was in a few weeks' time to be the principal actor on a similar occasion. Alas! my own wife fell sick and died. I made every remonstrance I could to the king not to expose me, a foreigner, to this inhuman law. I appealed in vain. The king and all his court, with the most considerable persons in the city, sought to soften my sorrow by honoring the funeral ceremony with their presence; and, at the termination of the ceremony, I was lowered into the pit, with a vessel full of water and seven loaves. As I approached the bottom, I discovered, by the aid of the little light that came from above, the nature of this subterranean place. It seemed an endless cavern, and might be about fifty fathoms deep. I lived for some time there upon my bread and water, when one day, just as it was on the point of exhaustion, I heard something tread, and breathing or panting as it moved. I followed the sound. The animal seemed to stop sometimes, but always fled and breathed hard as I approached. I pursued it for a considerable time, till at last I perceived a light, resembling a star. I went on, sometimes lost sight of it, but always found it again, and at last discovered that it came through a hole in the rock, which I got through, and found myself upon the seashore, at which I felt exceeding joy. I prostrated myself on the shore to thank God for this mercy, and shortly afterward I perceived a ship making for the place where I was. I made a sign with the linen of my turban, and called to the crew as loud as I could. They heard me, and sent a boat to bring me on board. It was fortunate for me that these people did not inspect the place where they found me, but without hesitation took me on board.

We passed by several islands, and, among others, that called the Isle of Bells, about ten days' sail from Serendib with a regular wind, and six from that of Kela, where we landed. Lead mines are found in the island; also Indian canes and excellent camphire.

The king of the Isle of Kela is very rich and powerful, and the Isle of Bells, which is about two days' journey in extent, is also subject to him.

The inhabitants are so barbarous that they still eat human flesh. After we had finished our traffic in that island we put to sea again, and touched at several other ports; at last I arrived happily at Bagdad. Out of gratitude to God for His mercies, I contributed liberally toward the support of several mosques and the subsistence of the poor, and enjoyed myself with friends in festivities and amusements.

Here Sindbad made a new present of one hundred sequins to Hindbad, whom he requested to return with the rest next day at the same hour, to dine with him and hear the story of his fifth voyage.

THE FIFTH VOYAGE

All the troubles and calamities I had undergone could not cure me of my inclination to make new voyages. I therefore bought goods, departed with them for the best seaport; and there, that I might not be obliged to depend upon a captain, but have a ship at my own command, I remained till one was built on purpose, at my own charge. When the ship was ready I went on board with my goods; but not having enough to load her, I agreed to take with me several merchants of different nations, with their merchandise.

We sailed with the first fair wind, and, after a long navigation, the first place we touched at was a desert island, where we found an egg of a roc, equal in size to that I formerly mentioned. There was a young roc in it, just ready to be hatched, and its beak had begun to break the egg. The merchants who landed with me broke the egg with hatchets, and made a hole in it, pulled out the young roc, piecemeal, and roasted it. I had in vain entreated them not to meddle with the egg.

Scarcely had they finished their repast, When there appeared in the air, at a considerable distance, two great clouds. The captain of my ship, knowing by experience what they meant, said they were the male and female parents of the roc, and pressed us to re-embark with all speed, to prevent the misfortune which he saw would otherwise befall us.

The two rocs approached with a frightful noise, which they redoubled when they saw the egg broken and their young one gone. They flew back in the direction they had come, and disappeared for some time, while we made all the sail we could to endeavor to prevent that which unhappily befell us.

They soon returned, and we observed that each of them carried between its talons an enormous rock. When they came directly over my ship, they hovered, and one of them let go his rock; but by the dexterity of the steersman it missed us, and fell into the sea. The other so exactly hit the middle of the ship as to split it into pieces. The mariners and passengers were all crushed to death, or fell into the sea. I myself was of the number of the latter; but, as I came up again, I fortunately caught hold of a piece of the wreck, and swimming, sometimes with one hand and sometimes with the other, but always holding fast the plank, the wind and the tide favoring me, I came to an island, and got safely ashore.

I sat down upon the grass, to recover myself from my fatigue, after which I went into the island to explore it. It seemed to be a delicious garden. I found trees everywhere, some of them bearing green and others ripe fruits, and streams of fresh pure water. I ate of the fruits, which I found excellent; and drank of the water, which was very light and good.

When I was a little advanced into the island, I saw an old man, who appeared very weak and infirm. He was sitting on the bank of a stream, and at first I took him to be one who had been shipwrecked like myself. I went toward him and saluted him, but he only slightly bowed his head. I asked him why he sat so still; but instead of answering me, he made a sign for me to take him upon my back, and carry him over the brook.

I believed him really to stand in need of my assistance, took him upon my back, and having carried him over, bade him get down, and for that end stooped, that he might get off with ease; but instead of doing so (which I laugh at every time I think of it), the old man, who to me appeared quite decrepit, threw his legs nimbly about my neck. He sat astride upon my shoulders, and held my throat so tight that I thought he would have strangled me, and I fainted away.

Notwithstanding my fainting, the ill-natured old fellow still kept his seat upon my neck. When I had recovered my breath, he thrust one of his feet against my side, and struck me so rudely with the other that he forced me to rise up against my will. Having arisen, he made me carry him under the trees, and forced me now and then to stop, that he might gather and eat fruit. He never left his seat all day; and when I lay down to rest at night, he laid himself down with me, holding still fast about my neck. Every morning he pinched me to make me awake, and afterward obliged me to get up and walk, and spurred me with his feet.

One day I found several dry calabashes that had fallen from a tree. I took a large one, and, after cleaning it, pressed into it some juice of grapes, which abounded in the island; having filled the calabash, I put it by in a convenient place, and going thither again some days after, I tasted it, and found the wine so good that it gave me new vigor, and so exhilarated my spirits that I began to sing and dance as I carried my burden.

The old man, perceiving the effect which this had upon me, and that I carried him with more ease than before, made me a sign to give him some of it. I handed him the calabash, and the liquor pleasing his palate, he drank it off. There being a considerable quantity of it, he soon began to sing, and to move about from side to side in his seat upon my shoulders, and by degrees to loosen his legs from about me. Finding that he did not press me as before, I threw him upon the ground, where he lay without motion; I then took up a great stone and slew him.

I was extremely glad to be thus freed for ever from this troublesome fellow. I now walked toward the beach, where I met the crew of a ship that had cast anchor to take in water; they were surprised to see me, but more so at hearing the particulars of my adventures. "You fell," said they, "into the hands of the Old Man of the Sea, and are the first who ever escaped strangling by his malicious embraces. He never quitted those he had once made himself master of till he had destroyed them, and he has made this island notorious by the number of men he has slain." They carried me with them to the captain, who received me with great kindness. He put out again to sea, and, after some days' sail, we arrived at the harbor of a great city, the houses of which overhung the sea.

One of the merchants who had taken me into his friendship invited me to go along with him. He gave me a large sack, and having recommended me to some people of the town, who used to gather cocoanuts, desired them to take me with them. "Go," said he, "follow them, and act as you see them do; but do not separate from them, otherwise you may endanger your life." Having thus spoken, he gave me provisions for the journey, and I went with them.

We came to a thick forest of cocoa trees, very lofty, with trunks so smooth that it was not possible to climb to the branches that bore the fruit. When we entered the forest we saw a great number of apes of several sizes, who fled as soon as they perceived us, and climbed to the tops of the trees with amazing swiftness.

The merchants with whom I was gathered stones, and threw them at the apes on the trees. I did the same; and the apes, out of revenge, threw coconuts at us so fast, and with such gestures, as sufficiently testified their anger and resentment. We gathered up the cocoanuts, and from time to time threw stones to provoke the apes; so that by this stratagem we filled our bags with cocoanuts. I thus gradually collected as many cocoanuts as produced me a considerable sum.

Having laden our vessel with cocoanuts, we set sail, and passed by the islands where pepper grows in great plenty. From thence we went to the Isle of Comari, where the best species of wood of aloes grows. I exchanged my cocoa in those two islands for pepper and wood of aloes, and went with other merchants a-pearl-fishing, I hired divers, who brought me up some that were very large and pure. I embarked in a vessel that happily arrived at Bussorah; from thence I returned to Bagdad, where I realized vast sums from my pepper, wood of aloes, and pearls. I gave the tenth of my gains in alms, as I had done upon my return from my other voyages, and rested from my fatigues.

Sindbad here ordered one hundred sequins to be given to Hindbad, and requested him and the other guests to dine with him the next day, to hear the account of his sixth voyage.

THE SIXTH VOYAGE

I know, my friends, that you will wish to hear how, after having been shipwrecked five times, and escaped so many dangers, I could resolve again to tempt fortune, and expose myself to new hardships. I am myself astonished at my conduct when I reflect upon it, and must certainly have been actuated by my destiny, from which none can escape. Be that as it may, after a year's rest I prepared for a sixth voyage, notwithstanding the entreaties of my kindred and friends, who did all in their power to dissuade me.

Instead of taking my way by the Persian Gulf, I travelled once more through several provinces of Persia and the Indies, and arrived at a seaport, where I embarked in a ship, the captain of which was bound on a long voyage, in which he and the pilot lost their course. Suddenly we saw the captain quit his rudder, uttering loud lamentations. He threw off his turban, pulled his beard, and beat his head like a madman. We asked him the reason; and he answered that we were in the most dangerous place in all the ocean. "A rapid current carries the ship along with it, and we shall all perish in less than a quarter of an hour. Pray to God to deliver us from this peril; we cannot escape if He do not take pity on us." At these words he ordered the sails to be lowered; but all the ropes broke, and the ship was carried by the current to the foot of an inaccessible mountain, where she struck and went to pieces; yet in such a manner that we saved our lives, our provisions, and the best of our goods.

The mountain at the foot of which we were was covered with wrecks, with a vast number of human bones, and with an incredible quantity of goods and riches of all kinds. These objects served only to augment our despair. In all other places it is usual for rivers to run from their channels into the sea; but here a river of fresh water runs from the sea into a dark cavern, whose entrance is very high and spacious. What is most remarkable in this place is that the stones of the mountain are of crystal, rubies, or other precious stones. Here is also a sort of fountain of pitch or bitumen, that runs into the sea, which the fish swallow, and evacuate soon afterward, turned into ambergris; and this the waves throw up on the beach in great quantities. Trees also grow here, most of which are of wood of aloes, equal in goodness to those of Comari.

To finish the description of this place, it is not possible for ships to get off when once they approach within a certain distance. If they be driven thither by a wind from the sea, the wind and the current impel them; and if they come into it when a land wind blows, which might seem to favor their getting out again, the height of the mountain stops the wind, and occasions a calm, so that the force of the current carries them ashore: and what completes the misfortune is that there is no possibility of ascending the mountain, or of escaping by sea.

We continued upon the shore, at the foot of the mountain, in a state of despair, and expected death every day. On our first landing we had divided our provisions as equally as we could, and thus every one lived a longer or shorter time, according to his temperance, and the use he made of his provisions.

I survived all my companions; and when I buried the last I had so little provisions remaining that I thought I could not long survive, and I dug a grave, resolving to lie down in it, because there was no one left to pay me the last offices of respect. But it pleased God once more to take compassion on me, and put it in my mind to go to the bank of the river which ran into the great cavern. Considering its probable course with great attention, I said to myself, "This river, which runs thus underground, must somewhere have an issue. If I make a raft, and leave myself to the current, it will convey me to some inhabited country, or I shall perish. If I be drowned I lose nothing, but only change one kind of death for another."

I immediately went to work upon large pieces of timber and cables, for I had a choice of them from the wrecks, and tied them together so strongly that I soon made a very solid raft. When I had finished, I loaded it with some chests of rubies, emeralds, ambergris, rock crystal and bales of rich stuffs. Having balanced my cargo exactly, and fastened it well to the raft, I went on board with two oars that I had made, and leaving it to the course of the river, resigned myself to the will of God.

As soon as I entered the cavern I lost all light, and the stream carried me I knew not whither. Thus I floated on in perfect darkness, and once, found the arch so low that it very nearly touched my head, which made me cautious afterward to avoid the like danger. All this while I ate nothing but what was just necessary to support nature; yet, notwithstanding my frugality, all my provisions were spent. Then I became insensible. I cannot tell how long I continued so; but when I revived, I was surprised to find myself in an extensive plain on the brink of a river, where my raft was tied, among a great number of negroes. I got up as soon as I saw them, and saluted them. They spoke to me, but I did not understand their language.

I was so transported with joy that I knew not whether I was asleep or awake; but being persuaded that I was not asleep, I recited the following words in Arabic aloud:

"Call upon the Almighty, He will help thee; thou needst not perplex thyself about anything else: shut thy eyes, and while thou art asleep God will change thy bad fortune into good."

One of the negroes, who understood Arabic, hearing me speak thus, came toward me, and said: "Brother, be not surprised to see us; we are inhabitants of this country, and water our fields from this river, which comes out of the neighboring mountain. We saw your raft, and one of us swam into the river, and brought it hither, where we fastened it, as you see, until you should awake. Pray tell us your history. Whence did you come?"

I begged of them first to give me something to eat, and then I would satisfy their curiosity. They gave me several sorts of food, and when I had satisfied my hunger, I related all that had befallen me, which they listened to with attentive surprise. As soon as I had finished they told me, by the person who spoke Arabic and interpreted to them what I said, that I must go along with them, and tell my story to their king myself; it being too extraordinary to be related by any other than the person to whom the events had happened.

They immediately sent for a horse, and having helped me to mount, some of them walked before to show the way, while the rest took my raft and cargo and followed.

We marched till we came to the capital of Serendib, for it was in that island I had landed. The negroes presented me to their king; I approached his throne, and saluted him as I used to do the kings of the Indies; that is to say, I prostrated myself at his feet. The prince ordered me to rise, received me with an obliging air, and made me sit down near him.

I concealed nothing from the king; but related to him all that I have told you. At last my raft was brought in, and the bales opened in his presence: he admired the quantity of wood of aloes and ambergris; but above all, the rubies and emeralds, for he had none in his treasury that equalled them.

Observing that he looked on my jewels with pleasure, and viewed the most remarkable among them, one after another, I fell prostrate at his feet, and took the liberty to say to him, "Sire, not only my person is at your majesty's service, but the cargo of the raft, and I would beg of you to dispose of it as your own."

He answered me with a smile, "Sindbad, I will take nothing of yours; far from lessening your wealth, I design to augment it, and will not let you quit my dominions without marks of my liberality."

He then charged one of his officers to take care of me, and ordered people to serve me at his own expense. The officer was very faithful in the execution of his commission, and caused all the goods to be carried to the lodgings provided for me.

I went every day at a set hour to make my court to the king, and spent the rest of my time in viewing the city, and what was most worthy of notice.

The capital of Serendib stands at the end of a fine valley, in the middle of the island, encompassed by high mountains. They are seen three days' sail off at sea. Rubies and several sorts of minerals abound. All kinds of rare plants and trees grow there, especially cedars and cocoanut. There is also a pearl-fishery in the mouth of its principal river; and in some of its valleys are found diamonds. I made, by way of devotion, a pilgrimage to the place where Adam was confined after his banishment from Paradise, and had the curiosity to go to the top of the mountain.

When I returned to the city I prayed the king to allow me to return to my own country, and he granted me permission in the most obliging and honorable manner. He would force a rich present upon me; and at the same time charged me with a letter for the Commander of the Faithful, our sovereign, saying to me, "I pray you give this present from me, and this letter, to the Caliph Haroun-al-Raschid, and assure him of my friendship."

The letter from the King of Serendib was written on the skin of a certain animal of great value, very scarce, and of a yellowish color. The characters of this letter were of azure, and the contents as follows:

"The King of the Indies, before whom march one hundred elephants, who lives in a palace that shines with one hundred thousand rubies, and who has in his treasury twenty thousand crowns enriched with diamonds, to Caliph Haroun-al-Raschid.

"Though the present we send you be inconsiderable, receive it, however, as a brother and a friend, in consideration of the hearty friendship which we bear for you, and of which we are willing to give you proof. We desire the same part in your friendship, considering that we believe it to be our merit, as we are both kings. We send you this letter as from one brother to another. Farewell."

The present consisted, first, of one single ruby made into a cup, about half a foot high, an inch thick, and filled with round pearls of half a drachm each. 2. The skin of a serpent, whose scales were as bright as an ordinary piece of gold, and had the virtue to preserve from sickness those who lay upon it. 3. Fifty thousand drachms of the best wood of aloes, with thirty grains of camphire as big as pistachios. And 4. A female slave of great beauty, whose robe was covered over with jewels.

The ship set sail, and after a very successful navigation we landed at Bussorah, and from thence I went to the city of Bagdad, where the first thing I did was to acquit myself of my commission.

I took the King of Serendib's letter, and went to present myself at the gate of the Commander of the Faithful, and was immediately conducted to the throne of the caliph. I made my obeisance, and presented the letter and gift. When he had read what the King of Serendib wrote to him, he asked me if that prince were really so rich and potent as he represented himself in his letter. I prostrated myself a second time, and, rising again, said, "Commander of the Faithful, I can assure your majesty he doth not exceed the truth. I bear him witness. Nothing is more worthy of admiration than the magnificence of his palace. When the prince appears in public he has a throne fixed on the back of an elephant, and rides between two ranks of his ministers, favorites, and other people of his court. Before him, upon the same elephant, an officer carries a golden lance in his hand; and behind him there is another, who stands with a rod of gold, on the top of which is an emerald, half a foot long and an inch thick. He is attended by a guard of one thousand men, clad in cloth of gold and silk, and mounted on elephants richly caparisoned. The officer who is before him on the same elephant cries from time to time, with a loud voice, 'Behold the great monarch, the potent and redoubtable Sultan of the Indies, the monarch greater than Solomon, and the powerful Maharaja.'

"After he has pronounced those words, the officer behind the throne cries in his turn, 'This monarch, so great and so powerful, must die, must die, must die!' And the officer before replies, 'Praise alone be to Him who liveth for ever and ever.'"

The caliph was much pleased with my account, and sent me home with a rich present.

Here Sindbad commanded another hundred sequins to be paid to Hindbad, and begged his return on the morrow to hear his seventh and last voyage.

THE SEVENTH AND LAST VOYAGE

On my return home from my sixth voyage, I had entirely given up all thoughts of again going to sea; for, besides that my age now required rest, I was resolved no more to expose myself to such risks as I had encountered, so that I thought of nothing but to pass the rest of my days in tranquillity. One day, however, an officer of the caliph's inquired for me. "The caliph," said he, "has sent me to tell you that he must speak with you." I followed the officer to the palace, where, being presented to the caliph, I saluted him by prostrating myself at his feet. "Sindbad," said he to me, "I stand in need of your services; you must carry my answer and present to the King of Serendib."

This command of the caliph was to me like a clap of thunder. "Commander of the Faithful," I replied, "I am ready to do whatever your majesty shall think fit to command; but I beseech you most humbly to consider what I have undergone. I have also made a vow never to leave Bagdad."

Perceiving that the caliph insisted upon my compliance, I submitted, and told him that I was willing to obey. He was very well pleased, and ordered me one thousand sequins for the expenses of my journey.

I prepared for my departure in a few days. As soon as the caliph's letter and present were delivered to me, I went to Bussorah, where I embarked, and had a very prosperous voyage. Having arrived at the Isle of Serendib, I was conducted to the palace with much pomp, when I prostrated myself on the ground before the king. "Sindbad," said the king, "you are welcome; I have many times thought of you; I bless the day on which I see you once more." I made my compliments to him, and thanked him for his kindness, and delivered the gifts from my august master.

The caliph's letter was as follows:

"Greeting, in the name of the Sovereign Guide of the Right Way, from the servant of God, Haroun-al-Raschid, whom God hath set in the place of vicegerent to His Prophet, after his ancestors of happy memory, to the potent and esteemed Raja of Serendib.

"We receive your letter with joy, and send you from our imperial residence, the garden of superior wits. We hope when you look upon it you will perceive our good intention, and be pleased with it. Farewell."

The caliph's present was a complete suit of cloth of gold, valued at one thousand sequins; fifty robes of rich stuff; a hundred of white cloth, the finest of Cairo, Suez, and Alexandria; a vessel of agate, more broad than deep, an inch thick, and half a foot wide, the bottom of which represented in bas-relief a man with one knee on the ground, who held a bow and an arrow, ready to discharge at a lion. He sent him also a rich tablet, which, according to tradition, belonged to the great Solomon.

The King of Serendib was highly gratified at the caliph's acknowledgment of his friendship. A little time after this audience I solicited leave to depart, and with much difficulty obtained it. The king, when he dismissed me, made me a very considerable present. I embarked immediately to return to Bagdad, but had not the good-fortune to arrive there so speedily as I had hoped. God ordered it otherwise.

Three or four days after our departure we were attacked by pirates, who easily seized upon our ship, because it was not a vessel of war. Some of the crew offered resistance, which cost them their lives. But for myself and the rest, who were not so imprudent, the pirates saved us, and carried us into a remote island, where they sold us.

I fell into the hands of a rich merchant, who, as soon as he bought me, took me to his house, treated me well, and clad me handsomely as a slave. Some days after he asked me if I understood any trade. I answered that I was no mechanic, but a merchant, and that the pirates who sold me had robbed me of all I possessed. "Tell me," replied he, "can you shoot with a bow?" I answered that the bow was one of my exercises in my youth. He gave me a bow and arrows, and, taking me behind him on an elephant, carried me to a thick forest some leagues from the town. We penetrated a great way into the wood, and when he thought fit to stop, he bade me alight; then showing me a great tree, "Climb up that," said he, "and shoot at the elephants as you see them pass by, for there is a prodigious number of them in this forest, and if any of them fall, come and give me notice." Having spoken thus, he left me victuals, and returned to the town, and I continued upon the tree all night.

I saw no elephant during the night, but next morning, at break of day, I perceived a great number. I shot several arrows among them, and at last one of the elephants fell, when the rest retired immediately, and left me at liberty to go and acquaint my patron with my success. When I had informed him, he commended my dexterity, and caressed me highly. We went afterward together to the forest, where we dug a hole for the elephant; my patron designing to return when it was rotten, and take his teeth to trade with.

I continued this employment for two months. One morning, as I looked for the elephants, I perceived with extreme amazement that, instead of passing by me across the forest as usual, they stopped, and came to me with a horrible noise, in such numbers that the plain was covered and shook under them. They surrounded the tree in which I was concealed, with their trunks uplifted, and all fixed their eyes upon me. At this alarming spectacle I continued immovable, and was so much terrified that my bow and arrows fell out of my hand.

My fears were not without cause; for after the elephants had stared upon me some time, one of the largest of them put his trunk round the foot of the tree, plucked it up, and threw it on the ground. I fell with the tree, and the elephant, taking me up with his trunk, laid me on his back, where I sat more like one dead than alive, with my quiver on my shoulder. He put himself at the head of the rest, who followed him in line, one after the other, carried me a considerable way, then laid me down on the ground, and retired with all his companions. After having lain some time, and seeing the elephants gone, I got up, and found I was upon a long and broad hill, almost covered with the bones and teeth of elephants. I doubted not but that this was the burial-place of the elephants, and that they carried me thither on purpose to tell me that I should forbear to kill them, as now I knew where to get their teeth without inflicting injury on them. I did not stay on the hill, but turned toward the city; and after having travelled a day and a night, I came to my patron.

As soon as my patron saw me, "Ah, poor Sindbad!" exclaimed he, "I was in great trouble to know what was become of you. I have been at the forest, where I found a tree newly pulled up, and your bow and arrows on the ground, and I despaired of ever seeing you more. Pray tell me what befell you." I satisfied his curiosity, and we both of us set out next morning to the hill. We loaded the elephant which had carried us with as many teeth as he could bear; and when we were returned, my master thus addressed me: "Hear now what I shall tell you. The elephants of our forest have every year killed us a great many slaves, whom we sent to seek ivory. For all the cautions we could give them, those crafty animals destroyed them one time or other. God has delivered you from their fury, and has bestowed that favor upon you only. It is a sign that He loves you, and has some use for your service in the world. You have procured me incredible wealth; and now our whole city is enriched by your means, without any more exposing the lives of our slaves. After such a discovery, I can treat you no more as a slave, but as a brother. God bless you with all happiness and prosperity. I henceforth give you your liberty; I will also give you riches."

To this I replied: "Master, God preserve you. I desire no other reward for the service I had the good-fortune to do to you and your city but leave to return to my own country." "Very well," said he, "the monsoon will in a little time bring ships for ivory. I will then send you home." I stayed with him while waiting for the monsoon; and during that time we made so many journeys to the hill, that we filled all our warehouses with ivory. The other merchants who traded in it did the same, for my master made them partakers of his good-fortune.

The ships arrived at last, and my master himself having made choice of the ship wherein I was to embark, loaded half of it with ivory on my account, laid in provisions in abundance for my passage, and besides obliged me to accept a present of some curiosities of the country of great value. After I had returned him a thousand thanks for all his favors I went aboard. We stopped at some islands to take in fresh provisions. Our vessel being come to a port on the mainland in the Indies, we touched there, and, not being willing to venture by sea to Bussorah, I landed my proportion of the ivory, resolving to proceed on my journey by land. I realized vast sums by my ivory, bought several rarities, which I intended for presents, and when my equipage was ready, set out in company with a large caravan of merchants. I was a long time on the journey, and suffered much, but was happy in thinking that I had nothing to fear from the seas, from pirates, from serpents, or from the other perils to which I had been exposed.

I at last arrived safe at Bagdad, and immediately waited upon the caliph, to give him an account of my embassy. He loaded me with honors and rich presents, and I have ever since devoted myself to my family, kindred, and friends.

Sindbad here finished the relation of his seventh and last voyage, and then addressing himself to Hindbad, "Well, friend," said he, "did you ever hear of any person that suffered so much as I have done? Is it not reasonable that, after all this, I should enjoy a quiet and pleasant life?" As he said these words, Hindbad kissed his hand, and said, "Sir, my afflictions are not to be compared with yours. You not only deserve a quiet life, but are worthy of all the riches you possess, since you make so good a use of them. May you live happily for a long time." Sindbad ordered him to be paid another hundred sequins, and told him to give up carrying burdens as a porter, and to eat henceforth at his table, for he wished that he should all his life have reason to remember that he henceforth had a friend in Sindbad the Sailor.

ROBINSON CRUSOE

Although hundreds have tried, both at home and abroad, no one has been able to write a book that could take the place of Robinson Crusoe, the story of that sturdy, voyaging Englishman who was always on the lookout for adventures and was never discouraged by any circumstances in which he found himself. The picture of the brave captain in his hairy goatskin clothes, Poll on his shoulder, his faithful dog by his side, and Friday following along behind, is one that remains stamped for life on every reader's mind.

Like all great books, it interests people of all ages. To the child it is a fascinating fairy tale; to the older boys and girls it is a story of stirring adventure, while to the mature man it is a picture of civilization. And so it has come to be read again and again, and admired and cherished the world over.

Robinson Crusoe was written in 1719 by Daniel Defoe, the son of a butcher, when he was over sixty years of age. His son deserted and deceived him, as Robinson Crusoe deserted and deceived his father, and it almost broke the old man's heart.

ROBINSON CRUSOE IS SHIPWRECKED

By Daniel Defoe

Having lived almost four years in the Brazils, and beginning to thrive and prosper very well upon my plantation, I had not only learned the language, but had contracted acquaintance and friendship among my fellow-planters, as well as among the merchants at St. Salvador, which was our port; and in my discourses among them, I had frequently given them an account of my two voyages to the coast of Guinea, the manner of trading with the negroes there, and how easy it was to purchase upon the coast for trifles, such as beads, toys, knives, scissors, hatchets, bits of glass, and the like, not only gold dust, Guinea grains, elephants' teeth, etc., but negroes, for the service of the Brazils, in great numbers.

They listened very attentively to my discourses on these heads, but especially to that part which related to the buying of negroes, which was a trade at that time, not far entered into.

Being in company with some merchants and planters of my acquaintance, and talking of things very earnestly, three of them came to me next morning, and told me they had been musing very much upon what I had discoursed with them of the last night, and they came to make a secret proposal to me; and, after enjoining me secrecy, they told me that they had a mind to fit out a ship to go to Guinea; that they had all plantations as well as I, and for which they needed nothing so much as servants; that as it was a trade that could not be carried on, because they could not publicly sell the negroes when they came home, so they desired to make but one voyage, to bring the negroes on shore privately, and divide them among their own plantations; and, in a word, the question was, whether I would go to manage the trading part upon the coast of Guinea; and they offered me that I should have my equal share of the negroes, without providing any part of the stock.

This was a fair proposal, it must be confessed, had it been made to any one that had not had a settlement and a plantation of his own to look after, which was in a fair way of coming to be very considerable, and with a good stock upon it; but for me, that was thus entered and established, and had nothing to do but to go on as I had begun for three or four years more, and to have sent for the other hundred pounds from England, and who in that time, and with that little addition, could scarce have failed of being worth three or four thousand pounds sterling, and that increasing, too; for me to think of such a voyage was the most preposterous thing that ever man in such circumstances could be guilty of.

But I, that was born to be my own destroyer, could no more resist the offer than I could restrain my first rambling designs when my father's good counsel was lost upon me. In a word, I told them I would go with all my heart, if they would undertake to look after my plantation in my absence, and would dispose of it to such as I should direct, if I miscarried. This they all engaged to do, and entered into writings or covenants to do so; and I made a formal will disposing of my plantation and effects in case of my death, making the captain of the ship that had saved my life, as before, my universal heir, but obliging him to dispose of my effects as I had directed in my will, one-half of the produce being to himself, and the other to be shipped to England.

In short, I took all possible caution to preserve my effects, and to keep up my plantation; had I used half as much prudence to have looked into my own interest, and have made a judgment of what I ought to have done and ought not to have done, I had certainly never gone away from so prosperous an undertaking, and gone upon a voyage to sea, attended with all its hazards.

But I was hurried on, and obeyed blindly the dictates of my fancy rather than my reason; and, accordingly, the ship being fitted out, and the cargo furnished, and all things done as by agreement, by my partners in the voyage, I went on board in an evil hour, the 1st of September, 1659, being the same day eight years that I went from my father and mother at Hull.

Our ship was about 120 tons burden, carried six guns, and fourteen men, besides the master, his boy, and myself; we had on board no large cargo of goods, except of such toys as were fit for our trade with the negroes, such as beads, bits of glass, shells, and other trifles, especially little looking-glasses, knives, scissors, hatchets, and the like.

The same day I went on board we set sail, standing away to the northward upon our own coast, with design to stretch over for the African coast when we came about ten or twelve degrees of northern latitude, which, it seems, was the manner of their course in those days. We had very good weather, only excessively hot, all the way upon our own coast, till we came to the height of Cape St. Augustino; from whence, keeping further off at sea, we lost sight of land, and steered as if we were bound for the isle Fernando de Noronha, holding our course N. E. by N., and leaving those isles on the east. In this course we passed the line in about twelve days' time, and were, by our last observation, in 7 degrees 22' northern latitude, when a violent tornado, or hurricane, took us quite out of our knowledge. It blew in such a terrible manner, that for twelve days together we could do nothing but drive; and, scudding away before it, let it carry us wherever fate and the fury of the winds directed; and during these twelve days, I need not say that I expected every day to be swallowed up; nor did any in the ship expect to save their lives.

In this distress we had, besides the terror of the storm, one of our men die of the calenture, and a man and a boy washed overboard. About the twelfth day, the weather abating a little, the master made an observation as well as he could, and found that he was in about eleven degrees of north latitude, but that he was twenty-two degrees of longitude difference west from Cape St. Augustino; so that he found he was gotten upon the coast of Guiana, or the north part of Brazil, beyond the river Amazon, toward that of the river Orinoco, commonly called the Great River; and now he began to consult with me what course he should take; for the ship was leaky, and very much disabled, and he was for going directly back to the coast of Brazil.

I was positively against that; and looking over the charts of the sea-coast of America with him, we concluded there was no inhabited country for us to have recourse to till we came within the circle of the Caribbee Islands, and therefore resolved to stand away for Barbadoes; which, by keeping off at sea, to avoid the indraft of the bay or gulf of Mexico, we might easily perform, as we hoped, in about fifteen days' sail; whereas we could not possibly make our voyage to the coast of Africa without some assistance both to our ship and to ourselves.

With this design we changed our course, and steered away N.W. by W., in order to reach some of our English islands, where I hoped for relief; but our voyage was otherwise determined; for, being in the latitude of twelve degrees eighteen minutes, a second storm came upon us, which carried us away with the same impetuosity westward, and drove us so out of the way of all human commerce that, had all our lives been saved as to the sea, we were rather in danger of being devoured by savages than ever returning to our own country.

In this distress, the wind still blowing very hard, one of our men early one morning cried out, "Land!" and we had no sooner run out of the cabin to look out, in hopes of seeing whereabout in the world we were, than the ship struck upon the sand, and in a moment, her motion being so stopped, the sea broke over her in such a manner that we expected we should all have perished immediately; and we were even driven into our close quarters, to shelter us from the very foam and spray of the sea.

It is not easy for any one who has not been in the like condition to describe or conceive the consternation of men in such circumstances. We knew nothing where we were, or upon what land it was we were driven; whether an island or the main, whether inhabited or not inhabited. As the rage of the wind was still great, though rather less than at first, we could not so much as hope to have the ship hold many minutes without breaking in pieces, unless the winds, by a kind of miracle, should turn immediately about. In a word, we sat looking one upon another, and expecting death every moment, and every man acting accordingly, as preparing for another world; for there was little or nothing more for us to do in this; that which was our present comfort, and all the comfort we had, was that, contrary to our expectation, the ship did not break yet, and that the master said the wind began to abate.

Now, though we thought the wind did a little abate, yet the ship having thus struck upon the sand, and sticking too fast for us to expect her getting off, we were in a dreadful condition indeed, and had nothing to do but to think of saving our lives as well as we could. We had a boat at our stern just before the storm, but she was fast staved by dashing against the ship's rudder, and in the next place she broke away, and either sunk, or was driven off to sea; so there was no hope from her. We had another boat on board; but how to get her off into the sea was a doubtful thing; however, there was no room to debate, for we fancied the ship would break in pieces every minute, and some told us she was actually broken already.

In this distress, the mate of our vessel lays hold of the boat, and with the help of the rest of the men, they got her flung over the ship's side; and getting all into her, we let go, and committed ourselves, being eleven in number, to God's mercy and the wild sea: for though the storm was abated considerably, yet the sea went dreadfully high upon the shore, and might be well called *den wild zee*, as the Dutch call the sea in a storm.

And now our case was very dismal indeed; for we all saw plainly that the sea went so high that the boat could not escape, and that we should be inevitably drowned. As to making sail, we had none, nor, if we had, could we have done anything with it; so we worked at the oar toward the land, though with heavy hearts, like men going to execution; for we all knew that when the boat came near the shore, she would be dashed in a thousand pieces by the breach of the sea. However, we committed our souls to God in the most earnest manner; and the wind driving us toward the shore, we hastened our destruction with our own hands, pulling as well as we could toward land.

What the shore was, whether rock or sand, whether steep or shoal, we knew not; the only hope that could rationally give us the least shadow of expectation was, if we might happen into some bay or gulf, or the mouth of some river, where by great chance we might have run our boat in, or got under the lee of the land, and perhaps made smooth water. But there was nothing of this appeared; but as we made nearer and nearer the shore, the land looked more frightful than the sea.

After we had rowed, or rather driven, about a league and a half, as we reckoned it, a raging wave, mountain-like, came rolling astern of us, and plainly bade us expect the *coup de grace*. In a word, it took us with such a fury that it overset the boat at once; and separating us as well from the boat as from one another, gave us not time hardly to say, "O God!" for we were all swallowed up in a moment.

Nothing can describe the confusion of thought which I felt when I sank into the water; for though I swam very well, yet I could not deliver myself from the waves so as to draw breath, till that wave having driven me, or rather carried me, a vast way on toward the shore, and having spent itself, went back and left me upon the land, almost dry, but half dead with the water I took in. I had so much presence of mind, as well as breath left, that seeing myself nearer the mainland than I expected, I got upon my feet, and endeavored to make on toward the land as fast as I could, before another wave should return and take me up again; but I soon found it was impossible to avoid it; for I saw the sea come after me as high as a great hill, and as furious as an enemy, which I had no means or strength to contend with: my business was to hold my breath, and raise myself upon the water, if I could; and so by swimming to preserve my breathing, and pilot myself toward the shore if possible, my greatest concern now being that the wave, as it would carry me a great way toward the shore when it came on, might not carry me back again with it when it gave back toward the sea.

The wave that came upon me again buried me at once twenty or thirty feet deep in its own body, and I could feel myself carried with a mighty force and swiftness toward the shore a very great way; but I held my breath and assisted myself to swim still forward with all my might. I was ready to burst with holding my breath when, as I felt myself rising up, so, to my immediate relief, I found my head and hands shoot out above the surface of the water; and though it was not two seconds of time that I could keep myself so, yet it relieved me greatly, gave me breath and new courage. I was covered again with water a good while, but not so long but I held it out; and finding the water had spent itself, and began to return, I struck forward against the return of the waves, and felt ground again with my feet. I stood still a few moments to recover breath, and till the waters went from me, and then took to my heels and ran with what strength I had farther toward the shore. But neither would this deliver me from the fury of the sea, which came pouring in after me again; and twice more I was lifted up by the waves and carried forward as before, the shore being very flat. The last time of these two had wellnigh been fatal to me; for the sea having hurried me along, as before, landed me, or rather dashed me, against a piece of a rock, and that with such force as it left me senseless, and, indeed, helpless as to my own deliverance; for the blow, taking my side and breast, beat the breath as it were quite out of my body; and had it returned again immediately, I must have been strangled in the water; but I recovered a little before the return of the waves, and seeing I should be covered again with water, I resolved to hold fast by a piece of the rock, and so to hold my breath, if possible, till the wave went back. Now, as the waves were not so high as at first, being nearer land, I held my hold till the wave abated, and then fetched another run, which brought me so near the shore, that the next wave, though it went over me, yet did not so swallow me up as to carry me away; and the next run I took I got to the mainland; where, to my great comfort, I clambered up the clifts and sat upon the grass, free from danger and quite out of the reach of the water,

I was now landed and safe on shore, and began to look up and thank God that my life was saved, in a case wherein there was some minutes before scarce any room to hope. I believe it is impossible to express, to the life, what the ecstasies and transports of the soul are, when it is so saved, as I may say, out of the very grave: and I do not wonder now at that custom, when a malefactor, who has the halter about his neck, is tied up, and just going to be turned off, and has a reprieve brought to him—I say I do not wonder that they bring a surgeon with it, to let him bleed that very moment they tell him of it, that the surprise may not drive the animal spirits from the heart, and overwhelm him,

For sudden joys, like griefs, confound at first.

I walked about on the shore, lifting up my hands, and my whole being, as I may say, wrapped up in a contemplation of my deliverance; making a thousand gestures and motions, which I cannot describe; reflecting upon all my comrades that were drowned, and that there should not be one soul saved but myself; for, as for them, I never saw them afterward, or any sign of them, except three of their hats, one cap, and two shoes that were not fellows.

I cast my eyes to the stranded vessel when, the breach and froth of the sea being so big, I could hardly see it, it lay so far off; and considered, Lord! how was it possible I could get on shore?

After I had solaced my mind with the comfortable part of my condition, I began to look round me, to see what kind of place I was in, and what was next to be done: and I soon found my comforts abate, and that, in a word, I had a dreadful deliverance: for I was wet, had no clothes to shift me, nor anything either to eat or drink, to comfort me; neither did I see any prospect before me but that of perishing with hunger, or being devoured by wild beasts: and that which was particularly afflicting to me was that I had no weapon, either to hunt and kill any creature for my sustenance, or to defend myself against any other creature that might desire to kill me for theirs. In a word, I had nothing about me but a knife, a tobacco-pipe, and a little tobacco in a box. This was all my provision; and this threw me into terrible agonies of mind, that for a while I ran about like a madman. Night coming upon me, I began, with a heavy heart, to consider what would be my lot if there were any ravenous beasts in that country, seeing at night they always come abroad for their prey.

All the remedy that offered to my thoughts, at that time, was to get up into a thick, bushy tree, like a fir, but thorny, which grew near me, and where I resolved to sit all night, and consider the next day what death I should die, for as yet I saw no prospect of life. I walked about a furlong from the shore, to see if I could find any fresh water to drink, which I did, to my great joy; and having drunk, and put a little tobacco in my mouth to prevent hunger, I went to the tree, and getting up into it, endeavored to place myself so that if I should sleep I might not fall. And having cut me a short stick like a truncheon, for my defence, I took up my lodging; and being excessively fatigued, I fell fast asleep, and slept as comfortably as, I believe, few could have done in my condition, and found myself more refreshed with it than I think I ever was on such an occasion.

ALONE ON A DESOLATE ISLAND

By Daniel Defoe

When I waked it was broad day, the weather clear, and the storm abated, so that the sea did not rage and swell as before. But that which surprised me most was, that the ship was lifted off in the night from the sand where she lay by the swelling of the tide, and was driven up almost as far as the rock which I at first mentioned, where I had been so bruised by the wave dashing me against it. This being within about a mile from the shore where I was, and the ship seeming to stand upright still, I wished myself on board, that at least I might save some necessary things for my use.

When I came down from my apartment in the tree, I looked about me again, and the first thing I found was the boat, which lay, as the wind and the sea had tossed her up, upon the land, about two miles on my right hand. I walked as far as I could upon the shore to have got to her; but found a neck or inlet of water between me and the boat which was about half a mile broad; so I came back for the present, being more intent upon getting at the ship, where I hoped to find something for my present subsistence.

A little after noon I found the sea very calm, and the tide ebbed so far out that I could come within a quarter of a mile of the ship. And here I found a fresh renewing of my grief; for I saw evidently that if we had kept on board we had been all safe — that is to say, we had all got safe on shore, and I had not been so miserable as to be left entirely destitute of all comfort and company as I now was. This forced tears to my eyes again; but as there was little relief in that, I resolved, if possible, to get to the ship; so I pulled off my clothes — for the weather was hot to extremity — and took the water. But when I came to the ship my difficulty was still greater to know how to get on board; for, as she lay aground, and high out of the water, there was nothing within my reach to lay hold of. I swam round her twice, and the second time I spied a small piece of rope, which I wondered I did not see at first, hung down by the fore-chains so low as that with great difficulty I got hold of it, and by the help of that rope I got up into the forecastle of the ship. Here I found that the ship was bulged, and had a great deal of water in her hold, but that she lay so on the side of a bank of hard sand, or rather earth, that her stern lay lifted up upon the bank, and her head low, almost to the water. By this means all her quarter was free, and all that was in that part was dry; for you may be sure my first work was to search, and to see what was spoiled and what was free. And, first, I found that all the ship's provisions were dry and untouched by the water, and, being very well disposed to eat, I went to the bread-room and filled my pockets with biscuit, and ate it as I went about other things, for I had no time to lose. I also found some rum in the great cabin, of which I took a large dram, and which I had, indeed, need enough of to spirit me for what was before me. Now I wanted nothing but a boat to furnish myself with many things which I foresaw would be very necessary to me.

It was in vain to sit still and wish for what was not to be had; and this extremity roused my application. We had several spare yards, and two or three large spars of wood, and a spare topmast or two in the ship; I resolved to fall to work with these, and I flung as many of them overboard as I could manage for their weight, tying every one with a rope, that they might not drive away. When this was done I went down the ship's side, and pulling them to me, I tied four of them together at both ends as well as I could, in the form of a raft, and laying two or three short pieces of plank upon them crossways, I found I could walk upon it very well, but that it was not able to bear any great weight, the pieces being too light. So I went to work, and with a carpenter's saw I cut a spare topmast into three lengths, and added them to my raft, with a great deal of labor and pains. But the hope of furnishing myself with necessaries encouraged me to go beyond what I should have been able to have done upon another occasion.

My raft was now strong enough to bear any reasonable weight. My next care was what to load it with, and how to preserve what I laid upon it from the surf of the sea; but I was not long considering this. I first laid all the planks or boards upon it that I could get, and having considered well what I most wanted, I got three of the seamen's chests, which I had broken open, and emptied, and lowered them down upon my raft; the first of these I filled with provisions; viz., bread, rice, three Dutch cheeses, five pieces of dried goat's flesh (which we lived much upon), and a little remainder of European corn, which had been laid by for some fowls which we brought to sea with us, but the fowls were killed. There had been some barley and wheat together; but, to my great disappointment, I found afterwards that the rats had eaten or spoiled it all. As for liquors, I found several cases of bottles belonging to our skipper, in which were some cordial waters; and, in all, about five or six gallons of rack. These I stowed by themselves, there being no need to put them into the chest, nor any room for them. While I was doing this, I found the tide begin to flow, though very calm; and I had the mortification to see my coat, shirt, and waistcoat, which I had left on the shore, upon the sand, swim away. As for my breeches, which were only linen, and open-kneed, I swam on board in them and my stockings. However, this set me on rummaging for clothes, of which I found enough, but took no more than I wanted for present use, for I had other things which my eye was more upon — as, first, tools to work with on shore. And it was after long searching that I found out the carpenter's chest, which was, indeed, a very useful prize to me, and much more valuable than a ship-load of gold would have been at that time. I got it down to my raft, whole as it was, without losing time to look into it, for I knew in general what it contained.

My next care was for some ammunition and arms.

There were two very good fowling-pieces in the great cabin, and two pistols. These I secured first, with some powder-horns and a small bag of shot, and two old rusty swords. I knew there were three barrels of powder in the ship, but knew not where our gunner had stowed them; but with much search I found them, two of them dry and good, the third had taken water. Those two I got to my raft, with the arms. And now I thought myself pretty well freighted, and began to think how I should get to shore with them, having neither sail, oar, nor rudder; and the least capful of wind would have overset all my navigation.

I had three encouragements — 1st, a smooth calm sea; 2ndly, the tide rising, and setting in to the shore; 3dly, what little wind there was blew me towards the land. And thus, having found two or three broken oars belonging to the boat — and, besides the tools which were in the chest, I found two saws, an axe, and a hammer — with this cargo I put to sea. For a mile or thereabouts my raft went very well, only that I found it drive a little distant from the place where I had landed before; by which I perceived that there was some indraft of the water, and consequently I hoped to find some creek or river there, which I might make use of as a port to get to land with my cargo.

As I imagined, so it was. There appeared before me a little opening of the land, and I found a strong current of the tide set into it; so I guided my raft as well as I could, to keep in the middle of the stream.

But here I had like to have suffered a second shipwreck, which, if I had, I think verily would have broken my heart; for, knowing nothing of the coast, my raft ran aground at one end of it upon a shoal, and, not being aground at the other end, it wanted but a little that all my cargo had slipped off towards the end that was afloat, and so fallen into the water. I did my utmost, by setting my back against the chests, to keep them in their places, but could not thrust off the raft with all my strength; neither durst I stir from the posture I was in; but, holding up the chests with all my might, I stood in that manner near half an hour, in which time the rising of the water brought me a little more upon a level; and a little after, the water still rising, my raft floated again, and I thrust her off with the oar I had into the channel, and then driving up higher I at length found myself in the mouth of a little river, with land on both sides, and a strong current of tide running up. I looked on both sides for a proper place to get to shore, for I was not willing to be driven too high up the river: hoping in time to see some ships at sea, and therefore resolved to place myself as near the coast as I could.

At length I spied a little cove on the right shore of the creek, to which with great pain and difficulty I guided my raft, and at last got so near that, reaching ground with my oar, I could thrust her directly in. But here I had like to have dipped all my cargo into the sea again; for that shore lying pretty steep — that is to say sloping — there was no place to land, but where one end of my float, if it ran on shore, would lie so high, and the other sink lower, as before, that it would endanger my cargo again. All that I could do was to wait till the tide was at the highest, keeping the raft with my oar like an anchor, to hold the side of it fast to the shore, near a flat piece of ground, which I expected the water would flow over; and so it did. As soon as I found water enough — for my raft drew about a foot of water — I thrust her upon that flat piece of ground, and there fastened or moored her, by sticking my two broken oars into the ground, one on one side, near one end, and one on the other side near the other end; and thus I lay till the water ebbed away and left my raft and all my cargo safe on shore.

My next work was to view the country, and seek a proper place for my habitation, and where to stow my goods to secure them from whatever might happen. Where I was, I yet knew not; whether on the continent or on an island; whether inhabited or not inhabited; whether in danger of wild beasts or not. There was a hill not above a mile from me, which rose up very steep and high, and which seemed to overtop some other hills, which lay as in a ridge from it northward. I took out one of the fowling-pieces, and one of the pistols, and a horn of powder; and thus armed I travelled for discovery up to the top of that hill, where, after I had with great labor and difficulty got to the top, I saw my fate, to my great affliction — viz., that I was in an island environed every way with the sea: no land to be seen except some rocks, which lay a great way off; and two small islands, less than this, which lay about three leagues to the west.

I found also that the island I was in was barren, and, as I saw good reason to believe, uninhabited except by wild beasts, of whom, however, I saw none. Yet I saw abundance of fowls, but knew not their kinds; neither when I killed them could I tell what was fit for food, and what not. At my coming back, I shot at a great bird which I saw sitting upon a tree on the side of a great wood.

I believe it was the first gun that had been fired there since the creation of the world. I had no sooner fired than from all parts of the wood there arose an innumerable number of fowls, of many sorts, making a confused screaming and crying, and every one according to his usual note, but not one of them of any kind that I knew. As for the creature I killed, I took it to be a kind of hawk, its color and beak resembling it, but it had no talons or claws more than common. Its flesh was carrion, and fit for nothing.

Contented with this discovery, I came back to my raft, and fell to work to bring my cargo on shore, which took me up the rest of that day. What to do with myself at night I knew not, nor indeed where to rest, for I was afraid to lie down on the ground, not knowing but some wild beast might devour me, though, as I afterwards found, there was really no need for those fears.

However, as well as I could, I barricaded myself round with the chests and boards that I had brought on shore, and made a kind of hut for that night's lodging. As for food, I yet saw not which way to supply myself, except that I had seen two or three creatures like hares run out of the wood where I shot the fowl.

I now began to consider that I might yet get a great many things out of the ship which would be useful to me, and particularly some of the rigging and sails, and such other things as might come to land; and I resolved to make another voyage on board the vessel, if possible. And as I knew that the first storm that blew must necessarily break her all in pieces, I resolved to set all other things apart till I had got everything out of the ship that I could get. Then I called a council — that is to say, in my thoughts — whether I should take back the raft; but this appeared impracticable; so I resolved to go as before, when the tide was down; and I did so, only that I stripped before I went from my hut, having nothing on but my chequered shirt, a pair of linen drawers, and a pair of pumps on my feet.

I got on board the ship as before, and prepared a second raft; and, having had experience of the first, I neither made this so unwieldy nor loaded it so hard, but yet I brought away several things very useful to me; as first, in the carpenter's stores I found two or three bags full of nails and spikes, a great screwjack, a dozen or two of hatchets, and, above all, that most useful thing called a grindstone. All these I secured, together with several things belonging to the gunner, particularly two or three iron crows, and two barrels of musket bullets, seven muskets, another fowling-piece, with some small quantity of powder more; a large bagful of small shot, and a great roll of sheet- lead; but this last was so heavy I could not hoist it up to get it over the ship's side.

Besides these things, I took all the men's clothes that I could find, and a spare fore-topsail, a hammock, and some bedding, and with this I loaded my second raft, and brought them all safe on shore, to my very great comfort.

I was under some apprehension, during my absence from the land, that at least my provisions might be devoured on shore: but when I came back I found no sign of any visitor; only there sat a creature like a wild cat upon one of the chests, which, when I came towards it, ran away a little distance, and then stood still. She sat very composed and unconcerned, and looked full in my face, as if she had a mind to be acquainted with me. I presented my gun at her, but, as she did not understand it, she was perfectly unconcerned at it, nor did she offer to stir away; upon which I tossed her a bit of biscuit, though, by the way, I was not very free of it, for my store was not great: however, I spared her a bit, I say, and she went to it, smelled at it, and ate it, and looked (as if pleased) for more; but I thanked her, and could spare no more, so she marched off.

Having got my second cargo on shore—though I was fain to open the barrels of powder, and bring them by parcels, for they were too heavy, being large casks—I went to work to make me a little tent with the sail and some poles which I cut for that purpose, and into this tent I brought everything that I knew would spoil either with rain or sun; and I piled all the empty chests and casks up in a circle round the tent, to fortify it from any sudden attempt, either from man or beast.

When I had done this, I blocked up the door of the tent with some boards within, and an empty chest set up on end without; and spreading one of the beds upon the ground, laying my two pistols just at my head, and my gun at length by me, I went to bed for the first time, and slept very quietly all night, for I was very weary and heavy; for the night before I had slept little, and had labored very hard all day to fetch all those things from the ship, and to get them on shore.

I had the biggest magazine of all kinds now that ever was laid up, I believe, for one man; but I was not satisfied still, for while the ship sat upright in that posture I thought I ought to get everything out of her that I could: so every day at low water I went on board, and brought away something or other; but particularly the third time I went I brought away as much of the rigging as I could, as also all the small ropes and rope-twines I could get, with a piece of spare canvas, which was to mend the sails upon occasion, and the barrel of wet gunpowder. In a word, I brought away all the sails, first and last; only that I was fain to cut them in pieces, and bring as much at a time as I could, for they were no more useful to be sails, but as mere canvas only.

But that which comforted me more still was that last of all, after I had made five or six such voyages as these, and thought I had nothing more to expect from the ship that was worth my meddling with—I say, after all this, I found a great hogshead of bread, three large runlets of rum, or spirits, a box of sugar, and a barrel of fine flour; this was surprising to me, because I had given over expecting any more provisions, except what was spoiled by the water. I soon emptied the hogshead of the bread, and wrapped it up, parcel by parcel, in pieces of the sails, which I cut out; and, in a word, I got all this safe on shore also.

The next day I made another voyage, and now, having plundered the ship of what was portable and fit to hand out, I began with the cables. Cutting the great cable into pieces, such as I could move, I got two cables and a hawser on shore, with all the ironwork I could get; and having cut down the spritsail-yard, and the mizzen- yard, and everything I could, to make a large raft, I loaded it with all these heavy goods, and came away. But my good luck began now to leave me; for this raft was so unwieldy, and so overladen, that, after I had entered the little cove where I had landed the rest of my goods, not being able to guide it so handily as I did the other, it overset, and threw me and all my cargo into the water. As for myself, it was no great harm, for I was near the shore; but as to my cargo, it was a great part of it lost, especially the iron, which I expected would have been of great use to me; however, when the tide was out, I got most of the pieces of the cable ashore, and some of the iron, though with infinite labor; for I was fain to dip for it into the water, a work which fatigued me very much. After this, I went every day on board, and brought away what I could get.

I had been now thirteen days on shore, and had been eleven times on board the ship, in which time I had brought away all that one pair of hands could well be supposed capable to bring; though I believe verily, had the calm weather held, I should have brought away the whole ship, piece by piece. But preparing the twelfth time to go on board, I found the wind began to rise; however, at low water I went on board, and, though I thought I had rummaged the cabin so effectually that nothing more could be found, yet I discovered a locker with drawers in it, in one of which I found two or three razors, and one pair of large scissors, with some ten or a dozen of good knives and forks: in another I found about thirty-six pounds value in money—some European coin, some Brazil, some pieces of eight, some gold, and some silver.

I smiled to myself at the sight of this money: "O drug!" said I, aloud, "what art thou good for? Thou art not worth to me—no, not the taking off the ground; one of those knives is worth all this heap; I have no manner of use for thee—e'en remain where thou art, and go to the bottom, as a creature whose life is not worth saving." However, upon second thoughts I took it away;

and, wrapping all this in a piece of canvas, I began to think of making another raft; but while I was preparing this, I found the sky overcast, and the wind began to rise, and in a quarter of an hour it blew a fresh gale from the shore. It presently occurred to me that it was in vain to pretend to make a raft with the wind off shore; and that it was my business to be gone before the tide of flood began, otherwise I might not be able to reach the shore at all. Accordingly, I let myself down into the water, and swam across the channel which lay between the ship and the sands, and even that with difficulty enough, partly with the weight of the things I had about me, and partly the roughness of the water; for the wind rose very hastily, and before it was quite high water it blew a storm.

But I had got home to my little tent, where I lay, with all my wealth about me, very secure. It blew very hard all night, and in the morning, when I looked out, behold, no more ship was to be seen! I was a little surprised, but recovered myself with the satisfactory reflection that I had lost no time, nor abated any diligence, to get everything out of her that could be useful to me; and that, indeed, there was little left in her that I was able to bring away, if I had had more time.

THE BUILDING OF THE BOAT

By Daniel Defoe

Having now brought my mind a little to relish my condition, and given over looking out to sea, to see if I could spy a ship—I say, giving over these things, I began to apply myself to arrange my way of living, and to make things as easy to me as I could.

My habitation was a tent under the side of a rock, surrounded with a strong pale of posts and cables; but I might now rather call it a wall, for I raised a kind of wall up against it of turfs, about two feet thick, on the outside; and after some time (I think it was a year and a half) I raised rafters from it, leaning to the rock, and thatched or covered it with boughs of trees, and such things as I could get, to keep out the rain; which I found at some times of the year very violent.

I have already observed how I brought all my goods into this pale, and into the cave which I had made behind me. But I must observe, too, that at first this was a confused heap of goods, which, as they lay in no order, so they took up all my place—I had no room to turn myself; so I set myself to enlarge my cave, and work farther into the earth, for it was a loose sandy rock, which yielded easily to the labor I bestowed on it; and so, when I found I was pretty safe as to beasts of prey, I worked sideways, to the right hand, into the rock; and then, turning to the right again, worked quite out, and made me a door to come out on the outside of my pale or fortification. This gave me not only egress and regress, as it was a back way to my tent and to my storehouse, but gave me room to store my goods.

And now I began to apply myself to make such necessary things as I found I most wanted, particularly a chair and a table; for without these I was not able to enjoy the few comforts I had in the world— I could not write or eat, or do several things, with so much pleasure without a table; so I went to work. And here I must needs observe that, as reason is the substance and origin of the mathematics, so by stating and squaring everything by reason, and by making the most rational judgment of things, every man may be, in time, master of every mechanic art. I had never handled a tool in my life; and yet, in time, by labor, application, and contrivance, I found at last that I wanted nothing but I could have made it, especially if I had had tools. However, I made abundance of things, even without tools; and some with no more tools than an adze and a hatchet, which perhaps were never made that way before, and that with infinite labor. For example, if I wanted a board, I had no other way but to cut down a tree, set it on an edge before me, and hew it flat on either side with my axe, till I brought it to be thin as a plank, and then dub it smooth with my adze. It is true, by this method I could make but one board out of a whole tree; but this I had no remedy for but patience, any more than I had for the prodigious deal of time and labor which it took me up to make a plank or board; but my time or labor was little worth, and so it was as well employed one way as another.

However, I made me a table and a chair, as I observed above, in the first place; and this I did out of the short pieces of boards that I brought on my raft from the ship. But when I had wrought out some boards as above, I made large shelves, of the breadth of a foot and a half, one over another all along one side of my cave, to lay all my tools, nails, and ironwork on; and, in a word, to separate everything at large into their places, that I might come easily at them. I knocked pieces into the wall of the rock to hang my guns and all things that would hang up; so that, had my cave been to be seen, it looked like a general magazine of all necessary things; and I had everything so ready at my hand that it was a great pleasure to me to see all my goods in such order, and especially to find my stock of all necessaries so great.

And now it was that I began to keep a journal of every day's employment; for, indeed, at first I was in too much hurry, and not only hurry as to labor, but in too much discomposure of mind; and my journal would have been full of many dull things.

You may be sure my thoughts ran many times upon the prospect of land which I had seen from the other side of the island; and I was not without secret wishes that I were on shore there, fancying that, seeing the mainland, and an inhabited country, I might find some way or other to convey myself further, and perhaps at last find some means of escape.

But all this while I made no allowance for the dangers of such an undertaking, and how I might fall into the hands of savages, and perhaps such as I might have reason to think far worse than the lions and tigers of Africa: that if I once came in their power, I should run a hazard of more than a thousand to one of being killed, and perhaps of being eaten; for I had heard that the people of the Caribbean coast were cannibals or man-eaters, and I knew by the latitude that I could not be far from that shore. Then, supposing they were not cannibals, yet they might kill me, as many Europeans who had fallen into their hands had been served, even when they had been ten or twenty together—much more I, that was but one, and could make little or no defence; all these things, I say, which I ought to have considered well, and did come into my thoughts afterwards, yet gave me no apprehensions at first, and my head ran mightily upon the thought of getting over to the shore.

Now I wished for my boy Xury, and the longboat with shoulder-of-mutton sail, with which I sailed above a thousand miles on the coast of Africa; but this was in vain. Then I thought I would go and look at our ship's boat, which, as I have said, was blown up upon the shore a great way, in the storm, when we were first cast away. She lay almost where she did at first, but not quite; and was turned, by the force of the waves and the winds, almost bottom upward, against a high ridge of beachy, rough sand, but no water about her. If I had had hands to have refitted her, and to have launched her into the water, the boat would have done well enough, and I might have gone back into the Brazils with her easily enough; but I might have foreseen that I could no more turn her and set her upright upon her bottom than I could remove the island; however, I went to the woods, and cut levers and rollers, and brought them to the boat, resolving to try what I could do; suggesting to myself that if I could but turn her down, I might repair the damage she had received, and she would be a very good boat, and I might go to sea in her very easily.

I spared no pains, indeed, in this piece of fruitless toil, and spent, I think, three or four weeks about it; at last, finding it impossible to heave it up with my little strength, I fell to digging away the sand, to undermine it, and so to make it fall down, setting pieces of wood to thrust and guide it right in the fall.

But when I had done this, I was unable to stir it up again, or to get under it, much less to move it forward towards the water; so I was forced to give it over; and yet, though I gave over the hopes of the boat, my desire to venture over to the mainland increased, rather than decreased, as the means for it seemed impossible.

This at length put me upon thinking whether it was not possible to make myself a canoe, or periagua, such as the natives of those climates make, even without tools, or, as I might say, without hands, of the trunk of a great tree. This I not only thought possible, but easy, and pleased myself extremely with the thoughts of making it, and with my having much more convenience for it than any of the negroes or Indians; but not at all considering the particular inconvenience which I lay under more than the Indians did, viz., want of hands to move it, when it was made, into the water—a difficulty much harder for me to surmount than all the consequences of want of tools could be to them; for what was it to me if, when I had chosen a vast tree in the woods, and with much trouble cut it down, if I had been able with my tools to hew and dub the outside into the proper shape of a boat, and burn or cut out the inside to make it hollow, so as to make a boat of it—if, after all this, I must leave it just there where I found it, and not be able to launch it into the water?

One would have thought I could not have had the least reflection upon my mind of my circumstances while I was making this boat but I should have immediately thought how I should get it into the sea; but my thoughts were so intent upon my voyage over the sea in it that I never once considered how I should get it off the land; and it was really, in its own nature, more easy for me to guide it over forty-five miles of sea than about forty-five fathoms of land, where it lay, to set it afloat in the water.

I went to work upon this boat the most like a fool that ever man did who had any of his senses awake. I pleased myself with the design, without determining whether I was ever able to undertake it; not but that the difficulty of launching my boat came often into my head, but I put a stop to my inquiries into it by this foolish answer which I gave myself—"Let me first make it; I warrant I will find some way or other to get it along when it is done."

This was a most preposterous method; but the eagerness of my fancy prevailed, and to work I went. I felled a cedar-tree, and I question much whether Solomon ever had such a one for the building of the Temple of Jerusalem; it was five feet ten inches diameter at the lower part next the stump, and four feet eleven inches diameter at the end of twenty-two feet; after which it lessened for a while, and then parted into branches. It was not without infinite labor that I felled this tree; I was twenty days hacking and hewing at it at the bottom; I was fourteen more getting the branches and limbs and the vast spreading head cut off, which I hacked and hewed through with axe and hatchet, and inexpressible labor; after this, it cost me a month to shape it and dub it to a proportion, and to something like the bottom of a boat, that it might swim upright as it ought to do. It cost me near three months more to clear the inside, and work it out so as to make an exact boat of it; this I did, indeed, without fire, by mere mallet and chisel, and by the dint of hard labor, till I had brought it to be a very handsome periagua, and big enough to have carried six-and- twenty men, and consequently big enough to have carried me and all my cargo.

When I had gone through this work I was extremely delighted with it. The boat was really much bigger than ever I saw a canoe or periagua, that was made of one tree, in my life. Many a weary stroke it had cost, you may be sure; and had I gotten it into the water, I make no question but I should have begun the maddest voyage, and the most unlikely to be performed, that ever was undertaken.

But all my devices to get it into the water failed me; though they cost me infinite labor, too. It lay about one hundred yards from the water, and not more; but the first inconvenience was, it was up hill towards the creek. Well, to take away this discouragement, I resolved to dig into the surface of the earth, and so make a declivity: this I began, and it cost me a prodigious deal of pains (but who grudge pains who have their deliverance in view?); but when this was worked through, and this difficulty managed, it was still much the same, for I could no more stir the canoe than I could the other boat. Then I measured the distance of ground, and resolved to cut a dock or canal, to bring the water up to the canoe, seeing I could not bring the canoe down to the water. Well, I began this work; and when I began to enter upon it, and calculate how deep it was to be dug, how broad, how the stuff was to be thrown out, I found that, by the number of hands I had, being none but my own, it must have been ten or twelve years before I could have gone through with it; for the shore lay so high, that at the upper end it must have been at least twenty feet deep; so at length, though with great reluctancy, I gave this attempt over also.

This grieved me heartily; and now I saw, though too late, the folly of beginning a work before we count the cost, and before we judge rightly of our own strength to go through with it.

In the middle of this work I finished my fourth year in this place, and kept my anniversary with the same devotion, and with as much comfort as ever before.

In the first place, I was removed from all the wickedness of the world here; I had neither the lusts of the flesh, the lusts of the eye, nor the pride of life. I had nothing to covet, for I had all that I was now capable of enjoying; I was lord of the whole manor; or, if I pleased, I might call myself king or emperor over the whole country which I had possession of: there were no rivals; I had no competitor, none to dispute sovereignty or command with me; I might have raised ship-loadings of corn, but I had no use for it; so I let as little grow as I thought enough for my occasion. I had tortoise or turtle enough, but now and then one was as much as I could put to any use; I had timber enough to have built a fleet of ships; and I had grapes enough to have made wine, or to have cured into raisins, to have loaded that fleet when it had been built.

But all I could make use of was all that was valuable: I had enough to eat and supply my wants, and what was all the rest to me? If I killed more flesh than I could eat, the dog must eat it, or vermin; if I sowed more corn than I could eat, it must be spoiled; the trees that I cut down were lying to rot on the ground; I could make no more use of them but for fuel, and that I had no occasion for but to dress my food.

In a word, the nature and experience of things dictated to me, upon just reflection, that all the good things of this world are no farther good to us than they are for our use; and that, whatever we may heap up to give others, we enjoy just as much as we can use, and no more. The most covetous, griping miser in the world would have been cured of the vice of covetousness if he had been in my case; for I possessed infinitely more than I knew what to do with.

FINDS THE PRINT OF A MAN'S FOOT ON THE SAND

By Daniel Defoe

It would have made a Stoic smile to have seen me and my little family sit down to dinner. There was my majesty, the prince and lord of the whole island; I had the lives of all my subjects at my absolute command; I could hang, draw, give liberty, and take it away, and no rebels among all my subjects. Then, to see how like a king I dined, too, all alone, attended by my servants! Poll, as if he had been my favorite, was the only person permitted to talk to me. My dog, who was now grown old, sat always at my right hand; and two cats, one on one side of the table and one on the other, expecting now and then a bit from my hand, as a mark of especial favor. With this attendance and in this plentiful manner I lived; neither could I be said to want anything but society; and of that, some time after this, I was likely to have too much.

I was something impatient, as I have observed, to have the use of my boat, though very loath to run any more hazards; and therefore sometimes I sat contriving ways to get her about the island, and at other times I sat myself down contented enough without her. But I had a strange uneasiness in my mind to go down to the point of the island: this inclination increased upon me every day, and at length I resolved to travel thither by land, following the edge of the shore. I did so; but had any one in England met such a man as I was, it must either have frightened him, or raised a great deal of laughter; and as I frequently stood still to look at myself, I could not but smile at the notion of my travelling through Yorkshire with such an equipage, and in such a dress. Be pleased to take a sketch of my figure, as follows:

I had a great high shapeless cap, made of a goat's skin, with a flap hanging down behind, as well to keep the sun from me as to shoot the rain off from running into my neck, nothing being so hurtful in these climates as the rain upon the flesh under the clothes.

I had a short jacket of goat's skin, the skirts coming down to about the middle of the thighs, and a pair of open-kneed breeches of the same; the breeches were made of the skin of an old he-goat, whose hair hung down such a length on either side that, like pantaloons, it reached to the middle of my legs; stockings and shoes I had none, but had made me a pair of somethings, I scarce knew what to call them, like buskins, to flap over my legs, and lace on either side like spatterdashes, but of a most barbarous shape, as indeed were all the rest of my clothes.

I had on a broad belt of goat's skin dried, which I drew together with two thongs of the same instead of buckles, and in a kind of a frog on either side of this, instead of a sword and dagger, hung a little saw and a hatchet, one on one side and one on the other. I had another belt not so broad, and fastened in the same manner, which hung over my shoulder, and at the end of it, under my left arm, hung two pouches, both made of goat's skin, too, in one of which hung my powder, in the other my shot. At my back I carried my basket, and on my shoulder my gun, and over my head a great clumsy, ugly, goat's-skin umbrella, but which, after all, was the most necessary thing I had about me next to my gun. As for my face, the color of it was really not so mulatto-like as one might expect from a man not at all careful of it, and living within nine or ten degrees of the equinox. My beard I had once suffered to grow till it was about a quarter of a yard long; but, as I had both scissors and razors sufficient, I had cut it pretty short, except what grew on my upper lip, which I had trimmed into a large pair of Mahometan whiskers, such as I had seen worn by some Turks at Sallee, for the Moors did not wear such, though the Turks did; of these mustachios, or whiskers, I will not say they were long enough to hang my hat upon them, but they were of a length and shape monstrous enough, and such as in England would have passed for frightful.

But all this is by the by; for as to my figure, I had so few to observe me that it was of no manner of consequence, so I say no more of that. In this kind of dress I went my new journey, and was out five or six days. I travelled first along the seashore, directly to the place where I first brought my boat to an anchor to get upon the rocks; and, having no boat now to take care of, I went over the land a nearer way to the same height that I was upon before, when, looking forward to the points of the rocks which lay out, and which I was obliged to double with my boat, as is said above, I was surprised to see the sea all smooth and quiet—no rippling, no motion, no current, any more there than in other places. I was at a strange loss to understand this, and resolved to spend some time in the observing it, to see if nothing from the sets of the tide had occasioned it; but I was presently convinced how it was; viz., that the tide of ebb setting from the west, and joining with the current of waters from some great river on the shore, must be the occasion of this current, and that, according as the wind blew more forcibly from the west or from the north, this current came nearer or went farther from the shore; for, waiting thereabouts till evening, I went up to the rock again, and then, the tide of ebb being made, I plainly saw the current again as before, only that it ran farther off, being near half a league from the shore, whereas in my case it set close upon the shore, and hurried me and my canoe along with it, which at another time it would not have done.

This observation convinced me that I had nothing to do but to observe the ebbing and the flowing of the tide, and I might very easily bring my boat about the island again; but when I began to think of putting it in practice, I had such terror upon my spirits at the remembrance of the danger I had been in, that I could not think of it again with any patience, but, on the contrary, I took up another resolution, which was more safe, though more laborious — and this was, that I would build, or rather make, me another perigaua or canoe, and so have one for one side of the island, and one for the other.

You are to understand that now I had, as I may call it, two plantations in the island — one my little fortification or tent, with the wall about it, under the rock, with the cave behind me, which by this time I had enlarged into several apartments or caves, one within another. One of these, which was the driest and largest, and had a door out beyond my wall or fortification — that is to say, beyond where my wall joined to the rock — was all filled up with the large earthen pots of which I have given an account, and with fourteen or fifteen great baskets, which would hold five or six bushels each, where I laid up my stores of provisions, especially my corn, some in the ear, cut off short from the straw, and the other rubbed out with my hand.

As for my wall, made, as before, with long stakes or piles, those piles grew all like trees, and were by this time grown so big, and spread so very much, that there was not the least appearance, to any one's view, of any habitation behind them.

Near this dwelling of mine, but a little farther within the land, and upon lower ground, lay my two pieces of corn land, which I kept duly cultivated and sowed, and which duly yielded me their harvest in its season; and whenever I had occasion for more corn, I had more land adjoining as fit as that.

Besides this, I had my country-seat, and I had now a tolerable plantation there also; for, first, I had my little bower as I called it, which I kept in repair — that is to say, I kept the hedge which encircled it in constantly fitted up to its usual height, the ladder standing always in the inside. I kept the trees, which at first were no more than stakes, but were now grown very firm and tall, always cut, so that they might spread and grow thick and wild, and make the more agreeable shade, which they did effectually to my mind. In the middle of this I had my tent always standing, being a piece of a sail spread over poles, set up for that purpose, and which never wanted any repair or renewing; and under this I had made me a squab or couch with the skins of the creatures I had killed, and with other soft things, and a blanket laid on them, such as belonged to our sea-bedding, which I had saved; and a great watch-coat to cover me. And there, whenever I had occasion to be absent from my chief seat, I took up my country habitation.

Adjoining to this I had my enclosures for my cattle, that is to say my goats, and I had taken an inconceivable deal of pains to fence and enclose this ground. I was so anxious to see it kept entire, lest the goats should break through, that I never left off till, with infinite labor, I had stuck the outside of the hedge so full of small stakes, and so near to one another, that it was rather a pale than a hedge, and there was scarce room to put a hand through between them; which afterwards, when those stakes grew, as they all did in the next rainy season, made the enclosure strong like a wall, indeed stronger than any wall.

This will testify for me that I was not idle, and that I spared no pains to bring to pass whatever appeared necessary for my comfortable support, for I considered the keeping up a breed of tame creatures thus at my hand would be a living magazine of flesh, milk, butter, and cheese for me as long as I lived in the place, if it were to be forty years; and that keeping them in my reach depended entirely upon my perfecting my enclosures to such a degree that I might be sure of keeping them together; which by this method, indeed, I so effectually secured that, when these little stakes began to grow, I had planted them so very thick that I was forced to pull some of them up again.

In this place also I had my grapes growing, which I principally depended on for my winter store of raisins, and which I never failed to preserve very carefully, as the best and most agreeable dainty of my whole diet; and indeed they were not only agreeable, but medicinal, wholesome, nourishing, and refreshing to the last degree.

As this was also about half-way between my other habitation and the place where I had laid up my boat, I generally stayed and lay here in my way thither, for I used frequently to visit my boat; and I kept all things about or belonging to her in very good order. Sometimes I went out in her to divert myself, but no more hazardous voyages would I go, scarcely ever above a stone's cast or two from the shore, I was so apprehensive of being hurried out of my knowledge again by the currents or winds, or any other accident. But now I come to a new scene of my life.

It happened one day, about noon, going towards my boat, I was exceedingly surprised with the print of a man's naked foot on the shore, which was very plain to be seen on the sand. I stood like one thunderstruck, or as if I had seen an apparition. I listened, I looked round me, but I could hear nothing, nor see anything; I went up to a rising ground to look farther; I went up the shore and down the shore, but it was all one; I could see no other impression but that one. I went to it again to see if there were any more, and to observe if it might not be my fancy; but there was no room for that, for there was exactly the print of a foot— toes, heel, and every part of a foot. How it came thither I knew not, nor could I in the least imagine; but after innumerable fluttering thoughts, like a man perfectly confused and out of myself, I came home to my fortification, not feeling, as we say, the ground I went on, but terrified to the last degree, looking behind me at every two or three steps, mistaking every bush and tree, and fancying every stump at a distance to be a man. Nor is it possible to describe how many various shapes my affrighted imagination represented things to me in, how many wild ideas were found every moment in my fancy, and what strange, unaccountable whimsies came into my thoughts by the way.

When I came to my castle (for so I think I called it ever after this), I fled into it like one pursued. Whether I went over by the ladder, as first contrived, or went in at the hole in the rock, which I had called a door, I cannot remember; no, nor could I remember the next morning, for never frightened hare fled to cover, or fox to earth, with more terror of mind than I to this retreat.

I slept none that night; the farther I was from the occasion of my fright, the greater my apprehensions were, which is something contrary to the nature of such things, and especially to the usual practice of all creatures in fear; but I was so embarrassed with my own frightful ideas of the thing, that I formed nothing but dismal imaginations to myself, even though I was now a great way off. Sometimes I fancied it must be the devil, and reason joined in with me in this supposition, for how should any other thing in human shape come into the place? Where was the vessel that brought them? What marks were there of any other footstep? And how was it possible a man should come there? But then, to think that Satan should take human shape upon him in such a place, where there could be no manner of occasion for it, but to leave the print of his foot behind him, and that even for no purpose, too, for he could not be sure I should see it—this was an amusement the other way. I considered that the devil might have found out abundance of other ways to have terrified me than this of the single print of a foot; that as I lived quite on the other side of the island, he would never have been so simple as to leave a mark in a place where it was ten thousand to one whether I should ever see it or not, and in the sand, too, which the first surge of the sea, upon a high wind, would have defaced entirely. All this seemed inconsistent with the thing itself, and with all the notions we usually entertain of the subtlety of the devil.

Abundance of such things as these assisted to argue me out of all apprehensions of its being the devil; and I presently concluded then that it must be some more dangerous creature; viz., that it must be some of the savages of the mainland opposite who had wandered out to sea in their canoes, and, either driven by the currents or by contrary winds, had made the island, and had been on shore, but were gone away again to sea; being as loath, perhaps, to have stayed in this desolate island as I would have been to have had them.

While these reflections were rolling in my mind, I was very thankful in my thoughts that I was so happy as not to be thereabouts at that time, or that they did not see my boat, by which they would have concluded that some inhabitants had been in the place, and perhaps have searched farther for me. Then terrible thoughts racked my imagination about their having found out my boat, and that there were people here; and that, if so, I should certainly have them come again in greater numbers and devour me; that if it should happen that they should not find me, yet they would find my enclosure, destroy all my corn, and carry away all my flock of tame goats, and I should perish at last for mere want.

Thus my fear banished all my religious hope, all that former confidence in God, which was founded upon such wonderful experience as I had had of His goodness; as if He that had fed me by miracle hitherto could not preserve, by His power, the provision which He had made for me by His goodness. I reproached myself with my laziness, that would not sow any more corn one year than would just serve me till the next season, as if no accident could intervene to prevent my enjoying the crop that was upon the ground; and this I thought so just a reproof, that I resolved for the future to have two or three years' corn beforehand; so that, whatever might come, I might not perish for want of bread.

How strange a chequer-work of Providence is the life of man! and by what secret different springs are the affections hurried about, as different circumstances present! To-day we love what to-morrow we hate; to-day we seek what to-morrow we shun; to-day we desire what to-morrow we fear, nay, even tremble at the apprehensions of. This was exemplified in me, at this time, in the most lively manner imaginable; for I whose only affliction was that I seemed banished from human society, that I was alone, circumscribed by the boundless ocean, cut off from mankind, and condemned to what I call silent life; that I was as one whom Heaven thought not worthy to be numbered among the living, or to appear among the rest of His creatures; that to have seen one of my own species would have seemed to me a raising me from death to life, and the greatest blessing that Heaven itself, next to the supreme blessing of salvation, could bestow—I say, that I should now tremble at the very apprehensions of seeing a man, and was ready to sink into the ground at but the shadow or silent appearance of a man having set his foot in the island.

Such is the uneven state of human life; and it afforded me a great many curious speculations afterwards, when I had recovered from my first surprise. I considered that this was the station of life the infinitely wise and good providence of God had determined for me; that as I could not foresee what the ends of Divine wisdom might be in all this, so I was not to dispute His sovereignty; who, as I was His creature, had an undoubted right, by creation, to govern and dispose of me absolutely as He thought fit; and who, as I was a creature that had offended Him, had likewise a judicial right to condemn me to what punishment He thought fit; and that it was my part to submit to bear His indignation, because I had sinned against Him. I then reflected, that as God, who was not only righteous but omnipotent, had thought fit thus to punish and afflict me, so He was able to deliver me: that if He did not think fit to do so, it was my unquestioned duty to resign myself absolutely and entirely to His will; and, on the other hand, it was my duty also to hope in Him, pray to Him, and quietly to attend to the dictates and directions of His daily providence.

These thoughts took me up many hours, days, nay, I may say weeks and months: and one particular effect of my cogitations on this occasion I cannot omit. One morning early, lying in my bed, and filled with thoughts about my danger from the appearances of savages, I found it discomposed me very much; upon which these words of the Scripture came into my thoughts, "Call upon Me in the day of trouble, and I will deliver thee, and thou shalt glorify Me." Upon this, rising cheerfully out of my bed, my heart was not only comforted, but I was guided and encouraged to pray earnestly to God for deliverance; when I had done praying I took up my Bible, and, opening it to read, the first words that presented to me were, "Wait on the Lord, and be of good cheer, and He shall strengthen thy heart; wait, I say, on the Lord." It is impossible to express the comfort this gave me. In answer, I thankfully laid down the book, and was no more sad, at least on that occasion.

In the middle of these cogitations, apprehensions, and reflections, it came into my thoughts one day that all this might, be a mere chimera of my own, and that this foot might be the print of my own foot, when I came on shore from my boat: this cheered me up a little, too, and I began to persuade myself it was all a delusion; that it was nothing else but my own foot, and why might I not come that way from the boat, as well as I was going that way to the boat? Again, I considered also that I could by no means tell for certain where I had trod, and where I had not; and that if, at last, this was only the print of my own foot, I had played the part of those fools who try to make stories of spectres and apparitions, and then are frightened at them more than anybody.

Now I began to take courage, and to peep abroad again, for I had not stirred out of my castle for three days and nights so that I began to starve for provisions; for I had little or nothing within doors but some barley-cakes and water; then I knew that my goats wanted to be milked, too, which usually was my evening diversion, and the poor creatures were in great pain and inconvenience for want of it; and, indeed, it almost spoiled some of them, and almost dried up their milk. Encouraging myself, therefore, with the belief that this was nothing but the print of one of my own feet, and that I might be truly said to start at my own shadow, I began to go abroad again, and went to my country house to milk my flock; but to see with what fear I went forward, how often I looked behind me, how I was ready every now and then to lay down my basket and run for my life, it would have made any one have thought I was haunted with an evil conscience, or that I had been lately most terribly frightened; and so, indeed, I had.

However, I went down thus two or three days, and, having seen nothing, I began to be a little bolder, and to think there was really nothing in it but my own imagination; but I could not persuade myself fully of this till I should go down to the shore again, and see this print of a foot, and measure it by my own, and see if there was any similitude or fitness, that I might be assured it was my own foot: but when I came to the place, first, it appeared evidently to me that when I laid up my boat I could not possibly be on shore anywhere thereabouts; secondly, when I came to measure the mark with my own foot, I found my foot not so large by a great deal. Both these things filled my head with new imaginations, and gave me the vapors again to the highest degree, so that I shook with cold like one in an ague; and I went home again, filled with the belief that some man or men had been on shore there; or, in short, that the island was inhabited, and I might be surprised before I was aware; and what course to take for my security I knew not.

Oh, what ridiculous resolutions men take when possessed with fear! It deprives them of the use of those means which reason offers for their relief. The first thing I proposed to myself was, to throw down my enclosures, and turn all my tame cattle wild into the woods, lest the enemy should find them, and then frequent the island in prospect of the same or the like booty; then the simple thing of digging up my two corn-fields, lest they should find such a grain there, and still be prompted to frequent the island; then to demolish my bower and tent, that they might not see any vestiges of habitation, and be prompted to look farther, in order to find out the persons inhabiting.

These were the subjects of the first night's cogitations after I was come home again, while the apprehensions which had so overrun my mind were fresh upon me, and my head was full of vapors. Thus, fear of danger is ten thousand times more terrifying than danger itself, when apparent to the eyes, and we find the burden of anxiety greater, by much, than the evil which we are anxious about; and what was worse than all this, I had not that relief in this trouble that from the resignation I used to practise I hoped to have. I looked, I thought, like Saul, who complained not only that the Philistines were upon him, but that God had forsaken him; for I did not now take due ways to compose my mind, by crying to God in my distress, and resting upon His providence, as I had done before, for my defence and deliverance; which, if I had done, I had at least been more cheerfully supported under this new surprise, and perhaps carried through it with more resolution.

This confusion of my thoughts kept me awake all night; but in the morning I fell asleep; and having, by the amusement of my mind, been as it were tired, and my spirits exhausted, I slept very soundly, and waked much better composed than I had ever been before. And now I began to think sedately; and, upon debate with myself, I concluded that this island (which was so exceedingly pleasant, fruitful, and no farther from the mainland than as I had seen) was not so entirely abandoned as I might imagine; that, although there were no stated inhabitants who lived on the spot, yet that there might sometimes come boats off from the shore, who, either with design, or perhaps never but when they were driven by cross winds, might come to this place; that I had lived there fifteen years now and had not met with the least shadow or figure of any people yet; and that, if at any time they should be driven here, it was probable they went away again as soon as ever they could, seeing they had never thought fit to fix here upon any occasion; that the most I could suggest any danger from was from any casual accidental landing of straggling people from the main, who, as it was likely, if they were driven hither, were here against their wills, so they made no stay here, but went off again with all possible speed; seldom staying one night on shore, lest they should not have the help of the tides and daylight back again; and that, therefore, I had nothing to do but consider of some safe retreat, in case I should see any savages land upon the spot.

Now I began sorely to repent that I had dug my cave so large as to bring a door through again, which door, as I said, came out beyond where my fortification joined to the rock; upon maturely considering this, therefore, I resolved to draw me a second fortification; in the manner of a semicircle, at a distance from my wall, just where I had planted a double row of trees about twelve years before, of which I made mention; these trees having been planted so thick before, they wanted but few piles to be driven between them, that they might be thicker and stronger, and my wall would be soon finished. So that I had now a double wall; and my outer wall was thickened with pieces of timber, old cables, and everything I could think of, to make it strong; having in it seven little holes, about as big as I might put my arm out at. In the inside of this I thickened my wall to about ten feet thick with continually bringing earth out of my cave, and laying it at the foot of the wall, and walking upon it; and through the seven holes I contrived to plant the muskets, of which I took notice that I had got seven on shore out of the ship; these I planted like my cannon, and fitted them into frames, that held them like a carriage, so that I could fire all the seven guns in two minutes' time; this wall I was many a weary month in finishing, and yet never thought myself safe till it was done.

When this was done I stuck all the ground without my wall, for a great length every way, as full with stakes or sticks of the osier-like wood, which I found so apt to grow, as they could well stand; insomuch that I believe I might set in near twenty thousand of them, leaving a pretty large space between them and my wall, that I might have room to see an enemy, and they might have no shelter from the young trees, if they attempted to approach my outer wall.

Thus in two years' time I had a thick grove; and in five or six years' time I had a wood before my dwelling, growing so monstrously thick and strong that it was indeed perfectly impassable; and no men, of what kind soever, could ever imagine that there was anything beyond it, much less a habitation. As for the way which I proposed to myself to go in and out (for I left no avenue), it was by setting two ladders, one to a part of the rock which was low, and then broke in, and left room to place another ladder upon that; so when the two ladders were taken down no man living could come down to me without doing himself mischief; and if they had come down, they were still on the outside of my outer wall.

Thus I took all the measures human prudence could suggest for my own preservation; and it will be seen at length that they were not altogether without just reason; though I foresaw nothing at that time more than my mere fear suggested to me.

FRIDAY RESCUED FROM THE CANNIBALS

By Daniel Defoe

I was surprised one morning by seeing no less than five canoes all on shore together on my side the island, and the people who belonged to them all landed and out of my sight. The number of them broke all my measures; for seeing so many, and knowing that they always came four or six or sometimes more in a boat, I could not tell what to think of it, or how to take my measures to attack twenty or thirty men single-handed; so lay still in my castle perplexed and discomforted. However, I put myself into the same position for an attack that I had formerly provided, and was just ready for action if anything had presented. Having waited a good while listening to hear if they made any noise, at length, being very impatient, I set my guns at the foot of my ladder, and clambered up to the top of the hill, by my two stages, as usual; standing so, however, that my head did not appear above the hill, so that they could not perceive me by any means. Here I observed, by the help of my perspective glass, that they were no less than thirty in number; that they had a fire kindled, and that they had meat dressed. How they had cooked it I knew not, or what it was, but they were all dancing, in I know not how many barbarous gestures and figures, their own way, round the fire.

While I was thus looking on them, I perceived, by my perspective, two miserable wretches dragged from the boats, where, it seems, they were laid by, and were now brought out for the slaughter. I perceived one of them immediately fall, being knocked down, I suppose, with a club or wooden sword, for that was their way; and two or three others were at work immediately, cutting him open for their cookery, while the other victim was left standing by himself, till they should be ready for him. In that very moment, this poor wretch seeing himself a little at liberty and unbound, nature inspired him with hopes of life, and he started away from them, and ran with incredible swiftness along the sands, directly towards me; I mean towards that part of the coast where my habitation was.

I was dreadfully frightened, I must acknowledge, when I perceived him run my way, and especially when, as I thought, I saw him pursued by the whole body; and now I expected that part of my dream was coming to pass, and that he would certainly take shelter in my grove; but I could not depend, by any means, upon my dream that the other savages would not pursue him thither and find him there. However, I kept my station, and my spirits began to recover when I found that there was not above three men that followed him; and still more was I encouraged when I found that he outstripped them exceedingly in running, and gained ground on them; so that, if he could but hold out for half an hour, I saw easily he would fairly get away from them all.

There was between them and my castle the creek, which I mentioned often in the first part of my story, where I landed my cargoes out of the ship, and this I saw plainly he must necessarily swim over, or the poor wretch would be taken there; but when the savage escaping came thither he made nothing of it, though the tide was then up, but, plunging in, swam through in about thirty strokes, or thereabouts, landed, and ran with exceeding strength and swiftness.

When the three persons came to the creek, I found that two of them could swim, but the third could not, and that, standing on the other side, he looked at the others, but went no farther, and soon after went softly back again; which, as it happened, was very well for him in the end. I observed that the two who swam were yet more than twice as long swimming over the creek as the fellow was that fled from them. It came very warmly upon my thoughts, and indeed irresistibly, that now was the time to get me a servant, and, perhaps, a companion or assistant; and that I was plainly called by Providence to save this poor creature's life. I immediately ran down the ladders with all possible expedition, fetched my two guns, for they were both at the foot of the ladders, as I observed before, and getting up again with the same haste to the top of the hill, I crossed towards the sea; and having a very short cut, and all down hill, placed myself in the way between the pursuers and the pursued, hallooing aloud to him that fled, who, looking back, was at first perhaps as much frightened at me as at them; but I beckoned with my hand to him to come back and, in the meantime, I slowly advanced towards the two that followed; then rushing at once upon the foremost, I knocked him down with the stock of my piece. I was loath to fire, because I would not have the rest hear; though, at that distance, it would not have been easily heard, and being out of sight of the smoke, too, they would not have known what to make of it. Having knocked this fellow down, the other who pursued him stopped, as if he had been frightened, and I advanced towards him; but as I came nearer, I perceived presently he had a bow and arrow, and was fitting it to shoot at me: so I was then obliged to shoot at him first, which I did, and killed him at the first shot.

The poor savage who fled, but had stopped, though he saw both his enemies fallen and killed, as he thought, yet was so frightened with the fire and noise of my piece that he stood stock still and neither came forward nor went backward, though he seemed rather inclined still to fly than to come on. I hallooed again to him, and made signs to come forward, which he easily understood, and came a little way; then stopped again, and then a little farther, and stopped again; and I could then perceive that he stood trembling, as if he had been taken prisoner, and had just been sentenced to be killed, as his two enemies were. I beckoned to him again to come to me, and gave him all the signs of encouragement that I could think of; and he came nearer and nearer, kneeling down every ten or twelve steps, in token of acknowledgment for saving his life. I smiled at him, and looked pleasantly, and beckoned to him to come still nearer; at length he came close to me, and then he kneeled down again, kissed the ground and laid his head upon the ground, and taking me by the foot set my foot upon his head; this, it seems, was in token of swearing to be my slave forever. I took him up and made much of him, and encouraged him all I could.

But there was more work to do yet, for I perceived the savage whom I had knocked down was not killed, but stunned with the blow, and began to come to himself; so I pointed to him, and showed him the savage, that he was not dead; upon this he spoke some words to me and, though I could not understand them, yet I thought they were pleasant to hear, for they were the first sound of a man's voice that I had heard, my own excepted, for above twenty-five years.

But there was no time for such reflections now; the savage who was knocked down recovered himself so far as to sit up upon the ground, and I perceived that my savage began to be afraid; but when I saw that, I presented my other piece at the man, as if I would shoot him; upon this my savage, for so I call him now, made a motion to me to lend him my sword, which hung naked in a belt by my side, which I did. He no sooner had it but he runs to his enemy, and at one blow cut off his head so cleverly no executioner in Germany could have done it sooner or better; which I thought very strange for one who, I had reason to believe, never saw a sword in his life before, except their own wooden swords. However, it seems, as I learned afterwards, they make their wooden swords so sharp, so heavy, and the wood is so hard, that they will even cut off heads with them, ay, and arms, and that at one blow, too. When he had done this, he comes laughing to me in sign of triumph, and brought me the sword again, and, with abundance of gestures which I did not understand, laid it down, with the head of the savage that he had killed, just before me. But that which astonished him most was to know how I killed the other Indian so far off; so, pointing to him, he made signs to me to let him go to him; and I bade him go, as well as I could. When he came to him, he stood like one amazed, looking at him, turning him first on one side, then on the other; looked at the wound the bullet had made, which it seems was just in his breast, where it had made a hole, and no great quantity of blood had followed; but he had bled inwardly, for he was quite dead. He took up his bow and arrows, and came back; so I turned to go away, and beckoned him to follow me, making sign to him that more might come after them. Upon this he made signs to me that he should bury them with sand, that they might not be seen by the rest, if they followed; and so I made signs to him again to do so. He fell to work; and in an instant he had scraped a hole in the sand with his hands big enough to bury the first in, and then dragged him into it, and covered him, and did so by the other also; I believe he had buried them both in a quarter of an hour. Then, calling him away, I carried him, not to my castle, but quite away to my cave, on the farther part of the island: so I did not let my dream come to pass in that part, that he came into my grove for shelter. Here I gave him bread and a bunch of raisins to eat, and a draught of water, which I found he was indeed in great distress for, from his running; and, having refreshed him, I made signs for him to go and lie down to sleep, showing him a place where I had laid some rice-straw, and a blanket upon it, which I used to sleep upon myself sometimes; so the poor creature lay down, and went to sleep.

He was a comely, handsome fellow, perfectly well made, with straight, strong limbs, not too large; tall, and well-shaped; and, as I reckon, about twenty-six years of age. He had a very good countenance, not a fierce and surly aspect, but seemed to have something very manly in his face; and yet he had all the sweetness and softness of a European in his countenance, too, especially when he smiled. His hair was long and black, not curled like wool; his forehead very high and large; and a great vivacity and sparkling sharpness in his eyes. The color of his skin was not quite black, but very tawny; and yet not an ugly, yellow, nauseous tawny, as the Brazilians and Virginians, and other natives of America are, but of a bright kind of a dun olive-color, that had in it something very agreeable, though not very easy to describe. His face was round and plump; his nose small, not flat, like the negroes; a very good mouth, thin lips, and his fine teeth well set, and as white as ivory.

After he had slumbered, rather than slept, about half an hour, he awoke again, and came out of the cave to me—for I had been milking my goats which I had in the enclosure just by; when he espied me he came running to me, laying himself down again upon the ground, with all the possible signs of an humble, thankful disposition, making a great many antic gestures to show it. At last he lays his head flat upon the ground, close to my foot, and sets my other foot upon his head, as he had done before; and after this made all the signs to me of subjection, servitude, and submission imaginable, to let me know how he would serve me so long as he lived. I understood him in many things, and let him know I was very well pleased with him. In a little time I began to speak to him, and teach him to speak to me; and first, I let him know his name should be Friday, which was the day I saved his life: I called him so for the memory of the time. I likewise taught him to say Master, and then let him know that was to be my name; I likewise taught him to say yes and no, and to know the meaning of them. I gave him some milk in an earthen pot, and let him see me drink it before him, and sop my bread in it; and gave him a cake of bread to do the like, which he quickly complied with, and made signs that it was very good for him.

I kept there with him all that night; but as soon as it was day I beckoned to him to come with me, and let him know I would give him some clothes; at which he seemed very glad, for he was stark naked. As we went by the place where he had buried the two men, he pointed exactly to the place, and showed me the marks that he had made to find them again, making signs to me that we should dig them up again and eat them. At this I appeared very angry, expressed my abhorrence of it, made as if I would vomit at the thoughts of it, and beckoned with my hand to him to come away, which he did immediately, with great submission.

I then led him up to the top of the hill, to see if his enemies were gone; and pulling out my glass I looked, and saw plainly the place where they had been, but no appearance of them or their canoes; so that it was plain they were gone, and had left their two comrades behind them, without any search after them.

We came back to our castle, and there I fell to work for my man Friday; and first of all I gave him a pair of linen drawers, which I had out of the poor gunner's chest I mentioned, which I found in the wreck, and which, with a little alteration, fitted him very well; and then I made him a jerkin of goat's skin, as well as my skill would allow (for I was now grown a tolerably good tailor); and I gave him a cap which I made of hare's skin, very convenient, and fashionable enough; and thus he was clothed, for the present, tolerably well, and was mighty well pleased to see himself almost as well clothed as his master. It is true he went awkwardly in these clothes at first: wearing the drawers was very awkward to him, and the sleeves of the waistcoat galled his shoulders and the inside of his arms; but a little easing them where he complained they hurt him, and using himself to them, he took to them at length very well.

The next day, after I came home to my hutch with him, I began to consider where I should lodge him; and that I might do well for him and yet be perfectly easy myself, I made a little tent for him in the vacant place between my two fortifications, in the inside of the last, and in the outside of the first. As there was a door or entrance there into my cave, I made a formal framed door-case, and a door to it, of boards, and set it up in the passage, a little within the entrance; and, causing the door to open in the inside, I barred it up in the night, taking in my ladders, too; so that Friday could no way come at me in the inside of my innermost wall without making so much noise in getting over that it must needs awaken me; for my first wall had now a complete roof over it of long poles, covering all my tent, and leaning up to the side of the hill; which was again laid across with smaller sticks, instead of laths, and then thatched over a great thickness with the rice-straw, which was strong, like reeds; and at the hole or place which was left to go in or out by the ladder I had placed a kind of trap-door, which, if it had been attempted on the outside, would not have opened at all, but would have fallen down and made a great noise. As to weapons, I took them all into my side every night. But I needed none of all this precaution; for never man had a more faithful, loving, sincere servant than Friday was to me; without passions, sullenness, or designs, perfectly obliged and engaged; his very affections were tied to me, like those of a child to a father, and I dare say he would have sacrificed his life to save mine upon any occasion whatsoever; the many testimonies he gave me of this put it out of doubt, and soon convinced me that I needed to use no precautions for my safety on his account.

I was greatly delighted with him, and made it my business to teach him everything that was proper to make him useful, handy, and helpful; but especially to make him speak, and understand me when I spoke; and he was the aptest scholar that ever was; and particularly was so merry, so constantly diligent, and so pleased when he could but understand me, or make me understand him, that it was very pleasant to me to talk to him.

Now my life began to be so easy that I began to say to myself that could I but have been safe from more savages, I cared not if I was never to remove from the place where I lived.

ROBINSON CRUSOE RESCUED

By Daniel Defoe

[After having been on his island for twenty-seven years, an English vessel at last arrives. The crew had mutinied, and brought the captain and several of the men ashore. Crusoe saves the captain and two of the crew, and seizes the ship's boat.]

While we were thus preparing our designs, and had first, by main strength, heaved the boat upon the beach so high that the tide would not float her off at high-water mark, and besides had broke a hole in her bottom too big to be quickly stopped, and were set down musing what we should do, we heard the ship fire a gun, and make a waft with her ensign as a signal for the boat to come on board-but no boat stirred; and they fired several times, making other signals for the boat. At last, when all their signals and firing proved fruitless, and they found the boat did not stir, we saw them, by the help of my glasses, hoist another boat out and row towards the shore; and we found, as they approached, that there were no less than ten men in her, and that they had firearms with them.

As the ship lay almost two leagues from the shore, we had a full view of them as they came, and a plain sight even of their faces; because, the tide having set them a little to the east of the other boat, they rowed up under shore, to come to the same place where the other had landed, and where the boat lay; by this means, I say, we had a full view of them, and the captain knew the persons and characters of all the men in the boat, of whom, be said, there were three very honest fellows, who, he was sure, were led into this conspiracy by the rest, being overpowered and frightened; but that as for the boatswain, who it seems was the chief officer among them, and all the rest, they were as outrageous as any of the ship's crew, and were no doubt made desperate in their new enterprise; and terribly apprehensive he was that they would be too powerful for us. I smiled at him, and told him that men in our circumstances were past the operation of fear; that, seeing almost every condition that could be was better than that which we were supposed to be in, we ought to expect that the consequence, whether death or life, would be sure to be a deliverance. I asked him what he thought of the circumstances of my life, and whether a deliverance were not worth venturing for.

"And where, sir," said I, "is your belief of my being preserved here on purpose to save your life, which elevated you a little while ago? For my part," said I, "there seems to be but one thing amiss in all the prospect of it."

"What is that?" says he.

"Why," said I, "it is that, as you say, there are three or four honest fellows among them which should be spared; had they been all of the wicked part of the crew I should have thought God's providence had singled them out to deliver them into your hands; for depend upon it, every man that comes ashore is our own, and shall die or live as they behave to us."

As I spoke this with a raised voice and cheerful countenance, I found it greatly encouraged him; so we set vigorously to our business.

We had, upon the first appearance of the boat's coming from the ship, considered of separating our prisoners; and we had, indeed, secured them effectually. Two of them, of whom the captain was less assured than ordinary, I sent with Friday, and one of the three delivered men, to my cave, where they were remote enough, and out of danger of being heard or discovered, or of finding their way out of the woods if they could have delivered themselves. Here they left them bound, but gave them provisions, and promised them, if they continued there quietly, to give them their liberty in a day or two; but that if they attempted their escape they should be put to death without mercy. They promised faithfully to bear their confinement with patience, and were very thankful that they had such good usage as to have provisions and light left them; for Friday gave them candles (such as we made ourselves) for their comfort; and they did not know but that he stood sentinel over them at the entrance.

The other prisoners had better usage; two of them were kept pinioned, indeed, because the captain was not able to trust them; but the other two were taken into my service, upon the captain's recommendation, and upon their solemnly engaging to live and die with us; so with them and the three honest men we were seven men, well armed; and I made no doubt we should be able to deal well enough with the ten that were coming, considering that the captain had said there were three or four honest men among them also. As soon as they got to the place where their other boat lay, they ran their boat into the beach and came all on shore, hauling the boat up after them, which I was glad to see, for I was afraid they would rather have left the boat at an anchor some distance from the shore, with some hands in her to guard her, and so we should not be able to seize the boat.

Being on shore, the first thing they did, they ran all to their other boat; and it was easy to see they were under a great surprise to find her stripped, as above, of all that was in her, and a great hole in her bottom. After they had mused a while upon this, they set up two or three great shouts, hallooing with all their might, to try if they could make their companions hear; but all was to no purpose. Then they came all close in a ring, and fired a volley of their small arms, which indeed we heard, and the echoes made the woods ring. But it was all one; those in the cave, we were sure, could not hear; and those in our keeping, though they heard it well enough, yet durst give no answer to them. They were so astonished at the surprise of this, that, as they told us afterwards, they resolved to go all on board again to their ship, and let them know that the men were all murdered, and the long-boat staved; accordingly, they immediately launched their boat again, and got all of them on board.

The captain was terribly amazed, and even confounded, at this, believing they would go on board the ship again and set sail, giving their comrades over for lost, and so he should still lose the ship, which he was in hopes we should have recovered; but he was quickly as much frightened the other way.

They had not been long put off the boat, when we perceived them all coming on shore again; but with this new measure in their conduct, which it seems they consulted together upon, viz., to leave three men in the boat, and the rest to go on shore, and go up into the country to look for their fellows. This was a great disappointment to us, for now we were at a loss what to do, as our seizing those seven men on shore would be no advantage to us if we let the boat escape; because they would row away to the ship, and then the rest of them would be sure to weigh and set sail, and so our recovering the ship would be lost. However, we had no remedy but to wait and see what the issue of things might present. The seven men came on shore, and the three who remained in the boat put her off to a good distance from the shore, and came to an anchor to wait for them; so that it was impossible for us to come at them in the boat. Those that came on shore kept close together, marching towards the top of the little hill under which my habitation lay; and we could see them plainly, though they could not perceive us.

We should have been very glad if they would have come nearer us, so that we might have fired at them, or that they would have gone farther off, that we might come abroad. But when they were come to the brow of the hill where they could see a great way into the valleys and woods, which lay towards the northeast part, and where the island lay lowest, they shouted and hallooed till they were weary; and not caring, it seems, to venture far from the shore, nor far from one another, they sat down together under a tree to consider it. Had they thought fit to have gone to sleep there, as the other part of them had done, they had done the job for us; but they were too full of apprehensions of danger to venture to go to sleep, though they could not tell what the danger was they had to fear.

The captain made a very just proposal to me upon this consultation of theirs, viz., that perhaps they would all fire a volley again, to endeavor to make their fellows hear, and that we should all sally upon them just at the juncture when their pieces were all discharged, and they would certainly yield, and we should have them without bloodshed. I liked this proposal, provided it was done while we were near enough to come up to them before they could load their pieces again. But this event did not happen; and we lay still a long time, very irresolute what course to take. At length I told them there would be nothing done, in my opinion, till night; and then, if they did not return to the boat, perhaps we might find a way to get between them and the shore, and so might use some stratagem with them in the boat to get them on shore. We waited a great while, though very impatient for their removing; and were very uneasy when, after long consultation, we saw them all start up and march down towards the sea; it seems they had such dreadful apprehension of the danger of the place that they resolved to go on board the, ship again, give their companions over for lost, and so go on with their intended voyage with the ship.

As soon as I perceived them go towards the shore, I imagined it to be as it really was, that they had given over their search, and were going back again, and the captain, as soon as I told him my thoughts, was ready to sink at the apprehensions of it; but I presently thought of a stratagem to fetch them back again, and which answered my end to a title. I ordered Friday and the captain's mate to go over the little creek westward, towards the place where the savages came on shore when Friday was rescued, and so soon as they came to a little rising ground, at about half a mile distant, I bid them halloo out, as loud as they could, and wait till they found the seamen heard them; that as soon as ever they heard the seamen answer them, they should return it again; and then, keeping out of sight, take a round, always answering when the others hallooed, to draw them as far into the island and among the woods as possible, and then wheel about again to me by such ways as I directed them.

They were just going into the boat when Friday and the mate hallooed; and they presently heard them, and answering ran along the shore westward, towards the voice they heard, when they were stopped by the creek, where, the water being up, they could not get over, and called for the boat to come up and set them over; as, indeed, I expected. When they had set themselves over, I observed that the boat being gone a good way into the creek, and, as it were, in a harbor within the land, they took one of the three men out of her, to go along with them, and left only two in the boat, having fastened her to the stump of a little tree on the shore. This was what I wished for, and, immediately leaving Friday and the captain's mate to their business, I took the rest with me; and, crossing the creek out of their sight, we surprised the two men before they were aware—one of them lying on the shore, and the other being in the boat. The fellow on shore was between sleeping and waking, and going to start up; the captain, who was foremost, ran in upon him, and knocked him down; and then called out to him in the boat to yield, or he was a dead man.

They needed very few arguments to persuade a single man to yield when he saw five men upon him and his comrade knocked down; besides, this was, it seems, one of the three who were not so hearty in the mutiny as the rest of the crew, and therefore was easily persuaded not only to yield, but afterwards to join very sincerely with us. In the meantime, Friday and the captain's mate so well managed their business with the rest that they drew them, by hallooing and answering from one hill to another, and from one wood to another, till they not only heartily tired them, but left them where they were, very sure they could not reach back to the boat before it was dark; and, indeed, they were heartily tired themselves also, by the time they came back to us.

We had nothing now to do but to watch for them in the dark, and to fall upon them, so as to make sure work with them. It was several hours after Friday came back to me before they came back to their boat; and we could hear the foremost of them, long before they came quite up, calling to those behind to come along, and could also hear them answer, and complain how lame and tired they were, and not able to come any faster, which was very welcome news to us. At length they came up to the boat; but it is impossible to express their confusion when they found the boat fast aground in the creek, the tide ebbed out, and their two men gone. We could hear them call one to another in a most lamentable manner, telling one another they were got into an enchanted island; that either there were inhabitants in it, and they should all be murdered, or else there were devils and spirits in it, and they should be all carried away and devoured. They hallooed, again, and called their two comrades by their names a great many times; but no answer. After some time we could see them, by the little light there was, run about, wringing their hands like men in despair, and sometimes they would go and sit down in the boat to rest themselves, then come ashore again, and walk about again, and so the same thing over again.

My men would fain have had me give them leave to fall upon them at once in the dark; but I was willing to take them at some advantage, so as to spare them, and kill as few of them as I could; and especially I was unwilling to hazard the killing of any of our men, knowing the others were very well armed. I resolved to wait, to see if they did not separate; and therefore, to make sure of them, I drew my ambuscade nearer, and ordered Friday and the captain to creep upon their hands and feet, as close to the ground as they could, that they might not be discovered, and get as near them as they could possibly before they offered to fire.

They had not been long in that posture when the boatswain, who was the principal ringleader of the mutiny, and had now shown himself the most dejected and dispirited of all the rest, came walking towards them, with two more of the crew; the captain was so eager at having this principal rogue so much in his power, that he could hardly have patience to let him come so near as to be sure of him, for they only heard his tongue before; but when they came nearer, the captain and Friday, starting up on their feet, let fly at them. The boatswain was killed upon the spot; the next man was shot, in the body, and fell just by him, though he did not die till an hour or two after; and the third ran for it.

At the noise of the fire I immediately advanced with my whole army, which was now eight men, viz., myself, generalissimo; Friday, my lieutenant-general; the captain and his two men, and the three prisoners of war whom we had trusted with arms. We came upon them, indeed, in the dark, so that they could not see our number; and I made the man they had left in the boat, who was now one of us, to call them by name, to try if I could bring them to a parley, and so perhaps might reduce them to terms; which fell out just as we desired, for indeed it was easy to think, as their condition then was, they would be very willing to capitulate. So he calls out as loud as he could to one of them, "Tom Smith! Tom Smith!"

Tom Smith answered immediately, "Is that Robinson?" for it seems he knew the voice. The other answered,

"Ay, ay; for God's sake, Tom Smith, throw down your arms and yield, or you are all dead men this moment,"

"Who must we yield to? Where are they?" says Smith again.

"Here they are," says he, "here's our captain and fifty men with him, have been hunting you these two hours; the boatswain is killed; Will Fry is wounded, and I am a prisoner; and if you do not yield you are all lost."

"Will they give us quarter, then?" says Tom Smith, "and we will yield."

"I'll go and ask, if you promise to yield," said Robinson: so he asked the captain, and the captain himself then calls out,

"You, Smith, you know my voice; if you lay down your arms immediately and submit, you shall have your lives, all but Will Atkins."

Upon this Will Atkins cried out, "For God's sake, captain, give me quarter; what have I done? They have all been as bad as I," which, by the way, was not true, for it seems this Will Atkins was the first man that laid hold of the captain when they first mutinied, and used him barbarously in tying his hands and giving him injurious language. However, the captain told him he must lay down his arms at discretion, and trust to the governor's mercy: by which he meant me, for they all called me governor. In a word, they all laid down their arms and begged their lives; and I sent the man that had parleyed with them, and two more, who bound them all; and then my great army of fifty men, which, with those three, were in all but eight, came up and seized upon them, and upon their boat; only that I kept myself and one more out of sight for reasons of state.

Our next work was to repair the boat, and think of seizing the ship; and as for the captain, now he had leisure to parley with them, he expostulated with them upon the villany of their practices with him, and upon the further wickedness of their design, and how certainly it must bring them to misery and distress in the end, and perhaps to the gallows. They all appeared very penitent, and begged hard for their lives. As for that, he told them they were not his prisoners, but the commander's of the island; that they thought they had set him on shore in a barren, uninhabited island, but it had pleased God so to direct them that it was inhabited, and that the governor was an Englishman; that he might hang them all there, if he pleased; but as he had given them all quarter, he supposed he would send them all to England, to be dealt with there as justice required, except Atkins, whom he was commanded by the governor to advise to prepare for death, for that he would be hanged in the morning.

Though this was all but a fiction of his own, yet it had its desired effect; Atkins fell upon his knees to beg the captain to intercede with the governor for his life; and all the rest begged of him, for God's sake, that they might not be sent to England.

It now occurred to me that the time of our deliverance was come, and that it would be a most easy thing to bring these fellows in to be hearty in getting possession of the ship; so I retired in the dark from them, that they might not see what kind of a governor they had, and called the captain to me; when I called, at a good distance, one of the men was ordered to speak again and say to the captain, "Captain, the commander calls for you;" and presently the captain replied,

"Tell his excellency I am just coming."

This more perfectly amazed them, and they all believed that the commander was just by, with his fifty men. Upon the captain coming to me,

I told him my project for seizing the ship, which he liked wonderfully well, and resolved to put it in execution the next morning. But, in order to execute it with more art, and to be secure of success, I told him we must divide the prisoners, and that he should go and take Atkins, and two more of the worst of them, and send them pinioned to the cave where the others lay. This was committed to Friday and the two other men who came on shore with the captain. They conveyed them to the cave as to a prison: and it was, indeed, a dismal place, especially to men in their condition. The others I ordered to my bower, as I called it, of which I have given a full description; and as it was fenced in, and they pinioned, the place was secure enough, considering they were upon their behavior.

To these in the morning I sent the captain, who was to enter into a parley with them; in a word, to try them, and tell me whether he thought they might be trusted or not to go on board and surprise the ship. He talked to them of the injury done him, of the condition they were brought to, and that, though the governor had given them quarter for their lives as to the present action, yet that if they were sent to England they would all be hanged in chains; but that if they would join in so just an attempt as to recover the ship, he would have the governor's engagement for their pardon.

Any one may guess how readily such a proposal would be accepted by men in their condition; they fell down on their knees to the captain, and promised, with the deepest imprecations, that they would be faithful to him to the last drop, and that they should owe their lives to him, and would go with him all over the world; that they would own him as a father to them as long as they lived.

"Well," says the captain, "I must go and tell the governor what you say, and see what I can do to bring him to consent to it."

So he brought me an account of the temper he found them in and that he verily believed they would be faithful. However, that we might be very secure, I told him he should go back again and choose out those five, and tell them that they might see he did not want men, that he would take out those five to be his assistants, and that the governor would keep the other two, and the three that were sent prisoners to the castle (my cave), as hostages for the fidelity of those five; and that if they proved unfaithful in the execution, the five hostages should be hanged in chains alive on the shore. This looked severe, and convinced them that the governor was in earnest; however, they had no way left them but accept it, and it was now the business of the prisoners, as much as of the captain, to persuade the other five to do their duty.

Our strength was now thus ordered for the expedition: first, the captain, his mate, and passenger; second, the two prisoners of the first gang, to whom, having their character from the captain, I had given their liberty, and trusted them with arms; third, the other two that I had kept till now in my bower, pinioned, but on the captain's motion had now released; fourth, these five released at last; so that there were twelve in all, besides five we kept prisoners in the cave for hostages.

I asked the captain if he were willing to venture with these hands on board the ship; but as for me and my man Friday, I did not think it was proper for us to stir, having seven men left behind; and it was employment enough for us to keep them asunder, and supply them with victuals. As to the five in the cave, I resolved to keep them fast, but Friday went in twice a day to them, to supply them with necessaries; and I made the other two carry provisions to a certain distance, where Friday was to take them.

When I showed myself to the two hostages it was with the captain, who told them I was the person the governor had ordered to look after them, and that it was the governor's pleasure they should not stir anywhere but at my direction; that if they did, they would be fetched into the castle, and be laid in irons: so that, as we never suffered them to see me as governor, I now appeared as another person, and spoke of the governor, the garrison, the castle, and the like, upon all occasions.

The captain now had no difficulty before him, but to furnish his two boats, stop the breach of one, and man them. He made his passenger captain of one, with four of the men; and himself, his mate, and five more went in the other; and they contrived their business very well, for they came up to the ship about midnight. As soon as they came within call of the ship, he made Robinson hail them, and tell them they had brought off the men and the boat, but that it was a long time before they had found them, and the like, holding them in a chat till they came to the ship's side; when the captain and the mate entering first, with their arms, immediately knocked down the second mate and carpenter with the butt-end of their muskets, being very faithfully seconded by their men; they secured all the rest that were upon the main and quarter decks, and began to fasten the hatches, to keep them down that were below; when the other boat and their men, entering at the forechains, secured the forecastle of the ship, and the scuttle which went down into the cook-room, making three men they found there prisoners.

When this was done, and all safe upon deck, the captain ordered the mate, with three men, to break into the round-house, where the new rebel captain lay, who, having taken the alarm, had got up, and with two men and a boy had got fire-arms in their hands; and when the mate, with a crow, split open the door, the new captain and his men fired boldly among them, and wounded the mate with a musket-ball, which broke his arm, and wounded two more of the men, but killed nobody. The mate, calling for help, rushed, however, into the round-house, wounded as he was, and, with his pistol, shot the new captain through the head, the bullet entering at his mouth, and came out again behind one of his ears, so that he never spoke a word more; upon which the rest yielded, and the ship was taken effectually, without any more lives lost.

As soon as the ship was thus secured, the captain ordered guns to be fired, which was the signal agreed upon with me to give me notice of his success, which, you may be sure, I was very glad to hear, having sat watching upon the shore for it till near two o'clock in the morning. Having thus heard the signal plainly, I laid me down; and, it having been a day of great fatigue to me, I slept sound, till I was surprised with the noise of a gun; and presently starting up, I heard a man call me by the name of "Governor! Governor!" and presently I knew the captain's voice; when, climbing up to the top of the hill, there he stood, and, pointing to the ship, he embraced me in his arms.

"My dear friend and deliverer," says he, "there's your ship; for she is all yours, and so are we, and all that belong to her."

I cast my eyes to the ship, and there she rode, within little more than half a mile of the shore; for they had weighed her anchor as soon as they were masters of her, and, the weather being fair, had brought her to an anchor just against the mouth of the little creek; and, the tide being up, the captain had brought the pinnace in near the place where I had first landed my rafts, and so landed just at my door. I was at first ready to sink down with the surprise; for I saw my deliverance indeed visibly put into my hands, all things easy, and a large ship just ready to carry me away whither I pleased to go. At first, for some time, I was not able to answer him one word; but as he had taken me in his arms, I held fast by him, or I should have fallen to the ground. He perceived the surprise, and immediately pulled a bottle out of his pocket and gave me a dram of cordial, which he had brought on purpose for me. After I had drunk it, I sat down upon the ground; and, though it brought me to myself, yet it was a good while before I could speak a word to him. All this time the poor man was in as great an ecstasy as I, only not under any surprise as I was, and he said a thousand kind and tender things to me, to compose and bring me to myself; but such was the flood of joy in my breast that it put all my spirits into confusion: at last it broke out into tears, and in a little while after I recovered my speech; I then took my turn, and embraced him as my deliverer, and we rejoiced together. I told him I looked upon him as a man sent from Heaven to deliver me, and that the whole transaction seemed to be a chain of wonders; that such things as these were the testimonies we had of a secret hand of Providence governing the world, and an evidence that the eye of an infinite Power could search into the remotest corner of the world, and send help to the miserable whenever He pleased. I forgot not to lift up my heart in thankfulness to Heaven; and what heart could forbear to bless Him who had not only in a miraculous manner provided for me in such a wilderness, and in such a desolate condition, but from whom every deliverance must always be acknowledged to proceed.

When we had talked a while, the captain told me he had brought me some little refreshment, such as the ship afforded, and such as the wretches that had been so long his masters had not plundered him of. Upon this, he called aloud to the boat, and bade his men bring the things ashore that were for the governor; and, indeed, it was a present as if I had been one that was not to be carried away with them, but as if I had been to dwell upon the island still. First, he had brought me a case of bottles full of excellent cordial waters, six large bottles of Madeira wine (the bottles held two quarts each), two pounds of excellent good tobacco, twelve good pieces of the ship's beef, and six pieces of pork, with a bag of peas, and about a hundred-weight of biscuit; he also brought me a box of sugar, a box of flour, a bag full of lemons, and two bottles of lime-juice, and abundance of other things. But besides these, and what was a thousand times more useful to me, he brought me six new clean shirts, six very good neckcloths, two pair of gloves, one pair of shoes, a hat, and one pair of stockings, with a very good suit of clothes of his own, which had been worn but very little: in a word, he clothed me from head to foot. It was a very kind and agreeable present, as any one may imagine, to one in my circumstances, but never was anything in the world of that kind so unpleasant, awkward, and uneasy as it was to me to wear such clothes at first.

After these ceremonies were past, and after all his good things were brought into my little apartment, we began to consult what was to be done with the prisoners we had; for it was worth considering whether we might venture to take them with us or no, especially two of them, whom he knew to be incorrigible and refractory to the last degree; and the captain said he knew they were such rogues that there was no obliging them, and if he did carry them away, it must be in irons, as malefactors, to be delivered over to justice at the first English colony he could come to; and I found that the captain himself was very anxious about it. Upon this, I told him that, if he desired it, I would undertake to bring the two men he spoke of to make it their own request that he should leave them upon the island.

"I should be very glad of that," says the captain, "with all my heart."

"Well," says I, "I will send for them up and talk with them for you."

So I caused Friday and the two hostages—for they were now discharged, their comrades having performed their promise—I say, I caused them to go to the cave, and bring up the five men, pinioned as they were, to the bower, and keep them there till I came. After some time, I came thither dressed in my new habit; and now I was called governor again. Being all met, and the captain with me, I caused the men to be brought before me, and I told them I had a full account of their villanous behavior to the captain, and how they had run away with the ship, and were preparing to commit further robberies, but that Providence had ensnared them in their own ways, and that they were fallen into the pit which they had dug for others. I let them know that by my direction the ship had been seized; that she lay now in the road; and they might see by and by that their new captain had received the reward of his villany, and that they would see him hanging at the yard-arm; that, as to them, I wanted to know what they had to say why I should not execute them as pirates taken in the fact, as by my commission they could not doubt but I had authority so to do.

One of them answered in the name of the rest, that they had nothing to say but this, that when they were taken the captain promised them their lives, and they humbly implored my mercy. But I told them I knew not what mercy to show them; for as for myself, I had resolved to quit the island with all my men, and had taken passage with the captain to go to England; and as for the captain, he could not carry them to England other than as prisoners in irons, to be tried for mutiny and running away with the ship; the consequence of which, they must needs know, would be the gallows; so that I could not tell what was best for them, unless they had a mind to take their fate in the island. If they desired that, as I had liberty to leave the island, I had some inclination to give them their lives, if they thought they could shift on shore. They seemed very thankful for it, and said they would much rather venture to stay there than be carried to England to be hanged. So I left it on that issue.

However, the captain seemed to make some difficulty of it, as if he durst not leave them there. Upon this I seemed a little angry with the captain, and told him that they were my prisoners, not his; and that seeing I had offered them so much favor, I would be as good as my word; and that if he did not think fit to consent to it I would set them at liberty, as I found them, and if he did not like it he might take them again if he could catch them. Upon this they appeared very thankful, and I accordingly set them at liberty, and bade them retire into the woods, to the place whence they came, and I would leave them some fire-arms, some ammunition, and some directions how they should live very well if they thought fit. Upon this I prepared to go on board the ship; but told the captain I would stay that night to prepare my things, and desired him to go on board in the meantime, and keep all right in the ship, and send the boat on shore next day for me; ordering him, at all events, to cause the new captain, who was killed, to be hanged at the yard-arm, that these men might see him.

When the captain was gone, I sent for the men up to me to my apartment, and entered seriously into discourse with them on their circumstances. I told them I thought they had made a right choice; that if the captain had carried them away they would certainly be hanged. I showed them the new captain hanging at the yard-arm of the ship, and told them they had nothing less to expect.

When they bad all declared their willingness to stay, I then told them I would let them into the story of my living there, and put them into the way of making it easy to them. Accordingly, I gave them the whole history of the place, and of my coming to it; showed them my fortifications, the way I made my bread, planted my corn, cured my grapes; and, in a word, all that was necessary to make them easy. I told them the story also of the seventeen Spaniards that were to be expected, for whom I left a letter, and made them promise to treat them in common with themselves. Here it may be noted that the captain, who had ink on board, was greatly surprised that I never hit upon a way of making ink of charcoal and water, or of something else, as I had done things much more difficult.

I left them my fire-arms; viz., five muskets, three fowling- pieces, and three swords. I had above a barrel and a half of powder left; for after the first year or two I used but little, and wasted none. I gave them a description of the way I managed the goats, and directions to milk and fatten them, and to make both butter and cheese. In a word, I gave them every part of my own story; and told them I should prevail with the captain to leave them two barrels of gunpowder more, and some garden-seeds, which I told them I would have been very glad of. Also, I gave them the bag of peas which the captain had brought me to eat, and bade them be sure to sow and increase them.

Having done all this I left them the next day and went on board the ship. We prepared immediately to sail, but did not weigh that night. The next morning early, two of the five men came swimming to the ship's side, and, making the most lamentable complaint of the other three, begged to be taken into the ship for God's sake, for they should be murdered, and begged the captain to take them on board, though he hanged them immediately. Upon this the captain pretended to have no power without me; but after some difficulty, and after their solemn promises of amendment, they were taken on board, and were, some time after, soundly whipped and pickled; after which they proved very honest and quiet fellows.

Some time after this, the boat was ordered on shore, the tide being up, with the things promised to the men; to which the captain, at my intercession, caused their chests and clothes to be added, which they took, and were very thankful for. I also encouraged them, by telling them that if it lay in my power to send any vessel to take them in, I would not forget them.

When I took leave of this island, I carried on board, for relics, the great goat-skin cap I had made, my umbrella, and one of my parrots; also, I forgot not to take the money I formerly mentioned, which had lain by me so long useless that it was grown rusty or tarnished, and could hardly pass for silver till it had been a little rubbed and handled, as also the money I found in the wreck of the Spanish ship. And thus I left the island, the 19th of December, as I found by the ship's account, in the year 1686, after I had been upon it eight-and-twenty years, two months, and nineteen days; being delivered from this second captivity the same day of the month that I first made my escape in the long-boat from among the Moors of Sallee. In this vessel, after a long voyage, I arrived in England the 11th of June, in the year 1687, having been thirty-five years absent.

GULLIVER'S TRAVELS

When the romance of Lemuel Gulliver appeared in 1727 it was immediately seized upon by an eager public. The first edition was gone in a week and was selling at an advanced price before the second edition could be printed. Many a reader at once got out his map to try and locate the Island of Lilliput, and the captain of a ship told Lord Scarborough that he knew Gulliver very well—had met him several times. Gulliver's Travels was written by Jonathan Swift, the Dean of St. Patrick's Cathedral in Dublin, one of the most original of writers, whose work was notably brilliant in the field of politics. From early youth he suffered from some disease of the body that made him cross and irritable, but he was much honored by the poor people of Ireland as their friend and champion. Daniel Defoe, who was about the same age as Swift, and lived at the same time, said Swift was a walking index of all books. It is interesting to note that two of the world's wonderful books, Robinson Crusoe and Gulliver's Travels, appeared when their authors were sixty years of age, and within three years of each other.

GULLIVER IS SHIPWRECKED AND SWIMS FOR HIS LIFE

By Daniel Defoe

My father had a small estate in Nottinghamshire; I was the third of five sons. He sent me to Emmanuel College in Cambridge, at fourteen years old, where I resided three years, and applied myself close to my studies; but the charge of maintaining me (although I had a very scanty allowance) being too great for a narrow fortune, I was bound apprentice to Mr. James Bates, an eminent surgeon in London, with whom I continued four years; and my father now and then sending me small sums of money, I laid them out in learning navigation, and other parts of the mathematics, useful to those who intend to travel, as I always believed it would be some time or other my fortune to do. When I left Mr. Bates, I went down to my father; where, by the assistance of him and my uncle John, and some other relations, I got forty pounds, and a promise of thirty pounds a year to maintain me at Leyden; there I studied physic two years and seven months, knowing it would be useful in long voyages. Soon after my return from Leyden, I was recommended by my good master, Mr. Bates, to be surgeon to the *Swallow,* Captain Abraham Pannell, commander; with whom I continued three years and a half, making a voyage or two into the Levant, and some other parts. When I came back, I resolved to settle in London, to which Mr. Bates, my master, encouraged me, and by him I was recommended to several patients. I took part of a small house in the Old Jewry; and being advised to alter my condition, I married Miss Mary Burton, second daughter to Mr. Edmund Burton, hosier, in Newgate Street, with whom I received four hundred pounds for a portion.

But, my good master Bates dying in two years after, and I having few friends, my business began to fail; for my conscience would not suffer me to imitate the bad practice of too many among my brethren. Having therefore consulted with my wife, and some of my acquaintance, I determined to go again to sea. I was surgeon successively in two ships, and made several voyages for six years to the East and West Indies, by which I got some addition to my fortune. My hours of leisure I spent in reading the best authors, ancient and modern, being always provided with a good number of books; and when I was ashore, in observing the manners and dispositions of the people, as well as learning their language, wherein I had a great facility by the strength of my memory.

The last of these voyages not proving very fortunate, I grew weary of the sea, and intended to stay at home with my wife and family. I removed from the Old Jewry to Fetter Lane, and from thence to Wapping, hoping to get business among the sailors; but it would not turn to account. After three years' expectation that things would mend, I accepted an advantageous offer from Captain William Prichard, master of the *Antelope*, who was making a voyage to the South Sea. We set sail from Bristol, May 4, 1699, and our voyage at first was very prosperous.

It would not be proper, for some reasons, to trouble the reader with the particulars of our adventures in those seas; let it suffice to inform him, that, in our passage from thence to the East Indies, we were driven by a violent storm to the northwest of Van Diemen's Land. By an observation we found ourselves in the latitude of 30 degrees 2 minutes south. Twelve of our crew were dead by immoderate labor, and ill food, the rest were in a very weak condition. On the fifth of November, which was the beginning of summer in those parts, the weather being very hazy, the seamen spied a rock, within half a cable's length of the ship; but the wind was so strong that we were driven directly upon it, and immediately split. Six of the crew, of whom I was one, having let down the boat into the sea, made a shift to get clear of the ship and the rock. We rowed, by my computation, about three leagues, till we were able to work no longer, being already spent with labor while we were in the ship. We therefore trusted ourselves to the mercy of the waves, and in about half an hour the boat was overset by a sudden flurry from the north. What became of my companions in the boat, as well as of those who escaped on the rock, or were left in the vessel, I cannot tell; but conclude they were all lost. For my own part, I swam as fortune directed me, and was pushed forward by wind and tide. I often let my legs drop, and could feel no bottom; but when I was almost gone, and able to struggle no longer, I found myself within my depth; and by this time the storm was much abated. The declivity was so small, that I walked near a mile before I got to the shore, which I conjectured was about eight o'clock in the evening. I then advanced forward near half a mile, but could not discover any sign of houses or inhabitants; at least I was in so weak a condition that I did not observe them. I was extremely tired, and with that, and the heat of the weather, and about half a pint of brandy that I drank as I left the ship, I found myself much inclined to sleep. I lay down on the grass, which was very short and soft, where I slept sounder than ever I remembered to have done in my life, and, as I reckoned, about nine hours; for when I awaked it was just daylight. I attempted to rise but was not able to stir; for as I happened to lie on my back, I found my arms and legs were strongly fastened on each side to the ground; and my hair, which was long and thick, tied down in the same manner. I likewise felt several slender ligatures across my body, from my arm-pits to my thighs. I could only look upwards, the sun began to grow hot, and the light offended my eyes. I heard a confused noise about me, but, in the posture I lay, could see nothing except the sky. In a little time I felt something alive moving on my left leg, which advancing gently forward, over my breast, came almost up to my chin; when bending my eyes downward as much as I could, I perceived it to be a human creature not six inches high, with a bow and arrow in his hands, and a quiver at his back. In the meantime, I felt at least forty more of the same kind (as I conjectured) following the first. I was in the utmost astonishment, and roared so loud, that they all ran back in a fright; and some of them, as I was afterwards told, were hurt with the falls they got by leaping from my sides upon the ground. However, they soon returned, and one of them, who ventured so far as to get a full sight of my face, lifting up his hands and eyes by way of admiration, cried out in a shrill but distinct voice, Hekinah degul; the others repeated the same words several times, but I then knew not what they meant. I lay all this while, as the reader may believe, in great uneasiness; at length, struggling to get loose, I had the fortune to break the strings, and wrench out the pegs that fastened my left arm to the ground; for, by lifting it up to my face, I discovered the methods they had taken to bind me, and, at the same time, with a violent pull, which gave me excessive pain, I a little loosened the strings that tied down my hair on the left side, so that I was just able to turn my head about two inches. But the creatures ran off a second time, before I could seize them; whereupon there was a great shout in a very shrill accent, and after it ceased, I heard one of them cry-aloud, Tolgo phonac; when in an instant I felt above an hundred arrows discharged on my left hand, which pricked me like so many needles; and besides, they shot another flight into the air, as we do bombs in Europe, whereof many I suppose fell on my body (though I felt them not), and some on my face, which I immediately covered with my left hand. When this shower of arrows was over, I fell a-groaning with grief and pain, and then striving again to get loose, they discharged another volley larger than the first, and some of them attempted with spears to stick me in the sides; but, by good luck, I had on me a buff jerkin, which they could not pierce. I thought it the most prudent method to lie still, and my design was to continue so till night, when my left hand being already loose, I could easily free myself; and as for the inhabitants, I had reason to believe I might be a match for the greatest army they could bring against me, if they were all of the same size with him that I saw. But fortune disposed otherwise of me. When the people observed I was quiet, they discharged no more arrows; but, by the noise I heard, I knew their numbers increased; and about four yards from me, over against my right ear, I heard a knocking for above an hour, like that of people at work; when turning my head that way, as well as the pegs and strings would permit me, I saw a stage erected, about a foot and a half from the ground, capable of holding four of the inhabitants, with two or three ladders to mount it; from whence one of them, who seemed to be a person of quality, made me a long speech, whereof I understood not one syllable. But I should have mentioned, that before the principal person began his oration, he cried out three times, *Langro dehul san* (these words and the former were afterwards repeated and explained to me). Whereupon immediately about fifty of the inhabitants came and cut the strings that fastened the left side of my head, which gave me the liberty of turning it to the right, and of observing the person and gesture of him that was to speak. He appeared to be of a middle age, and taller than any of the other three who attended him, whereof one was a page that held up his train, and seemed to be somewhat longer than my middle finger; the other two stood one on each side to support him. He acted every part of an orator, and I could observe many periods of threatenings, and others of promises, pity, arid kindness. I answered in a few words, but in the most submissive manner, lifting up my left hand and both my eyes to the sun, as calling him for a witness; and, being almost famished with hunger, having not eaten a morsel for some hours before I left the ship, I found the demands of nature so strong upon me, that I could not forbear showing my impatience (perhaps against the strict rules of decency) by putting my finger frequently to my mouth, to signify that I wanted food. The *Hurgo* (for so they call a great lord, as I afterwards learnt) understood me very well. He descended from the stage, and commanded that several ladders should be applied to my sides, on which above an hundred of the inhabitants mounted, and walked towards my mouth, laden with baskets full of meat, which had been provided and sent thither by the king's orders, upon the first intelligence he received of me. I observed there was the flesh of several animals, but could not distinguish them by the taste. There were shoulders, legs, and loins, shaped like those of mutton, and very well dressed, but smaller than the wings of a lark. I ate them by two or three at a mouthful, and took three loaves at a time, about the bigness of musket bullets. They supplied me as they could, showing a thousand marks of wonder and astonishment at my bulk and appetite, I then made another sign that I wanted drink. They found by my eating, that a small quantity would not suffice me, and being a most ingenious people, they flung up with great dexterity one of their largest hogsheads, then rolled it towards my hand, and beat out the top; I drank it off at a draught, which I might well do for it did not hold half a pint, and tasted like a small wine of Burgundy, but much more delicious. They brought me a second hogshead, which I drank in the same manner, and made signs for more; but they had none to give me. When I had performed these wonders, they shouted for joy, and danced upon my breast, repeating several times as they did at first, *Hekinah degul*. They made me a sign that I should throw down the two hogsheads, but first warning the people below to stand out of the way, crying aloud, *Borach mevolah,* and when they saw the vessels in the air, there was a universal shout of *Hekinah degul.* I confess, I was often tempted, while they were passing backwards and forwards on my body, to seize forty or fifty of the first that came in my reach, and dash them against the ground. But the remembrance of what I had felt, which probably might not be the worst they could do, and the promise of honor I made them, for so I interpreted my submissive behavior, soon drove out these imaginations. Besides, I now considered myself as bound by the laws of hospitality to a people who had treated me with so much expense and magnificence. However, in my thoughts, I could not sufficiently wonder at the intrepidity of these diminutive mortals, who durst venture to mount and walk upon my body, while one of my hands was at liberty, without trembling at the very sight of so prodigious a creature, as I must appear to them. After some time, when they observed that I made no more demands for meat; there appeared before me a person of high rank from his Imperial Majesty. His Excellency, having mounted on the small of my right leg, advanced forwards up to my face, with about a dozen of his retinue. And producing his credentials under the signet- royal, which he applied close to my eyes, spoke about ten minutes, without any signs of anger, but with a kind of determinate resolution; often pointing forwards, which, as I afterwards found, was towards the capital city, about half a mile distant, whither, it was agreed by his Majesty in council, that I must be conveyed. I answered in few words, but to no purpose, and made a sign with my hand that was loose, putting it to the other (but over his Excellency's head, for fear of hurting him or his train) and then to my own head and body, to signify that I desired my liberty. It appeared that he understood me well enough, for he shook his head by way of disapprobation, and held his hand in a posture, to show that I must be carried as a prisoner. However, he made other signs to let me understand that I should have meat and drink enough, and very good treatment. Whereupon I once more thought of attempting to break my bonds; but again, when I felt the smart of their arrows, upon my face and hands, which were all in blisters, and many of the darts still sticking in them; and observing likewise that the number of my enemies increased, I gave tokens, to let them know that they might do with me what they pleased. Upon this, the *Hurgo* and his train withdrew, with much civility and cheerful countenances. Soon after, I heard a general shout, with frequent repetitions of the words, *Peplom selan*, and I felt great numbers of people on my left side, relaxing the cords to such a degree, that I was able to turn upon my right. But before this, they had daubed my face, and both my hands, with a sort of ointment very pleasant to the smell, which in a few minutes removed all the smart of their arrows. These circumstances, added to the refreshment I had received by their victuals and drink, which were very nourishing, disposed me to sleep. I slept about eight hours, as I was afterwards assured; and it was no wonder, for the physicians, by the emperor's order had mingled a sleepy potion in the hogsheads of wine.

It seems that, upon the first moment I was discovered sleeping on the ground after my landing, the emperor had early notice of it by an express; and determined in council that I should be tied in the manner I have related (which was done in the night while I slept), that plenty of meat and drink should be sent to me, and a machine prepared to carry me to the capital city.

This resolution, perhaps, may appear very bold and dangerous, and I am confident, would not be imitated by any prince in Europe on the like occasion; however, in my opinion, it was extremely prudent, as well as generous; for, supposing these people had endeavored to kill me with their spears and arrows, while I was asleep, I should certainly have awaked with the first sense of smart, which might so far have roused my rage and strength, as to have enabled me to break the strings wherewith I was tied; after which, as they were not able to make resistance, so they could expect no mercy.

These people are most excellent mathematicians, and arrived to a great perfection in mechanics, by the countenance and encouragement of the emperor, who is a renowned patron of learning. This prince has several machines fixed on wheels, for the carriage of trees, and other great weights. He often builds his largest men-of-war, whereof some are nine feet long, in the woods, where the timber grows, and has them carried on these engines three or four hundred yards to the sea. Five hundred carpenters and engineers were immediately set at work to prepare the greatest engine they had. It was a frame of wood raised three inches from the ground, about seven feet long, and four wide, moving upon twenty-two wheels. The shout I heard was upon the arrival of this engine, which, it seems, set out in four hours after my landing. It was brought parallel to me as I lay. But the principal difficulty was, to raise and place me in this vehicle. Eighty poles, each of one foot high, were erected for this purpose, and very strong cords, of the bigness of packthread, were fastened by hooks to many bandages, which the workmen had girt round my neck, my hands, my body, and my legs. Nine hundred of the strongest men were employed to draw up these cords by many pulleys fastened on the poles, and thus, in less than three hours, I was raised, and flung into the engine, and there tied fast. All this I was told, for, while the whole operation was performing, I lay in a profound sleep, by the force of that soporiferous medicine infused into my liquor. Fifteen hundred of the emperor's largest horses, each about four inches and an half high, were employed to draw me towards the metropolis, which, as I said, was half a mile distant.

About four hours after we began our journey, I awaked by a very ridiculous accident; for the carriage being stopped a while to adjust something that was out of order, two or three of the young natives had the curiosity to see how I looked when I was asleep; they climbed up into the engine, and advancing very softly to my face, one of them, an officer in the guards, put the sharp end of his half-pike a good way up into my left nostril, which tickled my nose like a straw, and made me sneeze violently; whereupon they stole off unperceived, and it was three weeks before I knew the cause of my awaking so suddenly. We made a long march the remaining part of that day, and rested at night with five hundred guards on each side of me, half with torches, and half with bows and arrows, ready to shoot me, if I should offer to stir. The next morning at sunrise we continued our march, and arrived within two hundred yards of the city gates about noon. The emperor, and all his court, came out to meet us, but his great officers would by no means suffer his Majesty to endanger his person by mounting on my body.

At the place where the carriage stopped, there stood an ancient temple, esteemed to be the largest in the whole kingdom, which, having been polluted some years before by an unnatural murder, was, according to the zeal of those people, looked on as profane, and therefore had been applied to common use, and all the ornaments and furniture carried away. In this edifice it was determined I should lodge. The great gate fronting to the north, was about four feet high, and almost two feet wide, through which I could easily creep. On each side of the gate was a small window, not above six inches from the ground; into that on the left side, the king's smith conveyed fourscore and eleven chains, like those that hang to a lady's watch in Europe, and almost as large, which were locked to my left leg, with six and thirty padlocks. Over against this temple, on the other side of the great highway, at twenty feet distance, there was a turret at least five feet high. Here the emperor ascended, with many principal lords of his court, to have an opportunity of viewing me, as I was told, for I could not see them. It was reckoned, that above an hundred thousand inhabitants came out of the town upon the same errand; and, in spite of my guards, I believe there could not be fewer than ten thousand, at several times, who mounted my body by the help of ladders. But a proclamation was soon issued to forbid it, upon pain of death. When the workmen found it was impossible for me to break loose, they cut all the strings that bound me; whereupon I rose up with as melancholy a disposition as ever I had in my life.

But the noise and astonishment of the people, at seeing me rise and walk, are not to be expressed. The chains that held my left leg were about two yards long, and gave me not only the liberty of walking backwards and forwards in a semicircle, but, being fixed within four inches of the gate, allowed me to creep in, and lie at my full length in the temple.

GULLIVER AT THE COURT OF LILLIPUT

By Jonathan Swift

My gentleness and good behavior had gained so far on the emperor and his court, and indeed upon the army and people in general, that I began to conceive hopes of getting my liberty in a short time. I took all possible methods to cultivate this favorable disposition. The natives came, by degrees, to be less apprehensive of any danger from me. I would sometimes lie down and let five or six of them dance on my hand; and, at last, the boys and girls would venture to come and play at hide-and-seek in my hair. I had now made a good progress in understanding and speaking their language. The emperor had a mind, one day, to entertain me with several of the country shows, wherein they exceed all nations I have known, both for dexterity and magnificence. I was diverted with none so much as that of the rope-dances, performed upon a slender white thread, extended about two feet, and twelve inches from the ground. Upon which I shall desire liberty, with the reader's patience, to enlarge a little.

This diversion is only practised by those persons who are candidates for great employments, and high favor at court. They are trained in this art from their youth, and are not always of noble birth, or liberal education. When a great office is vacant, either by death or disgrace (which often happens), five or six of those candidates petition the emperor to entertain his Majesty and the court with a dance on the rope, and whoever jumps the highest, without falling, succeeds in the office. Very often the chief ministers themselves are commanded to show their skill, and to convince the emperor that they have not lost their faculty. Flimnap, the treasurer, is allowed to cut a caper on the strait rope at least an inch higher than any other lord in the whole empire. I have seen him do the somerset several times together, upon a trencher fixed on the rope, which is no thicker than a common packthread in England. My friend Reldresal, principal secretary for private affairs, is, in my opinion, if I am not partial, the second after the treasurer; the rest of the great officers are much upon a par.

These diversions are often attended with fatal accidents, whereof great numbers are on record. I myself have seen two or three candidates break a limb. But the danger is much greater when the ministers themselves are commanded to show their dexterity; for, by contending to excel themselves and their fellows, they strain so far, that there is hardly one of them who has not received a fall, and some of them two or three. I was assured, that, a year or two before my arrival, Flimnap would have infallibly broke his neck, if one of the king's cushions, that accidentally lay on the ground, had not weakened the force of his fall.

There is likewise another diversion, which is only shown before the emperor and empress, and first minister, upon particular occasions. The emperor lays on the table three fine silken threads of six inches long: one is blue, the other red, and the third green. These threads are proposed as prizes for those persons whom the emperor hath a mind to distinguish by a peculiar mark of his favor. The ceremony is performed in his Majesty's great chamber of state, where the candidates are to undergo a trial of dexterity very different from the former, and such as I have not observed the least resemblance of in any other country of the old or new world. The emperor holds a stick in his hands, both ends parallel to the horizon, while the candidates advancing, one by one, sometimes leap over the stick, sometimes creep under it backwards and forwards several times, according as the stick is advanced or depressed. Sometimes the emperor holds one end of the stick, and his first minister the other; sometimes the minister has it entirely to himself. Whoever performs his part with most agility, and holds out the longest in leaping and creeping, is rewarded with the blue-colored silk, the red is given to the next, and the green to the third, which they all wear girt twice round about the middle, and you see few great persons about this court who are not adorned with one of these girdles.

The horses of the army, and those of the royal stables, having been daily led before me, were no longer shy, but would come up to my very feet without starting, The riders would leap them over my hand as I held it on the ground, and one of the emperor's huntsmen, upon a large courser, took my foot, shoe and all; which was, indeed, a prodigious leap. I had the good fortune to divert the emperor, one day, after a very extraordinary manner: I desired he would order several sticks of two feet high, and the thickness of an ordinary cane, to be brought me; whereupon his Majesty commanded the master of his woods to give directions accordingly, and the next morning six woodmen arrived with as many carriages, drawn by eight horses to each. I took nine of these sticks, and fixing them firmly in the ground, in a quadrangular figure, two feet and a half square, I took four other sticks, and tied them parallel at each corner, about two feet from the ground; then I fastened my handkerchief to the nine sticks that stood erect, and extended it on all sides till it was as tight as the top of a drum; and the four parallel sticks, rising about five inches higher than the handkerchief, served as ledges on each side. When I had finished my work, I desired the emperor to let a troop of his best horse, twenty-four in number, come and exercise upon this plain. His Majesty approved of the proposal, and I took them up one by one in my hands, ready mounted and armed, with the proper officers to exercise them. As soon as they got in order, they divided into two parties, performed mock skirmishes, discharged blunt arrows, drew their swords, fled and pursued, attacked and retired, and in short discovered the best military discipline I ever beheld. The parallel sticks secured them and their horses from falling over the stage; and the emperor was so much delighted, that he ordered this entertainment to be repeated several days, and once was pleased to be lifted up, and give the word of command; and, with great difficulty, persuaded even the empress herself to let me hold her in her close chair within two yards of the stage, from whence she was able to take a full view of the whole performance. It was by good fortune that no ill accident happened in these entertainments, only once a fiery horse, that belonged to one of the captains, pawing with his hoof, struck a hole in my handkerchief, and his foot slipping, he overthrew his rider and himself; but I immediately relieved them both, and covering the hole with one hand, I set down the troop with the other, in the same manner as I took them up. The horse that fell was strained in the left shoulder, but the rider got no hurt, and I repaired my handkerchief as well as I could; however, I would not trust to the strength of it any more in such dangerous enterprises.

About two or three days before I was set at liberty, as I was entertaining the court with this kind of feats, there arrived an express to inform his Majesty that some of his subjects, riding near the place where I was first taken up, had seen a great black substance lying on the ground, very oddly shaped, extending its edges round as wide as his Majesty's bed-chamber, and rising up in the middle as high as a man; that it was no living creature, as they at first apprehended, for it lay on the grass without motion; and some of them had walked round it several times; that, by mounting upon each other's shoulders, they had got to the top, which was flat and even, and, stamping upon it, they found it was hollow within; that they humbly conceived it might be something belonging to the Man-Mountain; and if his Majesty pleased, they would undertake to bring it with only five horses. I presently knew what they meant, and was glad at heart to receive this intelligence. It seems upon my first reaching the shore, after our shipwreck, I was in such confusion, that, before I came to the place where I went to sleep, my hat, which I had fastened with a string to my head while I was rowing, and had stuck on all the time I was swimming, fell off after I came to land; the string, as I conjecture, breaking by some accident which I never observed, but thought my hat had been lost at sea. I intreated his Imperial Majesty to give orders it might be brought to me as soon as possible, describing to him the use and the nature of it; and the next day the wagoners arrived with it, but not in a very good condition; they had bored two holes in the brim, within an inch and a half of the edge, and fastened two hooks in the holes; these hooks were tied by a long cord to the harness, and thus my hat was dragged along for above half an English mile; but, the ground in that country being extremely smooth and level, it received less damage than I expected.

Two days after this adventure, the emperor having ordered that part of his army, which quarters in and about his metropolis, to be in readiness, took a fancy of diverting himself in a very singular manner; he desired I would stand like a colossus, with my legs as far asunder as I conveniently could; he then commanded his general (who was an old experienced leader, and a great patron of mine) to draw up the troops in close order, and march them under me; the foot by twenty-four in a-breast, and the horse by sixteen, with drums beating, colors flying, and pikes advanced. This body consisted of three thousand foot, and a thousand horse.

I had sent so many memorials and petitions for my liberty, that his Majesty at length mentioned the matter first in the cabinet, and then in a full council; where it was opposed by none, except Skyresh Bolgolam, who was pleased, without any provocation, to be my mortal enemy. But it was carried against him by the whole board, and confirmed by the emperor. That minister was *galbet,* or admiral of the realm, very much in his master's confidence, and a person well versed in affairs, but of a morose and sour complexion. However, he was at length persuaded to comply; but prevailed that the articles and conditions upon which I should be set free, and to which I must swear, should be drawn up by himself. These articles were brought to me by Skyresh Bolgolam in person, attended by two under-secretaries, and several persons of distinction. After they were read, I was demanded to swear to the performance of them; first in the manner of my own country, and afterwards in the method prescribed by their laws, which was to hold my right foot in my left hand, and to place the middle finger of my right hand on the crown of my head, and my thumb on the tip of my right ear.

But, because the reader may be curious to have some idea of the style and manner of expression peculiar to that people, as well as to know the articles upon which I recovered my liberty, I have made a translation of the whole instrument, word for word, as near as I was able, which I here offer to the public.

GOLBASTO MOMAREM EVLAME GURDILO SHEFIN MULLY ULLY GUE, most mighty Emperor of Lilliput, delight and terror of the universe, whose dominions extend five thousand *blustrugs* (about twelve miles in circumference), to the extremities of the globe; monarch of all monarchs, taller than the sons of men; whose feet press down to the centre, and whose head strikes against the sun; at whose nod the princes of the earth shake their knees; pleasant as the spring, comfortable as the summer, fruitful as autumn, dreadful as winter. His most sublime Majesty proposes to the Man-Mountain, lately arrived to our celestial dominions, the following articles, which, by a solemn oath, he shall be obliged to perform:

1st. The Man-Mountain shall not depart from our dominions without our licence under our great seal.

2d. He shall not presume to come into our metropolis without our express order; at which time the inhabitants shall have two hours' warning to keep within their doors.

3d. The said Man-Mountain shall confine his walks to our principal high roads, and not offer to walk or lie down in a meadow or field of corn.

4th. As he walks the said roads he shall take the utmost care riot to trample upon the bodies of any of our loving subjects, their horses, or carriages, nor take any of our subjects into his hands without their own consent.

5th. If an express requires extraordinary dispatch, the Man-Mountain shall be obliged to carry in his pocket the messenger and horse a six days' journey once in every moon, and return the said messenger back (if so required) safe to our imperial presence.

6th. He shall be our ally against our enemies in the Island of Blefuscu, and do his utmost to destroy their fleet, which is now preparing to invade us.

7th. That the said Man-Mountain shall, at his times of leisure, be aiding and assisting to our workmen, in helping to raise certain great stones, towards covering the wall of the principal park, and other our royal buildings.

8th. That the said Man-Mountain shall, in two moons' time, deliver in an exact survey of the circumference of our dominions, by a computation of his own paces round the coast.

Lastly, That, upon his solemn oath to observe all the above articles, the said Man-Mountain shall have a daily allowance of meat and drink sufficient for the support of 1724 of our subjects, with free access to our royal person, and other marks of our favor. Given at our palace at Belfaborac, the twelfth day of the ninety-first moon of our reign.

I swore and subscribed to these articles with great cheerfulness and content, although some of them were not so honorable as I could have wished; which proceeded wholly from the malice of Skyresh Bolgolam, the high admiral; whereupon my chains were immediately unlocked, and I was at full liberty; the emperor himself in person did me the honor to be by at the whole ceremony. I made my acknowledgments, by prostrating myself at his Majesty's feet, but he commanded me to rise; and after many gracious expressions, which, to avoid the censure of vanity, I shall not repeat, he added that he hoped I should prove a useful servant, and well deserve all the favors he had already conferred upon me, or might do for the future.

The reader may please to observe, that, in the last article for the recovery of my liberty, the emperor stipulates to allow me a quantity of meat and drink sufficient for the support of 1724 Lilliputians. Some time after, asking a friend at court how they came to fix on that determinate number; he told me that his Majesty's mathematicians, having taken the height of my body by the help of a quadrant, and finding it to exceed theirs in the proportion of twelve to one, they concluded, from the similarity of their bodies, that mine must contain, at least, 1724 of theirs, and, consequently, would require as much food as was necessary to support that number of Lilliputians. By which, the reader may conceive an idea of the ingenuity of that people, as well as the prudent and exact economy of so great a prince.

GULLIVER CAPTURES FIFTY
OF THE ENEMY'S SHIPS

By Jonathan Swift

The empire of Blefuscu is an island, situated to the northeast side of Lilliput, from whence it is parted only by a channel of eight hundred yards wide. I had not yet seen it, and upon this notice of an intended invasion, I avoided appearing on that side of the coast, for fear of being discovered by some of the enemy's ships, who had received no intelligence of me, all intercourse between the two empires having been strictly forbidden during the war, upon pain of death, and an embargo laid by our emperor upon all vessels whatsoever. I communicated to his Majesty a project I had formed of seizing the enemy's whole fleet; which, as our scouts assured us, lay at anchor in the harbor ready to sail with the first fair wind. I consulted the most experienced seamen upon the depth of the channel, which they had often plumbed, who told me, that in the middle, at high water, it was seventy *glumgluffs* deep, which is about six feet of European measure; and the rest of it fifty *glumgluffs* at most. I walked towards the northeast coast, over against Blefuscu; where, lying down behind a hillock, I took out my small perspective glass, and viewed the enemy's fleet at anchor, consisting of about fifty men-of-war, and a great number of transports; I then came back to my house, and gave order (for which I had a warrant) for a great quantity of the strongest cable and bars of iron. The cable was about as thick as packthread, and the bars of the length and size of a knitting needle. I trebled the cable to make it stronger, and, for the same reason, I twisted three of the iron bars together, binding the extremities into a hook. Having thus fixed fifty hooks to as many cables, I went back to the northeast coast, and putting off my coat, shoes, and stockings, walked into the sea, in my leathern jerkin, about an hour before high water. I waded with what haste I could, and swam in the middle about thirty yards, till I felt ground; I arrived at the fleet in less than half an hour. The enemy was so frighted when they saw me, that they leaped out of their ships, and swam to shore, where there could not be fewer than thirty thousand souls. I then took my tackling, and, fastening a hook to the hole at the prow of each, I tied all the cords together at the end. While I was thus employed, the enemy discharged several thousand arrows, many of which stuck in my hands and face; and, besides the excessive smart, gave me much disturbance in my work. My greatest apprehension was for mine eyes, which I should have infallibly lost, if I had not suddenly thought of an expedient. I kept among other little necessaries a pair of spectacles in a private pocket, which, as I observed before, had escaped the emperor's searchers. These I took out and fastened as strongly as I could upon my nose, and, thus armed, went on boldly with my work in spite of the enemy's arrows, many of which struck against the glasses of my spectacles, but without any other effect, further than a little to discompose them. I had now fastened all the hooks, and, taking the knot in my hand, began to pull, but not a ship would stir, for they were all too fast held by their anchors, so that the boldest part of my enterprise remained. I therefore let go the cord, and leaving the hooks fixed to the ships, I resolutely cut with my knife the cables that fastened the anchors, receiving above two hundred shots in my face and hands; then I took up the knotted end of the cables to which my hooks were tied, and with great ease drew fifty of the enemy's largest men-of-war after me.

The Blefuscudians, who had not the least imagination of what I intended, were at first confounded with astonishment. They had seen me cut the cables, and thought my design was only to let the ships run adrift, or fall foul on each other; but when they perceived the whole fleet moving in order, and saw me pulling at the end, they set up such a scream of grief and despair that it is almost impossible to describe or conceive. When I had got out of danger, I stopped a while to pick out the arrows that stuck in my hands and face; and rubbed on some of the same ointment that was given me at my first arrival, as I have formerly mentioned. I then took off my spectacles, and, waiting about an hour till the tide was a little fallen, I waded through the middle with my cargo, and arrived safe at the royal port of Lilliput.

The emperor and his whole court stood on the shore expecting the issue of this great adventure. They saw the ships move forward in a large half-moon, but could not discern me, who was up to my breast in water. When I advanced to the middle of the channel, they were yet in more pain, because I was under water to my neck. The emperor concluded me to be drowned, and that the enemy's fleet was approaching in a hostile manner; but he was soon eased of his fears, for the channel growing shallower every step I made, I came in a short time within hearing, and, holding up the end of the cable by which the fleet was fastened, I cried in a loud voice, "Long live the most puissant Emperor of Lilliput!" This great prince received me at my landing with all possible encomiums, and created me a *nardac* upon the spot, which is the highest title of honor among them.

His Majesty desired I would take some other opportunity of bringing all the rest of his enemy's ships into his ports. And so unmeasurable is the ambition of princes, that he seemed to think of nothing less than reducing the whole empire of Blefuscu into a province, and governing it by a viceroy; of destroying the Bigendian exiles and compelling that people to break the smaller end of their eggs, by which he would remain the sole monarch of the whole world. But I endeavored to divert him from his design, by many arguments drawn from the topics of policy as well as justice; and I plainly protested, that I would never be an instrument of bringing a free and brave people into slavery. And, when the matter was debated in council, the wisest part of the ministry were of my opinion.

This open bold declaration of mine was so opposite to the schemes and politics of his Imperial Majesty, that he could never forgive me; he mentioned it in a very artful manner at council, where I was told that some of the wisest appeared, at least, by their silence, to be of my opinion; but others, who were my secret enemies, could not forbear some expressions, which by a side-wind reflected on me. And from this time began an intrigue between his Majesty and a junto of ministers maliciously bent against me, which broke out in less than two months, and had like to have ended in my utter destruction. Of so little weight are the greatest services to princes, when put into the balance with a refusal to gratify their passions.

About three weeks after this exploit, there arrived a solemn embassy from Blefuscu, with humble offers of a peace; which was soon concluded upon conditions very advantageous to our emperor, wherewith I shall not trouble the reader. There were six ambassadors, with a train of about five hundred persons, and their entry was very magnificent, suitable to the grandeur of their master, and the importance of their business. When their treaty was finished, wherein I did them several good offices by the credit I now had, or at least appeared to have at court, their Excellencies, who were privately told how much I had been their friend, made me a visit in form. They began with many compliments upon my valor and generosity, invited me to that kingdom in the emperor their master's name, and desired me to show them some proofs of my prodigious strength, of which they had heard so many wonders; wherein I readily obliged them, but shall not trouble the reader with the particulars.

When I had for some time entertained their Excellencies to their infinite satisfaction and surprise, I desired they would do me the honor to present my most humble respects to the emperor their master, the renown of whose virtues had so justly filled the whole world with admiration, and whose royal person I resolved to attend before I returned to my own country; accordingly the next time I had the honor to see our emperor, I desired his general licence to wait on the Blefuscudian monarch, which he was pleased to grant me, as I could plainly perceive, in a very cold manner; but could not guess the reason, till I had a whisper from a certain person, that Flimnap and Bolgolam had represented my intercourse with these ambassadors as a mark of disaffection, from which I am sure my heart was wholly free. And this was the first time I began to conceive some imperfect idea of courts and ministers.

It is to be observed, that these ambassadors spoke to me by an interpreter, the languages of both empires differing as much from each other as any two in Europe, and each nation priding itself upon the antiquity, beauty, and energy of their own tongues, with an avowed contempt for that of their neighbor; yet our emperor, standing upon the advantage he had got by the seizure of their fleet, obliged them to deliver their credentials and make their speech in the Lilliputian tongue. And it must be confessed that, from the great intercourse of trade and commerce between both realms, from the continual reception of exiles, which is mutual among them, and from the custom in each empire to send their young nobility and richer gentry to the other, in order to polish themselves by seeing the world, and understanding men and manners, there are few persons of distinction, or merchants, or seamen, who dwell in the maritime parts, but what can hold conversation in both tongues; as I found some weeks after, when I went to pay my respects to the Emperor of Blefuscu, which, in the midst of great misfortunes through the malice of my enemies, proved a very happy adventure to me, as I shall relate in its proper place.

The reader may remember, that, when I signed those articles upon which I recovered my liberty, there were some which I disliked upon account of their being too servile, neither could anything but an extreme necessity have forced me to submit. But, being now a *nardac* of the highest rank in that empire, such offices were looked down upon as below my dignity, and the emperor (to do him justice) never once mentioned them to me.

GULLIVER LEAVES LILLIPUT

By Jonathan Swift

Three days after my arrival, walking out of curiosity to the northeast coast of the island, I observed, about half a league off, in the sea, somewhat that looked like a boat overturned. I pulled off my shoes and stockings, and, wading two or three hundred yards, I found the object to approach nearer by force of the tide; and then plainly saw it to be a real boat, which I supposed might, by some tempest, have been driven from a ship. Whereupon I returned immediately towards the city, and desired his Imperial Majesty to lend me twenty of the tallest vessels he had left after the loss of his fleet, and three thousand seamen, under the command of the vice-admiral. This fleet sailed round, while I went back the shortest way to the coast, where I first discovered the boat; I found the tide had driven it still nearer. The seamen were all provided with cordage, which I had beforehand twisted to a sufficient strength. When the ships came up, I stripped myself, and waded till I came within an hundred yards of the boat, after which I was forced to swim till I got up to it. The seamen threw me the end of the cord, which I fastened to a hole in the fore- part of the boat, and the other end to a man-of-war. But I found all my labor to little purpose; for, being out of my depth, I was not able to work. In this necessity, I was forced to swim behind, and push the boat forwards as often as I could, with one of my hands; and, the tide favoring me, I advanced so far, that I could just hold up my chin and feel the ground. I rested two or three minutes, and then gave the boat another shove, and so on, till the sea was no higher than my arm-pits; and now, the most laborious part being over, I took out my other cables, which were stowed in one of the ships, and fastened them first to the boat, and then to nine of the vessels which attended me; the wind being favorable, the seamen towed, and I shoved till we arrived within forty yards of the shore, and, waiting till the tide was out, I got dry to the boat, and by the assistance of two thousand men, with ropes, and engines, I made a shift to turn it on its bottom, and found it was but little damaged.

I shall not trouble the reader with the difficulties I was under, by the help of certain paddles, which cost me ten days making, to get my boat to the royal port of Blefuscu, where a mighty concourse of people appeared upon my arrival, full of wonder at the sight of so prodigious a vessel. I told the emperor that my good fortune had thrown this boat in my way, to carry me to some place from whence I might return into my native country, and begged his Majesty's orders for getting materials to fit it up, together with his licence to depart, which, after some kind expostulations, he was pleased to grant.

I did very much wonder, in all this time, not to have heard of any express relating to me from our emperor to the court of Blefuscu. But I was afterwards given privately to understand that his Imperial Majesty, never imagining I had the least notice of his designs, believed I was only gone to Blefuscu, in performance of my promise, according to the licence he had given me, which was well known at our court, and would return in a few days, when the ceremony was ended. But he was at last in pain at my long absence; and, after consulting with the treasurer and the rest of the cabal, a person of quality was dispatched with the copy of the articles against me. This envoy had instructions to represent to the monarch of Blefuscu the great lenity of his master, who was content to punish me no further than with the loss of my eyes; that I had fled from justice, and, if I did not return in two hours, I should be deprived of my title of *nardac*, and declared a traitor. The envoy further added, that in order to maintain the peace and amity between both empires, his master expected that his brother of Blefuscu would give orders to have me sent back to Lilliput, bound hand and foot, to be punished as a traitor.

The Emperor of Blefuscu, having taken three days to consult, returned an answer, consisting of many civilities and excuses. He said that as for sending me bound, his brother knew it was impossible; that although I had deprived him of his fleet, yet he owed great obligations to me for many good offices I had done him in making the peace; that, however, both their Majesties would soon be made easy; for I had found a prodigious vessel on the shore, able to carry me on the sea, which he had given orders to fit up with my own assistance and direction; and he hoped, in a few weeks, both empires would be freed from so insupportable an encumbrance.

With this answer the envoy returned to Lilliput, and the monarch of Blefuscu related to me all that had passed; offering me at the same time (but under the strictest confidence) his gracious protection, if I would continue in his service; wherein, although I believed him sincere, yet I resolved never more to put any confidence in princes or ministers, where I could possibly avoid it, and, therefore, with all due acknowledgments for his favorable intentions, I humbly begged to be excused. I told him, that since fortune, whether good or evil, had thrown a vessel in my way, I was resolved to venture myself on the ocean rather than be an occasion of difference between two such mighty monarchs. Neither did I find the emperor at all displeased, and I discovered, by a certain accident, that he was very glad of my resolution, and so were most of his ministers. These considerations moved me to hasten my departure somewhat sooner than I intended; to which the court, impatient to have me gone very readily contributed. Five hundred workmen were employed to make two sails to my boat, according to my directions, by quilting thirteen folds of their strongest linen together. I was at the pains of making ropes and cables by twisting ten, twenty, or thirty of the thickest and strongest of theirs. A great stone that I happened to find, after a long search by the sea-shore, served me for an anchor. I had the tallow of three hundred cows for greasing my boat and other uses. I was at incredible pains in cutting down some of the largest timber-trees for oars and masts, wherein I was, however, much assisted by his Majesty's ship-carpenters, who helped me in smoothing them after I had done the rough work.

In about a month, when all was prepared, I sent to receive his Majesty's commands, and to take my leave. The emperor and royal family came out of the palace; I lay down on my face to kiss his hand, which he very graciously gave me; so did the empress, and young princes of the blood. His Majesty presented me with fifty purses of two hundred *sprugs* apiece, together with his picture at full length, which I put immediately into one of my gloves, to keep it from being hurt. The ceremonies at my departure were too many to trouble the reader with at this time.

I stored the boat with the carcases of an hundred oxen, and three hundred sheep, with bread and drink proportionable, and as much meat ready dressed as four hundred cooks could provide. I took with me six cows and two bulls alive, with as many ewes and rams, intending to carry them into my own country and propagate the breed. And, to feed them on board, I had a good bundle of hay, and a bag of corn. I would gladly have taken a dozen of the natives, but this was a thing the emperor would by no means permit; and, besides a diligent search into my pockets, his Majesty engaged my honor not to carry away any of his subjects, although with their own consent and desire.

Having thus prepared all things as well as I was able, I set sail on the twenty-fourth day of September, 1701, at six in the morning; and when I had gone about four leagues to the northward, the wind being at southeast, at six in the evening I descried a small island about half a league to the northwest. I advanced forward, and cast anchor on the lee-side of the island, which seemed to be uninhabited. I then took some refreshment and went to my rest. I slept well, and I conjecture at least six hours, for I found the day broke in two hours after I awaked. It was a clear night. I ate my breakfast before the sun was up; and heaving anchor, the wind being favorable, I steered the same course that I had done the day before, wherein I was directed by my pocket-compass. My intention was to reach, if possible, one of those islands which I had reason to believe lay on the northeast of Van Diemen's Land. I discovered nothing all that day; but upon the next, about three in the afternoon, when I had by my computation made twenty-four leagues from Blefuscu, I descried a sail steering to the southeast; my course was due east. I hailed her, but could get no answer; yet I found I gained upon her, for the wind slackened. I made all the sail I could, and in half an hour she spied me, then hung out her ancient, and discharged a gun. It is not easy to express the joy I was in upon the unexpected hope of once more seeing my beloved country, and the dear pledges I had left in it. The ship slackened her sails, and I came up with her between five and six in the evening, September 26th; but my heart leaped within me to see her English colors. I put my cows and sheep into my coat-pockets, and got on board with all my little cargo of provisions. The vessel was an English merchantman, returning from Japan by the north and south seas; the captain, Mr. John Biddel of Deptford, a very civil man, and an excellent sailor. We were now in the latitude of 30 degrees south; there were about fifty men in the ship; and here I met an old comrade of mine, one Peter Williams, who gave me a good character to the captain. This gentleman treated me with kindness, and desired I would let him know what place I came from last and whither I was bound; which I did in few words, but he thought I was raving, and that the dangers I underwent had disturbed my head; whereupon I took my black cattle and sheep out of my pocket, which, after great astonishment, clearly convinced him of my veracity. I then showed him the gold given me by the Emperor of Blefuscu, together with his Majesty's picture at full length, and some other rarities of that country. I gave him two purses of two hundred *sprugs* each, and promised, when we arrived in England, to make him a present of a cow and a sheep.

I shall not trouble the reader with a particular account of this voyage, which was very prosperous for the most part. We arrived in the Downs on the 13th of April, 1702. I had only one misfortune, that the rats on board carried away one of my sheep; I found her bones in a hole, picked clean from the flesh. The rest of my cattle I got safe ashore, and set them a-grazing in a bowling- green at Greenwich, where the fineness of the grass made them feed very heartily, though I had always feared the contrary: neither could I possibly have preserved them in so long a voyage if the captain had not allowed me some of his best biscuit, which rubbed to powder, and mingled with water, was their constant food. The short time I continued in England, I made a considerable profit by showing my cattle to many persons of quality and others: and, before I began my second voyage, I sold them for six hundred pounds. Since my last return, I find the breed is considerably increased, especially the sheep, which I hope will prove much to the advantage of the woollen manufacture, by the fineness of the fleeces.

I stayed but two months with my wife and family; for my insatiable desire of seeing foreign countries would suffer me to continue no longer. I left fifteen hundred pounds with my wife, and fixed her in a good house at Redriff. My remaining stock I carried with me, part in money and part in goods, in hopes to improve my fortunes. My eldest uncle John had left me an estate in land, near Epping, of about thirty pounds a year; and I had a long lease of the Black Bull in Fetter Lane, which yielded me as much more: so that I was not in any danger of leaving my family upon the parish. My son Johnny, named so after his uncle, was at the grammar school, and a cowardly child. My daughter Betty (who is now well married, and has children) was then at her needlework. I took leave of my wife and boy and girl, with tears on both sides, and went on board the Adventure, a merchant ship, of three hundred tons, bound for Surat, Captain John Nicholas of Liverpool, commander.

GULLIVER IN THE LAND OF THE GIANTS

By Jonathan Swift

The Adventure had a very prosperous gale, till we arrived at the Cape of Good Hope, where we landed for fresh water; but discovering a leak, we unshipped our goods, and wintered there; for the captain falling sick of an ague, we could not leave the Cape till the end of March.

We then set sail, and had a good voyage till we passed the straits of Madagascar; but having got northward of that island, and to about five degrees south latitude, the winds, which in those seas are observed to blow a constant equal gale between the north and west, from the beginning of December to the beginning of May, on the 9th of April began to blow with much greater violence, and more westerly than usual, continuing so for twenty days together: during which time, we were driven a little to the east of the Molucca Islands, and about three degrees northward of the line, as our captain found by an observation he took the 2d of May, at which time the wind ceased, and it was a perfect calm, whereat I was not a little rejoiced. But he being a man well experienced in the navigation of those seas, bid us all prepare against a storm, which accordingly happened on the day following; for the southern wind, called the southern monsoon, began to set in.

Finding it was likely to overblow, we took in our sprit-sail, and stood by to hand the foresail; but, making foul weather, we looked the guns were all fast, and handed the mizzen. The ship lay very broad off, so we thought it better spooning before the sea, than trying or hulling. We reefed the foresail and set him, and hauled aft the foresheet; the helm was hard-a-weather. The ship wore bravely. We belayed the fore downhaul; but the sail was split, and we hauled down the yard, and got the sail into the ship, and unbound all the things clear of it. It was a very fierce storm; the sea broke strange and dangerous. We hauled off upon the lanyard of the whip-staff, and helped the man at the helm. We would not get down our topmast, but let all stand, because she scudded before the sea very well, and we knew that the topmast being aloft, the ship was the wholesomer, and made better way through the sea, seeing we had sea-room. When the storm was over, we set foresail and mainsail, and brought the ship to. Then we set the mizzen, maintopsail, and the foretopsail. Our course was east- northeast, the wind was at southwest. We got the starboard tacks aboard, we cast off our weather braces and lifts; we set in the lee braces, and hauled forward by the weather-bowlings, and hauled them tight, and belayed them, and hauled over the mizzen tack to windward, and kept her full and by as near as she would lie. During this storm, which was followed by a strong wind west- southwest, we were carried, by my computation, about five hundred leagues to the east, so that the oldest sailor on board could not tell in what part of the world we were. Our provisions held out well, our ship was stanch, and our crew all in good health; but we lay in the utmost distress for water. We thought it best to hold on the same course, rather than turn more northerly, which might have brought us to the northwest part of Great Tartary, and into the Frozen Sea.

On the 16th day of June, 1703, a boy on the topmast discovered land. On the 17th, we came in full view of a great island, or continent (for we knew not whether); on the south side whereof was a small neck of land jutting out into the sea, and a creek too shallow to hold a ship of above one hundred tons. We cast anchor within a league of the creek, and our captain sent a dozen of his men well armed in the long-boat, with vessels for water, if any could be found. I desired his leave to go with them, that I might see the country, and make what discoveries I could. When we came to land, we saw no river, or spring, nor any sign of inhabitants. Our men therefore wandered on the shore to find out some fresh water near the sea, and I walked alone about a mile on the other side, where I observed the country all barren and rocky. I now began to be weary, and seeing nothing to entertain my curiosity, I returned gently down toward the creek; and the sea being full in my view, I saw our men already got into the boat, and rowing for life to the ship. I was going to holla after them, although it had been to little purpose, when I observed a huge creature walking after them in the sea, as fast as he could: he waded not much deeper than his knees, and took prodigious strides: but our men had the start of him half a league, and the sea thereabout being full of sharp-pointed rocks, the monster was not able to overtake the boat. This I was afterward told, for I durst not stay to see the issue of the adventure, but ran as fast as I could the way I first went, and then climbed up a steep hill, which gave me some prospect of the country. I found it fully cultivated; but that which first surprised me was the length of the grass, which, in those grounds that seemed to be kept for hay, was about twenty feet high.

I fell into a highroad, for so I took it to be, though it served to the inhabitants only as a footpath through a field of barley. Here I walked on for some time, but could see little on either side, it being now near harvest, and the corn rising at least forty feet. I was an hour walking to the end of this field, which was fenced in with a hedge of at least one hundred and twenty feet high, and the trees so lofty that I could make no computation of their altitude. There was a stile to pass from this field into the next. It had four steps, and a stone to cross over when you come to the uppermost. It was impossible for me to climb this stile, because every step was six feet high, and the upper stone about twenty. I was endeavoring to find some gap in the hedge, when I discovered one of the inhabitants in the next field, advancing toward the stile, of the same size with him whom I saw in the sea pursuing our boat. He appeared as tall as an ordinary spire steeple, and took about ten yards at every stride, as near as I could guess. I was struck with the utmost fear and astonishment, and ran to hide myself in the corn, whence I saw him at the top of the stile looking back into the next field, on the right hand, and heard him call in a voice many degrees louder than a speaking- trumpet; but the noise was so high in the air, that at first I certainly thought it was thunder. Whereupon seven monsters, like himself, came toward him, with reaping-hooks in their hands, each hook about the largeness of six scythes. These people were not so well clad as the first, whose servants or laborers they seemed to be; for, upon some words he spoke, they went to reap the corn in the field where I lay. I kept from them at as great a distance as I could, but was forced to move with extreme difficulty, for the stalks of corn were sometimes not above a foot distant, so that I could hardly squeeze my body between them. However, I made a shift to go forward, till I came to a part of the field where the corn had been laid by the rain and wind. Here it was impossible for me to advance a step; for the stalks were so interwoven, that I could not creep through, and the beards of the fallen ears so strong and pointed, that they pierced through my clothes into my flesh. At the same time I heard the reapers not above a hundred yards behind me. Being quite dispirited with toil, and wholly overcome by grief and despair, I lay down between two ridges, and heartily wished I might there end my days. I bemoaned my desolate widow and fatherless children. I lamented my own folly and wilfulness, in attempting a second voyage, against the advice of all my friends and relations. In this terrible agitation of mind, I could not forbear thinking of Lilliput, whose inhabitants looked upon me as the greatest prodigy that ever appeared in the world; where I was able to draw an imperial fleet in my hand, and perform those other actions, which will be recorded forever in the chronicles of that empire, while posterity shall hardly believe them, although attested by millions. I reflected what a mortification it must prove to me to appear as inconsiderable in this nation, as one single Lilliputian would be among us. But this I conceived was to be the least of my misfortunes; for, as human creatures are observed to be more savage and cruel in proportion to their bulk, what could I expect but to be a morsel in the mouth of the first among these enormous barbarians that should happen to seize me? Undoubtedly philosophers are in the right when they tell us that nothing is great or little otherwise than by comparison. It might have pleased fortune, to have let the Lilliputians find some nation where the people were as diminutive with respect to them, as they were to me. And who knows but that even this prodigious race of mortals might be equally overmatched in some distant part of the world, whereof we have yet no discovery.

Scared and confounded as I was, I could not forbear going on with these reflections, when one of the reapers approaching within ten yards of the ridge where I lay, made me apprehend that with the next step I should be squashed to death under his foot, or cut in two with his reaping-hook. And therefore, when he was again about to move, I screamed as loud as fear could make me; whereupon the huge creature trod short, and looking round about under him for some time, at last espied me as I lay on the ground. He considered awhile, with the caution of one who endeavors to lay hold on a small dangerous animal in such a manner that it shall not be able either to scratch or bite him, as I myself have sometimes done with a weasel in England. At length he ventured to take me behind, by the middle, between his forefinger and thumb, and brought me within three yards of his eyes, that he might behold my shape more perfectly. I guessed his meaning, and my good fortune gave me so much presence of mind, that I resolved not to struggle in the least as he held me in the air above sixty feet from the ground, although he grievously pinched my sides, for fear I should slip through his fingers. All I ventured was to raise mine eyes toward the sun, and place my hands together in a supplicating posture, and to speak some words in an humble melancholy tone, suitable to the condition I then was in: for I apprehended every moment that he would dash me against the ground, as we usually do any little hateful animal which we have a mind to destroy. But my good star would have it, that he appeared pleased with my voice and gestures, and began to look upon me as a curiosity, much wondering to hear me pronounce articulate words, although he could not understand them. In the meantime I was not able to forbear groaning and shedding tears, and turning my head toward my sides; letting him know, as well as I could, how cruelly I was hurt by the pressure of his thumb and finger. He seemed to apprehend my meaning; for, lifting up the lappet of his coat, he put me gently into it, and immediately ran along with me to his master, who was a substantial farmer, and the same person I had first seen in the field.

The farmer having (as I suppose by their talk) received such an account of me as his servant could give him, took a piece of a small straw, about the size of a walking-staff, and therewith lifted up the lappets of my coat, which, it seems, he thought to be some kind of covering that nature had given me. He blew my hair aside to take a better view of my face. He called his hinds about him, and asked them, as I afterward learned, whether they had ever seen in the fields any little creature that resembled me? He then placed me softly on the ground on all fours, but I immediately got up, and walked slowly backward and forward, to let those people see I had no intent to run away. They all sat down in a circle about me, the better to observe my motions. I pulled off my hat, and made a low bow toward the farmer. I fell on my knees, and lifted up my hands and eyes, and spoke several words as loud as I could; I took a purse of gold out of my pocket, and humbly presented it to him. He received it on the palm of his hand, and then applied it close to his eye to see what it was, and afterward turned it several times with the point of a pin (which he took out of his sleeve), but could make nothing of it. Whereupon I made a sign that he should place his hand on the ground. I then took the purse, and opening it, poured all the gold into his palm. There were six Spanish pieces of four pistoles each, besides twenty or thirty smaller coins. I saw him wet the tip of his little finger upon his tongue, and take up one of my largest pieces, and then another; but he seemed to be wholly ignorant what they were. He made me a sign to put them again into my purse, and the purse again into my pocket, which, after offering it to him several times, I thought it best to do.

The farmer, by this time, was convinced I must be a rational creature. He spoke often to me, but the sound of his voice pierced my ears like that of a watermill, yet his words were articulate enough.

I answered as loud as I could in several languages, and he often laid his ear within two yards of me; but all in vain, for we were wholly unintelligible to each other. He then sent his servants to their work, and taking his handkerchief out of his pocket, he doubled and spread it on his left hand, which he placed flat on the ground with the palm upward, making me a sign to step into it, as I could easily do, for it was not above a foot in thickness. I thought it my part to obey, and, for fear of falling, laid myself at full length upon the handkerchief, with the remainder of which he lapped me up to the head for further security, and in this manner carried me home to his house. There he called his wife, and showed me to her; but she screamed and ran back, as women in England do at the sight of a toad or a spider. However, when she had awhile seen my behavior, and how well I observed the signs her husband made, she was soon reconciled, and by degrees grew extremely tender of me. It was about twelve at noon and a servant brought in dinner. It was only one substantial dish of meat (fit for the plain condition of a husbandman), in a dish of about four-and-twenty feet in diameter. The company were, the farmer and his wife, three children, and an old grandmother. When they were sat down, the farmer placed me at some distance from him on the table, which was thirty feet high from the floor. I was in a terrible fright, and kept as far as I could from the edge, for fear of falling. The wife minced a bit of meat, then crumbled some bread on a trencher, and placed it before me. I made her a low bow, took out my knife and fork, and fell to eat, which gave them exceeding delight. The mistress sent her maid for a small dram cup, which held about two gallons, and filled it with drink; I took up the vessel with much difficulty in both hands, and in a most respectful manner drank to her ladyship's health, expressing the words as loud as I could in English, which made the company laugh so heartily that I was almost deafened with the noise. This liquor tasted like a small cider, and was not unpleasant. Then the master made me a sign to come to his trencher side; but as I walked on the table, being at great surprise all the time, as the indulgent reader will easily conceive and excuse, I happened to stumble against a crust, and fell flat on my face, but received no hurt. I got up immediately, and observing the good people to be in much concern, I took my hat (which I held under my arm out of good manners), and waving it over my head, gave three huzzas, to show I had got no mischief by my fall. But advancing forward toward my master, (as I shall henceforth call him), his youngest son, who sat next to him, an arch boy of about ten years old, took me up by the legs, and held me so high in the air that I trembled in every limb; but his father snatched me from him, and at the same time gave him such a box on the left ear as would have felled an European troop of horse to the earth, ordering him to be taken from the table. But being afraid the boy might owe me a spite, and well remembering how mischievous all children among us naturally are to sparrows, rabbits, young kittens, and puppy dogs, I fell on my knees, and pointing to the boy, made my master to understand as well as I could, that I desired his son might be pardoned. The father complied, and the lad took his seat again, whereupon I went to him and kissed his hand, which my master took, and made him stroke me gently with it.

In the midst of dinner, my mistress's favorite cat leaped into her lap, I hearc a noise behind me like that of a dozen stocking- weavers at work; and turning my head, I found it proceeded from the purring of that animal, who seemed to be three times larger than an ox, as I computed by the view of her head, and one of her paws, while her mistress was feeding and stroking her. The fierceness of this creature's countenance altogether discomposed me; though I stood at the further end of the table, above fifty feet off; and though my mistress held her fast, for fear she might give a spring, and seize me in her talons. But it happened there was no danger, for the cat took not the least notice of me, when my master placed me within three yards of her. And as I have been always told, and found true by experience in my travels, that flying or discovering fear before a fierce animal is a certain way to make it pursue or attack you, so I resolved, in this dangerous juncture, to show no manner of concern. I walked with intrepidity five or six times before the very head of the cat, and came within half a yard of her; whereupon she drew herself back, as if she were more afraid of me. I had less apprehension concerning the dogs, whereof three or four came into the room, as is usual in farmers? houses; one of which was a mastiff, equal in bulk to four elephants, and a greyhound somewhat taller than the mastiff, but not so large.

When dinner was almost done, the nurse came in with a child of a year old in her arms, who immediately spied me, and began a squall that you might have heard from London Bridge to Chelsea, after the usual oratory of infants, to get me for a plaything. The mother, out of pure indulgence, took me up, and put me toward the child, who presently seized me by the middle, and got my head into his mouth, where I roared so loud that the urchin was frighted, and let me drop, and I should infallibly have broke my neck, if the mother had not held her apron under me. The nurse, to quiet her babe, made use of a rattle, which was a kind of hollow vessel filled with great stones, and fastened by a cable to the child's waist.

I remember, when I was at Lilliput, the complexions of those diminutive people appeared to me the fairest in the world; and talking upon the subject with a person of learning there, who was an intimate friend of mine, he said that my face appeared much fairer and smoother when he looked on me from the ground, than it did upon a nearer view, when I took him up in my hand and brought him close, which he confessed was at first a very shocking sight. He said "he could discover great holes in my skin; that the stumps of my beard were ten times stronger than the bristles of a boar, and my complexion made up of several colors, altogether disagreeable"; although I must beg leave to say for myself, that I am as fair as most of my sex and country, and very little sunburned by all my travels. On the other side, discoursing of the ladies in that emperor's court, he used to tell me, "one had freckles, another too wide a mouth, a third too large a nose"; nothing of which I was able to distinguish. I confess this reflection was obvious enough; which, however, I could not forbear, lest the reader might think those vast creatures were actually deformed: for I must do them the justice to say, they are a comely race of people; and particularly the features of my master's countenance, although he were but a farmer, when I beheld him from the height of sixty feet, appeared very well proportioned.

When dinner was done, my master went out to his laborers, and as I could discover by his voice and gesture gave his wife a strict charge to take care of me. I was very much tired and disposed to sleep, which my mistress perceiving, she put me on her own bed, covered me with a clean white handkerchief, but larger and coarser than the mainsail of a man-of-war.

I slept about two hours, and dreamed I was at home with my wife and children, which aggravated my sorrows when I awaked, and found myself alone, in a vast room, between two and three hundred feet wide, and about two hundred high, lying in a bed twenty yards wide. My mistress was gone about her household affairs, and had locked me in. The bed was eight yards from the floor. I durst not presume to call; and if I had, it would have been in vain, with such a voice as mine, at so great a distance as from the room where I lay to the kitchen where the family kept. While I was under these circumstances, two rats crept up the curtains, and ran smelling backward and forward on the bed. One of them came up almost to my face, whereupon I rose in a fright, and drew out my hanger to defend myself. These horrible animals had the boldness to attack me on both sides, and one of them held his forefeet at my collar; but I had the good fortune to rip up his belly before he could do me any mischief. He fell down at my feet; and the other, seeing the fate of his comrade, made his escape, but not without one good wound on the back, which I gave him as he fled, and made the blood run trickling from him. After this exploit, I walked gently to and fro on the bed, to recover my breath and loss of spirits. These creatures were of the size of a large mastiff, but infinitely more nimble and fierce; so that if I had taken off my belt before I went to sleep, I must have infallibly been torn to pieces and devoured. I measured the tail of the dead rat, and found it to be two yards long, wanting an inch; but it went against my stomach to draw the carcass off the bed, where it lay still bleeding. I observed it had yet some life, but with a strong slash across the neck, I thoroughly despatched it. Soon after, my mistress came into the room, who seeing me all bloody, ran and took me up in her hand. I pointed to the dead rat, smiling, and making other signs, to show I was not hurt; whereat she was extremely rejoiced, calling the maid to take up the dead rat with a pair of tongs, and throw it out of the window. Then she set me on a table, where I showed her my hanger all bloody, and wiping it on the lappet of my coat returned it to the scabbard.

I hope the gentle reader will excuse me for dwelling on these and the like particulars, which, however insignificant they may appear to grovelling vulgar minds, yet will certainly help a philosopher to enlarge his thoughts and imagination, and apply them to the benefit of public as well as private life, which was my sole design in presenting this, and other accounts of my travels, to the world; wherein I have been chiefly studious of truth, without affecting any ornaments of learning or of style. But the whole scene of this voyage made so strong an impression on my mind, and is so deeply fixed in my memory, that in committing it to paper I did not omit one material circumstance; however, upon strict review, I blotted out several passages of less moment, which were in my first copy, for fear of being censured as tedious and trifling, whereof travellers are often, perhaps not without justice, accused.

SOME OF GULLIVER'S ADVENTURES

By Jonathan Swift

Justly may I say, that I should have lived happy enough in the country, if my littleness had not exposed me to several ridiculous and troublesome accidents; some of which I shall venture to relate. Glumdalclitch often carried me into the gardens of the court in my smaller box, and would sometimes take me out of it, and hold me in her hand, or set me down to walk. I remember, before the dwarf left the queen, he followed us one day into those gardens, and my nurse having set me down, he and I being close together, near some dwarf apple-trees, I must needs show my wit, by a silly allusion between him and the trees, which happens to hold in their language as it does in ours. Whereupon, the malicious rogue, watching his opportunity, when I was walking under one of them, shook it directly over my head, by which a dozen apples, each of them near as large as a Bristol barrel, came tumbling about my ears; one of them hit me on the back as I chanced to stoop, and knocked me down flat on my face; but I received no other hurt, and the dwarf was pardoned at my desire, because I had given the provocation.

Another day, Glumdalelitch left me on a smooth grass plot to divert myself, while she walked at some distance with her governess. In the meantime, there suddenly fell such a violent shower of hail, that I was immediately, by the force of it, struck to the ground; and when I was down, the hailstones gave me such cruel bangs all over the body, as if I had been pelted with tennis-balls; however, I made a shift to creep on all fours, and shelter myself, by lying flat on my face, on the lee-side of a border of lemon-thyme; but so bruised from head to foot, that I could not go abroad in ten days. Neither is that at all to be wondered at, because nature, in that country, observing the same proportion through all her operations, a hailstone is near eighteen hundred times as large as one in Europe; which I can assert upon experience, having been so curious to weigh and measure them.

But a more dangerous accident happened to me in the same garden, when my little nurse, believing she had put me in a secure place (which I often entreated her to do, that I might enjoy my own thoughts), and having left my box at home, to avoid the trouble of carrying it, went to another part of the garden with her governess and some ladies of her acquaintance. While she was absent and out of hearing, a small white spaniel that belonged to one of the chief gardeners, having got by accident into the garden, happened to range near the place where I lay: the dog, following the scent, came directly up, and taking me in his mouth, ran straight to his master wagging his tail, and set me gently on the ground. By good fortune he had been so well taught, that I was carried between his teeth without the least hurt, or even tearing my clothes. But the poor gardener, who knew me well, and had a great kindness for me, was in a terrible fright; he gently took me up in both his hands, and asked me how I did; but I was so amazed and out of breath, that I could not speak a word. In a few minutes I came to myself, and he carried me safe to my little nurse, who, by this time, had returned to the place where she left me, and was in cruel agonies when I did not appear, nor answer when she called. She severely reprimanded the gardener on account of his dog. But the thing was hushed up, and never known at court, for the girl was afraid of the queen's anger; and truly, as to myself, I thought it would not be for my reputation that such a story should go about.

This accident absolutely determined Glumdalclitch never to trust me abroad for the future out of her sight. I had been long afraid of this resolution, and therefore concealed from her some little unlucky adventures, that happened in those times when I was left by myself. Once a kite, hovering over the garden, made a stoop at me, and if I had not resolutely drawn my hanger, and run under a thick espalier, he would have certainly carried me away in his talons. Another time, walking to the top of a fresh molehill, I fell to my neck in the hole, through which that animal had cast up the earth, and coined some lie, not worth remembering, to excuse myself for spoiling my clothes. I likewise broke my right shin against the shell of a snail, which I happened to stumble over, as I was walking alone and thinking of poor England.

I cannot tell whether I were more pleased or mortified to observe, in those solitary walks, that the smaller birds did not appear to be at all afraid of me, but would hop about within a yard's distance, looking for worms and other food, with as much indifference and security as if no creature at all were near them. I remember, a thrush had the confidence to snatch out of my hand, with his bill, a piece of cake that Glumdalclitch had just given me for my breakfast. When I attempted to catch any of these birds, they would boldly turn against me, endeavoring to peck my fingers, which I durst not venture within their reach; and then they would hop back unconcerned, to hunt for worms or snails, as they did before. But one day, I took a thick cudgel, and threw it with all my strength so luckily, at a linnet, that I knocked him down, and seizing him by the neck with both my hands, ran with him in triumph to my nurse. However, the bird, who had only been stunned, recovering himself, gave me so many boxes with his wings, on both sides of my head and body, though I held him at arm's length, and was out of the reach of his claws, that I was twenty times thinking to let him go. But I was soon relieved by one of our servants, who wrung off the bird's neck, and I had him next day for dinner, by the queen's command. This linnet, as near as I can remember, seemed to be somewhat larger than an English swan.

One day, a young gentleman, who was nephew to my nurse's governess, came and pressed them both to see an execution. It was of a man who had murdered one of that gentleman's intimate acquaintance. Glumdalclitch was prevailed on to be of the company, very much against her inclination, for she was naturally tender- hearted; and as for myself, although I abhorred such kind of spectacles, yet my curiosity tempted me to see something that I thought must be extraordinary. The malefactor was fixed on a chair upon a scaffold erected for that purpose, and his head cut off at one blow, with a sword of about forty feet long. The veins and arteries spouted up such a prodigious quantity of blood, and so high in the air, that the great fountain at Versailles was not equal for the time it lasted; and the head, when it fell on the scaffold floor, gave such a bounce as made me start, although I were at least half an English mile distant.

The queen, who often used to hear me talk of my sea-voyages, and took all occasions to divert me when I was melancholy, asked me whether I understood how to handle a sail or an oar, and whether a little exercise of rowing might not be convenient for my health? I answered that I understood both very well: for although my proper employment had been to be surgeon or doctor to the ship, yet often, upon a pinch, I was forced to work like a common mariner. But I could not see how this could be done in their country, where the smallest wherry was equal to a first-rate man-of-war among us; and such a boat as I could manage would never live in one of their rivers. Her Majesty said, if I would contrive a boat, her own joiner should make it, and she would provide a place for me to sail in. The fellow was an ingenious workman, and by my instructions, in ten days, finished a pleasure-boat, with all its tackling, able conveniently to hold eight Europeans. When it was finished, the queen was so delighted that she ran with it in her lap to the king, who ordered it to be put into a cistern full of water, with me in it, by way of trial; where I could not manage my two sculls, or little oars, for want of room. But the queen had before contrived another project. She ordered the joiner to make a wooden trough of three hundred feet long, fifty broad, and eight deep; which, being well pitched to prevent leaking, was placed on the floor along the wall, in an outer room of the palace. It had a cock near the bottom to let out the water, when it began to grow stale; and two servants could easily fill it in half an hour. Here I often used to row for my own diversion, as well as that of the queen and her ladies, who thought themselves well entertained with my skill and agility. Sometimes I would put up my sail and then my business was only to steer, while the ladies gave me a gale with their fans; and when they were weary, some of their pages would blow my sail forward with their breath, while I showed my art by steering starboard or larboard as I pleased. When I had done, Glumdalclitch always carried back my boat into her closet, and hung it on a nail to dry.

In this exercise I once met an accident, which had like to have cost me my life; for, one of the pages having put my boat into the trough, the governess who attended Glumdalclitch very officiously lifted me up, to place me in the boat; but I happened to slip through her fingers, and should infallibly have fallen down forty feet, upon the floor, if, by the luckiest chance in the world, I had not been stopped by a corking-pin that stuck in the good gentlewoman's stomacher; the head of the pin passed between my shirt and the waistband of my breeches, and thus I was held by the middle in the air, till Glumdalclitch ran to my relief.

Another time, one of the servants, whose office it was to fill my trough every third day with fresh water, was so careless to let a huge frog (not perceiving it) slip out of his pail. The frog lay concealed till I was put into my boat, but then seeing a resting- place, climbed up, and made it to lean so much on one side, that I was forced to balance it with all my weight on the other to prevent overturning. When the frog was got in, it hopped at once half the length of the boat, and then over my head, backward and forward, daubing my face and clothes with its odious slime. The largeness of its features made it appear the most deformed animal that can be conceived. However, I desired Glumdalclitch to let me deal with it alone. I banged it a good while with one of my sculls, and at last forced it to leap out of the boat.

But the greatest danger I underwent in that kingdom was from a monkey, who belonged to one of the clerks of the kitchen. Glumdalclitch had locked me up in her closet, while she went somewhere upon business, or a visit. The weather being very warm, the closet window was left open, as well as the windows and door of my bigger box, in which I usually lived, because of its largeness and conveniency. As I sat quietly meditating at my table, I heard something bounce in at the closet-window, and skip about from one side to the other; whereat, although I was much alarmed, yet I ventured to look out, but not stirring from my seat; and then I saw this frolicsome animal frisking and leaping up and down, till at last he came to my box, which he seemed to view with great pleasure and curiosity, peeping in at the door and every window. I retreated to the further corner of my room, or box; but the monkey, looking in at every side, put me into such a fright, that I wanted presence of mind to conceal myself under the bed, as I might easily have done. After some time spent in peeping, grinning, and chattering, he at last espied me; and reaching one of his paws in at the door, as a cat does when she plays with a mouse, although I often shifted place to avoid him, he at length seized the lappet of my coat (which being made of that country silk, was very thick and strong), and dragged me out. He took me up in his right forefoot, and held me as a nurse does a child; and when I offered to struggle, he squeezed me so hard, that I thought it more prudent to submit. I have good reason to believe that he took me for a young one of his own species, by his often stroking my face very gently with his other paw. In these diversions he was interrupted by a noise at the closet door, as if somebody were opening it; whereupon he suddenly leaped up to the window, at which he had come in, and thence upon the leads and gutters, walking upon three legs, and holding me in the fourth, till he clambered up to a roof that was next to ours. I heard Glumdalclitch give a shriek the moment he was carrying me out. The poor girl was almost distracted; that quarter of the palace was all in an uproar; the servants ran for ladders; the monkey was seen by hundreds in the court, sitting upon the ridge of a building, holding me like a baby in one of his fore-paws, and feeding me with the other, by cramming into my mouth some victuals he had squeezed out of the bag on one side of his chaps, and patting me when I would not eat; whereat many of the rabble below could not forbear laughing; neither do I think they justly ought to be blamed, for, without question, the sight was ridiculous enough to everybody but myself. Some of the people threw up stones, hoping to drive the monkey down; but this was strictly forbidden, or else, very probably, my brains had been dashed out.

The ladders were now applied, and mounted by several men; which the monkey observing, and finding himself almost encompassed, not being able to make speed enough with his three legs, let me drop on a ridge tile, and made his escape. Here I sat for some time, five hundred yards from the ground, expecting every moment to be blown down by the wind, or to fall by my own giddiness, and come tumbling over and over from the ridge to the eaves: but an honest lad, one of my nurse's footmen, climbed up, and putting me into his breeches pocket, brought me down — safe.

I was almost choked with the filthy stuff the monkey had crammed down my throat; but my dear little nurse picked it out of my mouth with a small needle, and then I fell a-vomiting, which gave me great relief. Yet I was so weak and bruised in the sides with the squeezes given me by this odious animal, that I was forced to keep my bed a fortnight. The king, queen, and all the court, sent every day to inquire after my health, and her Majesty made me several visits during my sickness. The monkey was killed, and an order made that no such animal should be kept about the palace.

When I attended the king after my recovery, to return him thanks for his favors, he was pleased to rally me a good deal upon this adventure. He asked me, what my thoughts and speculations were while I lay in the monkey's paw? how I liked the victuals he gave me? his manner of feeding? and whether the fresh air on the roof had sharpened my stomach? He desired to know what I would have done upon such an occasion in my own country? I told his Majesty, that in Europe we had no monkeys except such as were brought for curiosities from other places, and so small that I could deal with a dozen of them together, if they presumed to attack me. And as for that monstrous animal, with whom I was so lately engaged (it was indeed as large as an elephant), if my fears had suffered me to think so far as to make use of my hanger (looking fiercely, and clapping my hand upon the hilt, as I spoke) when he poked his paw into my chamber, perhaps I should have given him such a wound, as would have made him glad to withdraw it, with more haste than he put it in. This I delivered in a firm tone, like a person who was jealous lest his courage should be called in question. However, my speech produced nothing else beside a loud laughter, which all the respect due to his Majesty from those about him could not make them contain. This made me reflect, how vain an attempt it is for a man to endeavor to do himself honor among those who are out of all degree of equality or comparison with him. And yet I have seen the moral of my own behavior very frequently in England since my return; where a little contemptible varlet, without the least title to birth, person, wit, or common-sense, shall presume to look with importance, and put himself upon a foot with the greatest persons of the kingdom.

GULLIVER ESCAPES FROM THE EAGLE

By Jonathan Swift

Perilous circumstances, from which I had already escaped, inspired me with a strong impulse that I should some time recover my liberty, though it was impossible to conjecture by what means, or to form any project with the least hope of succeeding. The ship in which I sailed was the first known to be driven within sight of that coast, and the king had given strict orders, that if at any time another appeared, it should be taken ashore, and with all its crew and passengers brought in a tumbrel to Lorbrulgrud. I was indeed treated with much kindness: I was the favorite of a great king and queen, and the delight of the whole court; but it was upon such a foot as ill became the dignity of human-kind. I could never forget these domestic pledges I had left behind me. I wanted to be among people with whom I could converse upon even terms, and walk about the streets and fields without being afraid of being trod to death like a frog or a young puppy. But my deliverance came sooner than I expected, and in a manner not very common: the whole story and circumstances of which I shall faithfully relate.

I had now been two years in the country: and about the beginning of the third, Glumdalclitch and I attended the king and queen, in a progress to the south coast of the kingdom. I was carried as usual, in my travelling box, which, as I have already described, was a very convenient closet of twelve feet wide. And I had ordered a hammock to be fixed, by silken ropes, from the four corners at the top, to break the jolts when a servant carried me before him on horseback, as I sometimes desired; and would often sleep in my hammock, while we were upon the road. On the roof of my closet, not directly over the middle of the hammock, I ordered the joiner to cut a hole of a foot square, to give me air in hot weather as I slept; which hole I shut at pleasure, with a board that drew backward and forward through a groove.

When we came to our journey's end, the king thought proper to pass a few days at a palace he has near Flanflasnic, a city within eighteen English miles of the seaside. Glumdalclitch and I were much fatigued: I had gotten a small cold, but the poor girl was so ill as to be confined to her chamber. I longed to see the ocean, which must be the only scene of my escape, if ever it should happen. I pretended to be worse than I really was, and desired leave to take the fresh air of the sea, with a page whom I was very fond of, and who had sometimes been trusted with me. I shall never forget with what unwillingness Glumdalclitch consented, nor the strict charge she gave the page to be careful of me, bursting at the same time into a flood of tears, as if she had some foreboding of what was to happen. The boy took me out in my box, about half an hour's walk from the palace, toward the rocks on the sea-shore. I ordered him to set me down, and lifting up one of my sashes, cast many a wistful melancholy look toward the sea. I found myself not very well, and told the page that I had a mind to take a nap in my hammock, which I hoped would do me good. I got in, and the boy shut the window close down to keep out the cold. I soon fell asleep, and all I can conjecture is that, while I slept, the page, thinking no danger could happen, went among the rocks to look for birds' eggs, having before observed him from my window searching about, and picking up one or two in the clefts. Be that as it will, I found myself suddenly awakened with a violent pull upon the ring, which was fastened at the top of my box for the convenience of carriage. I felt my box raised very high in the air, and then borne forward with prodigious speed. The first jolt had like to have shaken me out of my hammock, but afterward the motion was easy enough. I called out several times as loud as I could raise my voice, but all to no purpose. I looked toward my windows, and could see nothing but the clouds and sky. I heard a noise over my head, like the clapping of wings, and then began to perceive the woful condition I was in: that some eagle had got the cord of my box in his beak, with an intent to let it fall on the rock, like a tortoise in a shell, and then pick out my body and devour it: for the sagacity and smell of this bird enable him to discover his quarry at a great distance, though better concealed than I could be within a two-inch board. In a little time I observed the noise and flutter of wings to increase very fast, and my box was tossed up and down, like a sign on a windy day. I heard several bangs or buffets, as I thought, given to the eagle (for such I am certain it must have been that held the cord of my box in his beak), and then, all on a sudden, felt myself falling perpendicularly down, for above a minute, but with such incredible swiftness, that I almost lost my breath. My fall was stopped by a terrible squash, that sounded louder to my ears than the cataract of Niagara; after which I was quite in the dark for another minute, and then my box began to rise so high that I could see light from the tops of the windows. I now perceived I was fallen into the sea. My box, by the weight of my body, the goods that were in it, and the broad plates of iron fixed for strength at the four corners of the top and bottom, floated about five feet deep in water. I did then, and do now suppose, that the eagle which flew away with my box was pursued by two or three others, and forced to let me drop, while he defended himself against the rest, who hoped to share in the prey. The plates of iron fastened at the bottom of the box (for those were the strongest) preserved the balance while it fell, and hindered it from being broken on the surface of the water. Every joint of it was well grooved; and the door did not move on hinges, but up and down like a sash, which kept my closet so tight that very little water came in. I got with much difficulty out of my hammock, having first ventured to draw back the slip-board on the roof already mentioned, contrived on purpose to let in air, for want of which I found myself almost stifled.

How often did I then wish myself with my dear Glumdalclitch, from whom one single hour had so far divided me! And I may say with truth, that in the midst of my own misfortunes I could not forbear lamenting my poor nurse, the grief she would suffer for my loss, the displeasure of the queen, and the ruin of her fortune. Perhaps many travellers have not been under greater difficulties and distress than I was at this juncture, expecting every moment to see my box dashed to pieces, or at least overset by the first violent blast or rising wave. A breach in one single pane of glass would have been immediate death: nor could anything have preserved the windows, but the strong lattice wires placed on the outside, against accidents in travelling. I saw the water ooze in at several crannies, although the leaks were not considerable, and I endeavored to stop them as well as I could. I was not able to lift up the roof of my closet, which otherwise I certainly should have done, and sat on the top of it: where I might at least preserve myself some hours longer, than by being shut up (as I may call it) in the hold. Or if I escaped these dangers for a day or two, what could I expect but a miserable death of cold and hunger? I was for four hours under these circumstances, expecting, and indeed wishing, every moment to be my last.

I have already told the reader that there were two strong staples fixed upon that side of my box which had no window; and into which the servant who used to carry me on horseback would put a leathern belt, and buckle it about his waist. Being in this disconsolate state, I heard, or at least thought I heard, some kind of grating noise on that side of my box where the staples were fixed; and soon after I began to fancy that the box was pulled or towed along the sea; for I now and then felt a sort of tugging, which made the waves rise near the tops of my windows, leaving me almost in the dark. This gave me some faint hopes of relief, although I was not able to imagine how it could be brought about. I ventured to unscrew one of my chairs, which were always fastened to the floor; and having made a hard shift to screw it down again directly under the shipping-board that I had lately opened, I mounted on the chair, and putting my mouth as near as I could to the hole, I called for help in a loud voice, and in all the languages I understood. I then fastened my handkerchief to a stick I usually carried, and thrusting it up the hole, waved it several times in the air, that if any boat or ship was near, the seamen might conjecture some unhappy mortal to be shut up in the box.

I found no effect from all I could do, but plainly perceived my closet to be moved along; and in the space of an hour, or better, that side of the box where the staples were, and had no windows, struck against something that was hard. I apprehended it to be a rock, and found myself tossed more than ever. I plainly heard a noise upon the cover of my closet, like that of a cable, and the grating of it as it passed through the ring. I then found myself hoisted up by degrees, at least three feet higher than I was before. Whereupon I again thrust up my stick and handkerchief, calling for help till I was almost hoarse. In return to which I heard a great shout repeated three times, giving me such transports of joy as are not to be conceived but by those who feel them. I now heard a trampling over my head, and somebody calling through the hole with a loud voice, in the English tongue, If there be anybody below, let them speak. I answered, I was an Englishman, drawn by ill fortune into the greatest calamity that ever any creature underwent, and begged, by all that was moving, to be delivered out of the dungeon I was in. The voice replied, I was safe, for my box was fastened to their ship; and the carpenter should immediately come and saw a hole in the cover, large enough to pull me out. I answered that was needless, and would take up too much time; for there was no more to be done, but let one of the crew put his finger into the ring, and take the box out of the sea into the ship, and so into the captain's cabin. Some of them, upon hearing me talk so wildly, thought I was mad; others laughed; for indeed it never came into my head, that I was now got among people of my own stature and strength. The carpenter came, and in a few minutes sawed a passage about four feet square, then let down a small ladder, upon which I mounted, and thence was taken into the ship in a very weak condition.

The sailors were all amazement, and asked me a thousand questions, which I had no inclination to answer, I was equally confounded at the sight of so many pygmies, for such I took them to be, after having so long accustomed mine eyes to the monstrous objects I had left. But the captain, Mr. Thomas Wilcocks, an honest worthy Shropshire man, observing I was ready to faint, took me into his cabin, gave me a cordial to comfort me, and made me turn in upon his own bed, advising me to take a little rest, of which I had great need. Before I went to sleep I gave him to understand that I had some valuable furniture in my box, too good to be lost: a fine hammock, a handsome field-bed, two chairs, a table, and a cabinet; that my closet was hung on all sides, or rather quilted, with silk and cotton; that if he would let one of the crew bring my closet into his cabin I would open it there before him and show him my goods. The captain, hearing me utter these absurdities, concluded I was raving; however (I suppose to pacify me), he promised to give order as I desired, and going upon deck, sent some of his men down into my closet, whence (as I afterward found) they drew up all my goods, and stripped off the quilting; but the chairs, cabinet, and bedstead, being screwed to the floor, were much damaged by the ignorance of the seamen, who tore them up by force. Then they knocked off some of the boards for the use of the ship, and when they had got all they had a mind for, let the hull drop into the sea, which, by reason of many breaches made in the bottom and sides, sunk outright. And, indeed, I was glad not to have been a spectator of the havoc they made; because I am confident it would have sensibly touched me, by bringing former passages into my mind which I would rather have forgot.

I slept some hours, but perpetually disturbed with dreams of the place I had left, and the dangers I had escaped. However, upon waking, I found myself much recovered. It was now about eight o'clock at night, and the captain ordered supper immediately, thinking I had already fasted too long. He entertained me with great kindness, observing me not to look wildly or talk inconsistently; and when we were left alone, desired I would give him a relation of my travels; and by what accident I came to be set adrift in that monstrous wooden chest. He said that about twelve o'clock at noon, as he was looking through his glass, he spied it at a distance, and thought it was a sail, which he had a mind to make, being not much out of his course, in hopes of buying some biscuit, his own beginning to fall short. That upon coming nearer, and finding his error, he sent out his long-boat, to discover what it was; that his men came back in fright, swearing they had seen a swimming house. That he laughed at their folly, and went himself in the boat, ordering his men to take a strong cable along with them. That the weather being calm, he rowed round me several times, observed my windows and wire lattices that defended them. That he discovered two staples upon one side, which was all of boards, without any passage for light. He then commanded his men to row up to that side, and fastening a cable to one of the staples, ordered them to tow my chest, as they called it, toward the ship. When it was there he gave directions to fasten another cable to the ring fixed in the cover, and to raise up my chest with pulleys, which all the sailors were not able to do above two or three feet. He said they saw my stick and handkerchief thrust out of the hole, and concluded that some unhappy man must be shut up in the cavity. I asked whether he or the crew had seen any prodigious birds in the air about the time he first discovered me? To which he answered, that discoursing this matter with the sailors while I was asleep, one of them said he had observed three eagles flying toward the north, but remarked nothing of their being larger than the usual size; which I suppose must be imputed to the great height they were at; and he could not guess the reason of my question. I then asked the captain how far he reckoned we might be from land? He said, by the best computation he could make, we were at least a hundred leagues. I assured him that he must be mistaken by almost half, for I had not left the country whence I came above two hours before I dropped into the sea. Whereupon he began again to think that my brain was disturbed, of which he gave me a hint, and advised me to go to bed in a cabin he had provided. I assured him I was well refreshed with his good entertainment and company, and as much in my senses as ever I was in my life. He then grew serious, and desired to ask me freely whether I were not troubled in my mind by the consciousness of some enormous crime, for which I was punished, at the command of some prince, by exposing me in that chest; as great criminals, in other countries, have been forced to sea in a leaky vessel without provisions: for although he should be sorry to have taken so ill a man into his ship, yet he would engage his word to set me safe ashore in the first port where we arrived? He added that his suspicions were much increased by some very absurd speeches I had delivered at first to his sailors, and afterward to himself, in relation to my closet or chest, as well as by my odd looks and behavior while I was at supper.

I begged his patience to hear me tell my story, which I faithfully did, from the last time I left England, to the moment he first discovered me. And as truth always forces its way into rational minds, so this honest worthy gentleman, who had some tincture of learning, and very good sense, was immediately convinced of my candor and veracity. But, further to confirm all I had said, I entreated him to give order that my cabinet should be brought, of which I had the key in my pocket; for he had already informed me how the seamen disposed of my closet. I opened it in his own presence, and showed him the small collection of rarities I made in the country from which I had been so strangely delivered. There was the comb I had contrived out of the stumps of the king's beard, and another of the same materials, but fixed into a paring of her Majesty's thumb-nail, which served for the back. There was a collection of needles and pins, from a foot to half a yard long; four wasp stings, like joiners' tacks; some combings of the queen's hair; a gold ring which one day she made me a present of, in a most obliging manner, taking it from her little finger and throwing it over my head like a collar. I desired the captain would please to accept this ring in return of his civilities, which he absolutely refused. I showed him a corn that I had cut off, with my own hand, from a maid of honor's toe; it was about the bigness of a Kentish pippin, and grown so hard that when I returned to England I got it hollowed into a cup, and set it in silver. Lastly, I desired him to see the breeches I had then on, which were made of a mouse's skin.

I could force nothing on him but a footman's tooth, which I observed him to examine with great curiosity, and found he had a fancy for it. He received it with abundance of thanks, more than such a trifle could deserve. It was drawn by an unskilful surgeon, in a mistake, from one of Glumdalclitch's men, who was afflicted with the toothache, but it was as sound as any in his head. I got it cleaned, and put it into my cabinet. It was about a foot long and four inches in diameter.

The captain was very well satisfied with this plain relation I had given him, and said he hoped, when we returned to England, I would oblige the world by putting it on paper, and making it public. My answer was that I thought we were overstocked with books of travels; that nothing could now pass which was not extraordinary; wherein I doubted some authors less consulted truth than their own vanity, or interest, or the diversion of ignorant readers; that my story could contain little besides common events, without those ornamented descriptions of strange plants, trees, birds, and other animals; or of the barbarous customs and idolatry of savage people, with which most writers abound. However, I thanked him for his good opinion, and promised to take the matter into my thoughts.

He said he wondered at one thing very much, which was to hear me speak so loud; asking me whether the king and queen of that country were thick of hearing? I told him it was what I had been used to for above two years past, and that I admired as much at the voices of him and his men, who seemed to me only to whisper, and yet I could hear them well enough. But when I spoke in that country it was like a man talking in the streets to another looking out from the top of a steeple, unless when I was placed on a table or held in any person's hand. I told him I had likewise observed another thing, that when I first got into the ship, and the sailors stood all about me, I thought they were the most contemptible little creatures I had ever beheld. For, indeed, while I was in that prince's country, I could never endure to look in a glass after mine eyes had been accustomed to such prodigious objects, because the comparisons gave me so despicable a conceit of myself. The captain said that while we were at supper he observed me to look at everything with a sort of wonder, and that I often seemed hardly able to contain my laughter, which he knew not well how to take, but imputed it to some disorder in my brain. I answered, it was very true; and I wondered how I could forbear, when I saw his dishes of the size of a silver threepence, a leg of pork hardly a mouthful, a cup not so big as a nutshell; and so I went on, describing the rest of his household stuff and provisions after the same manner. For, although the queen had ordered a little equipage of all things necessary for me while I was in her service, yet my ideas were wholly taken up with what I saw on every side of me, and I winked at my own littleness as people do at their own faults. The captain understood my raillery very well, and merrily replied with the old English proverb that he doubted mine eyes were bigger than my belly, for he did not observe my stomach so good, although I had fasted all day; and, continuing in his mirth, protested he would have gladly given a hundred pounds to have seen my closet in the eagle's bill, and afterward in its fall from so great a height into the sea: which would certainly have been a most astonishing object, worthy to have the description of it transmitted to future ages: and the comparison of Phaeton was so obvious that he could not forbear applying it, although I did not much admire the conceit.

The captain having been at Tonquin, was, in his return to England, driven northeastward to the latitude of 44 degrees and longitude of 143. But meeting a trade-wind two days after I came on board him, we sailed southward a long time, and, coasting New Holland, kept our course west-southwest, and then south-southwest, till we doubled the Cape of Good Hope. Our voyage was very prosperous, but I shall not trouble the reader with a journal of it. The captain called in at one or two ports, and sent in his longboat for provisions and fresh water; but I never went out of the ship till we came into the Downs, which was on the third day of June, 1706, about nine months after my escape. I offered to leave my goods in security for payment of my freight, but the captain protested he would not receive one farthing.

We took a kind leave of each other, and I made him promise he would come to see me at my house in Redriff. I hired a horse and guide for five shillings, which I borrowed of the captain.

As I was on the road, observing the littleness of the houses, the trees, the cattle, and the people, I began to think myself in Lilliput. I was afraid of trampling on every traveller I met, and often called aloud to them to have them stand out of the way, so that I had like to have gotten one or two broken heads for my impertinence.

When I came to my own house, for which I was forced to inquire, one of my servants opening the door, I bent down to go in (like a goose under a gate), for fear of striking my head. My wife ran out to embrace me, but I stooped lower than her knees, thinking she could otherwise never be able to reach my mouth. My daughter kneeled to ask my blessing, but I could not see her till she arose, having been so long used to stand with my head and eyes erect to above sixty feet; and then I went to take her up with one hand by the waist. I looked down upon the servants, and one or two friends who were in the house, as if they had been pygmies, and I a giant. I told my wife she had been too thrifty, for I found she had starved herself and daughter to nothing.

In short, I behaved myself so unaccountably that they were all of the captain's opinion when he first saw me, and concluded I had lost my wits.

This I mention as an instance of the great power of habit and prejudice.

In a little time I and my family and friends came to a right understanding: but my wife protested I should never go to sea any more; although my evil destiny so ordered, that she had not power to hinder me, as the reader may know hereafter. In the meantime, I here conclude the Second Part of my unfortunate Voyages.

THE PLAYS OF SHAKESPEARE

_William Shakespeare, the greatest of English writers, was born in 1564, and was pretty well educated for those days. The free school of the town was open to all boys, and his father could afford to send him to it. He early became an actor, and from correcting plays by other people he came to writing plays himself.

Shakespeare possessed a very unusual combination of two rare gifts. On the one side he had to a great degree the ability to understand men and women and read the thoughts that were passing through their minds.

But his second gift, which was more wonderful still, was his ability to write down on paper words that, as soon as we read them, make us feel just as he did, make us see just the pictures he saw.

Four of his plays are here represented by short stories, in which the plot of each play is briefly told. To play Shakespeare's plays is the height of an actor's ambition. To read and enjoy them has been for over three hundred years one of the greatest pleasures known to English-speaking people._

A MIDSUMMER-NIGHTS DREAM

Retold by E. Nesbit

HERMIA and Lysander were lovers; but Hermia's father wished her to marry another man, named Demetrius.

Now, in Athens, where they lived, there was a wicked law, by which any girl who refused to marry according to her father's wishes, might be put to death. Hermia's father was so angry with her for refusing to do as he wished, that he actually brought her before the Duke of Athens to ask that she might be killed, if she still refused to obey him.

The duke gave her four days to think about it, and, at the end of that time, if she still refused to marry Demetrius, she would have to die.

Lysander of course was nearly mad with grief, and the best thing to do seemed to him for Hermia to run away to his aunt's house at a place beyond the reach of that cruel law; and there he would come to her and marry her. But before she started, she told her friend, Helena, what she was going to do.

Helena had been Demetrius's sweetheart long before his marriage with Hermia had been thought of, and being very silly, like all jealous people, she could not see that it was not poor Hermia's fault that Demetrius wished to marry her instead of his own lady, Helena. She knew that if she told Demetrius that Hermia was going, as she was, to the wood outside Athens, he would follow her, "and I can follow him, and at least I shall see him," she said to herself. So she went to him, and betrayed her friend's secret.

Now this wood where Lysander was to meet Hermia, and where the other two had decided to follow them, was full of fairies, as most woods are, if one only had the eyes to see them, and in this wood on this night were the king and queen of the fairies, Oberon and Titania. Now fairies are very wise people, but now and then they can be quite as foolish as mortal folk. Oberon and Titania, who might have been as happy as the days were long, had thrown away all their joy in a foolish quarrel. They never met without saying disagreeable things to each other, and scolded each other so dreadfully that all their little fairy followers, for fear, would creep into acorn cups and hide them there.

So, instead of keeping one happy court and dancing all night through in the moonlight, as is fairies' use, the king with his attendants wandered through one part of the wood, while the queen with hers kept state in another. And the cause of all this trouble was a little Indian boy whom Titania had taken to be one of her followers. Oberon wanted the child to follow him and be one of his fairy knights; but the queen would not give him up.

On this night, in a mossy moonlit glade, the king and queen of the fairies met.

"Ill met by moonlight, proud Titania," said the king.

"What! jealous, Oberon?" answered the queen. "You spoil everything with your quarreling. Come, fairies, let us leave him. I am not friends with him now."

"It rests with you to make up the quarrel," said the king.

"Give me that little Indian boy, and I will again be your humble servant and suitor."

"Set your mind at rest," said the queen. "Your whole fairy kingdom buys not that boy from me. Come, fairies."

And she and her train rode off down the moonbeams.

"Well, go your ways," said Oberon. "But I'll be even with you before you leave this wood."

Then Oberon called his favorite fairy, Puck. Puck was the spirit of mischief. He used to slip into the dairies and take the cream away, and get into the churn so that the butter would not come, and turn the beer sour, and lead people out of their way on dark nights and then laugh at them, and tumble people's stools from under them when they were going to sit down, and upset their hot ale over their chins when they were going to drink.

"Now," said Oberon to this little sprite, "fetch me the flower called Love-in-idleness. The juice of that little purple flower laid on the eyes of those who sleep will make them, when they wake, to love the first thing they see. I will put some of the juice of that flower on my Titania's eyes, and when she wakes she will love the first thing she sees, were it lion, bear, or wolf, or bull, or meddling monkey, or a busy ape."

While Puck was gone, Demetrius passed through the glade followed by poor Helena, and still she told him how she loved him and reminded him of all his promises, and still he told her that he did not and could not love her, and that his promises were nothing. Oberon was sorry for poor Helena, and when Puck returned with the flower, he bade him follow Demetrius and put some of the juice on his eyes, so that he might love Helena when he woke and looked on her, as much as she loved him. So Puck set off, and wandering through the wood found, not Demetrius, but Lysander, on whose eyes he put the juice; but when Lysander woke, he saw not his own Hermia, but Helena, who was walking through the wood looking for the cruel Demetrius; and directly he saw her he loved her and left his own lady, under the spell of the purple flower.

When Hermia woke she found Lysander gone, and wandered about the wood trying to find him. Puck went back and told Oberon what he had done, and Oberon soon found that he had made a mistake, and set about looking for Demetrius, and having found him, put some of the juice on his eyes. And the first thing Demetrius saw when he woke was also Helena. So now Demetrius and Lysander were both following her through the wood, and it was Hermia's turn to follow her lover as Helena had done before. The end of it was that Helena and Hermia began to quarrel, and Demetrius and Lysander went off to fight.

Oberon was very sorry to see his kind scheme to help these lovers turn out so badly. So he said to Puck—

"These two young men are going to fight. You must overhang the night with drooping fog, and lead them so astray, that one will never find the other. When they are tired out, they will fall asleep. Then drop this other herb on Lysander's eyes. That will give him his old sight and his old love. Then each man will have the lady who loves him, and they will all think that this has been only a Midsummer-Night's Dream. Then when this is done, all will be well with them."

So Puck went and did as he was told, and when the two had fallen asleep without meeting each other, Puck poured the juice on Lysander's eyes, and said:—

"When thou wakest, Thou takest True delight In the sight Of thy former lady's eye: Jack shall have Jill; Nought shall go ill."

Meanwhile Oberon found Titania asleep on a bank where grew wild thyme, oxlips, and violets, and woodbine, musk-roses and eglantine. There Titania always slept a part of the night, wrapped in the enameled skin of a snake. Oberon stopped over her and laid the juice on her eyes, saying:—

"What thou seest when thou wake, Do it for thy true love take;" Now, it happened that when Titania woke the first thing she saw was a stupid clown, one of a party of players who had come out into the wood to rehearse their play. This clown had met with Puck, who had clapped an ass's head on his shoulders so that it looked as if it grew there. Directly Titania woke and saw this dreadful monster, she said, "What angel is this? Are you as wise as you are beautiful?"

"If I am wise enough to find my way out of this wood, that's enough for me," said the foolish clown.

"Do not desire to go out of the wood," said Titania. The spell of the love-juice was on her, and to her the clown seemed the most beautiful and delightful creature on all the earth. "I love you," she went on. "Come with me, and I will give you fairies to attend on you."

So she called four fairies, whose names were Peaseblossom, Cobweb, Moth, and Mustardseed.

"You must attend this gentleman," said the queen. "Feed him with apricots and dewberries, purple grapes, green figs, and mulberries. Steal honey-bags for him from the humble-bees, and with the wings of painted butterflies fan the moonbeams from his sleeping eyes."

"I will," said one of the fairies, and all the others said, "I will."

"Now, sit down with me," said the queen to the clown, "and let me stroke your dear cheeks, and stick musk-roses in your smooth, sleek head, and kiss your fair large ears, my gentle joy."

"Where's Peaseblossom?" asked the clown with the ass's head. He did not care much about the queen's affection, but he was very proud of having fairies to wait on him. "Ready," said Peaseblossom.

"Scratch my head, Peaseblossom," said the clown. "Where's Cobweb?" "Ready," said Cobweb.

"Kill me," said the clown, "the red bumble-bee on the top of the thistle yonder, and bring me the honey-bag. Where's Mustardseed?"

"Ready," said Mustardseed.

"Oh, I want nothing," said the clown. "Only just help Cobweb to scratch. I must go to the barber's, for methinks I am marvelous hairy about the face."

"Would you like anything to eat?" said the fairy queen.

"I should like some good dry oats," said the clown-for his donkey's head made him desire donkey's food—"and some hay to follow."

"Shall some of my fairies fetch you new nuts from the squirrel's house?" asked the queen.

"I'd rather have a handful or two of good dried peas," said the clown. "But please don't let any of your people disturb me; I am going to sleep."

Then said the queen, "And I will wind thee in my arms."

And so when Oberon came along he found his beautiful queen lavishing kisses and endearments on a clown with a donkey's head.

And before he released her from the enchantment, he persuaded her to give him the little Indian boy he so much desired to have. Then he took pity on her, and threw some juice of the disenchanting flower on her pretty eyes; and then in a moment she saw plainly the donkey-headed clown she had been loving, and knew how foolish she had been.

Oberon took off the ass's head from the clown, and left him to finish his sleep with his own silly head lying on the thyme and violets.

Thus all was made plain and straight again. Oberon and Titania loved each other more than ever. Demetrius thought of no one but Helena, and Helena had never had any thought of anyone but Demetrius.

As for Hermia and Lysander, they were as loving a couple as you could meet in a day's march, even through a fairy wood.

So the four mortal lovers went back to Athens and were married; and the fairy king and queen live happily together in that very wood at this very day.

THE TEMPEST

Retold by E. Nesbit

Prospero, the Duke of Milan, was a learned and studious man, who lived among his books, leaving the management of his dukedom to his brother Antonio, in whom indeed he had complete trust. But that trust was ill-rewarded, for Antonio wanted to wear the duke's crown himself, and, to gain his ends, would have killed his brother but for the love the people bore him. However, with the help of Prospero's great enemy, Alonso, King of Naples, he managed to get into his hands the dukedom with all its honor, power, and riches. For they took Prospero to sea, and when they were far away from land, forced him into a little boat with no tackle, mast, or sail. In their cruelty and hatred they put his little daughter, Miranda (not yet three years old), into the boat with him, and sailed away, leaving them to their fate.

But one among the courtiers with Antonio was true to his rightful master, Prospero. To save the duke from his enemies was impossible, but much could be done to remind him of a subject's love. So this worthy lord, whose name was Gonzalo, secretly placed in the boat some fresh water, provisions, and clothes, and what Prospero valued most of all, some of his precious books.

The boat was cast on an island, and Prospero and his little one landed in safety. Now this island was enchanted, and for years had lain under the spell of a fell witch, Sycorax, who had imprisoned in the trunks of trees all the good spirits she found there. She died shortly before Prospero was cast on those shores, but the spirits, of whom Ariel was the chief, still remained in their prisons.

Prospero was a great magician, for he had devoted himself almost entirely to the study of magic during the years in which he allowed his brother to manage the affairs of Milan. By his art he set free the imprisoned spirits, yet kept them obedient to his will, and they were more truly his subjects than his people in Milan had been. For he treated them kindly as long as they did his bidding, and he exercised his power over them wisely and well. One creature alone he found it necessary to treat with harshness: this was Caliban, the son of the wicked old witch, a hideous, deformed monster, horrible to look on, and vicious and brutal in all his habits.

When Miranda was grown up into a maiden, sweet and fair to see, it chanced that Antonio and Alonso, with Sebastian, his brother, and Ferdinand, his son, were at sea together with old Gonzalo, and their ship came near Prospero's island. Prospero, knowing they were there, raised by his art a great storm, so that even the sailors on board gave themselves up for lost; and first among them all Prince Ferdinand leaped into the sea, and, as his father thought in his grief, was drowned. But Ariel brought him safe ashore; and all the rest of the crew, although they were washed overboard, were landed unhurt in different parts of the island, and the good ship herself, which they all thought had been wrecked, lay at anchor in the harbor whither Ariel had brought her. Such wonders could Prospero and his spirits perform.

While yet the tempest was raging, Prospero showed his daughter the brave ship laboring in the trough of the sea, and told her that it was filled with living human beings like themselves. She, in pity of their lives, prayed him who had raised this storm to quell it. Then her father bade her to have no fear, for he intended to save every one of them.

Then, for the first time, he told her the story of his life and hers, and that he had caused this storm to rise in order that his enemies, Antonio and Alonso, who were on board, might be delivered into his hands.

When he had made an end of his story he charmed her into sleep, for Ariel was at hand, and he had work for him to do. Ariel, who longed for his complete freedom, grumbled to be kept in drudgery, but on being threateningly reminded of all the sufferings he had undergone when Sycorax ruled in the land, and of the debt of gratitude he owed to the master who had made those sufferings to end, he ceased to complain, and promised faithfully to do whatever Prospero might command.

"Do so," said Prospero, "and in two days I will discharge thee."

Then he bade Ariel take the form of a water nymph and sent him in search of the young prince. And Ariel, invisible to Ferdinand, hovered near him, singing the while—

"Come unto these yellow sands And then take hands: Court'sied when you have, and kiss'd (The wild waves whist), Foot it featly here and there; And, sweet sprites, the burden bear!"

And Ferdinand followed the magic singing, as the song changed to a solemn air, and the words brought grief to his heart, and tears to his eyes, for thus they ran—

"Full fathom five thy father lies; Of his bones are coral made. Those are pearls that were his eyes Nothing of him that doth fade, But doth suffer a sea-change Into something rich and strange. Sea-nymphs hourly ring his knell. Hark! now I hear them, — ding dong bell!"

And so singing, Ariel led the spell-bound prince into the presence of Prospero and Miranda. Then, behold! all happened as Prospero desired. For Miranda, who had never, since she could first remember, seen any human being save her father, looked on the youthful prince with reverence in her eyes, and love in her secret heart.

"I might call him," she said, "a thing divine, for nothing natural I ever saw so noble!"

And Ferdinand, beholding her beauty with wonder and delight, exclaimed —

"Most sure the goddess on whom these airs attend!"

Nor did he attempt to hide the passion which she inspired in him, for scarcely had they exchanged half a dozen sentences, before he vowed to make her his queen if she were willing. But Prospero, though secretly delighted, pretended wrath.

"You come here as a spy," he said to Ferdinand. "I will manacle your neck and feet together, and you shall feed on fresh water mussels, withered roots and husk, and have sea-water to drink. Follow."

"No," said Ferdinand, and drew his sword. But on the instant Prospero charmed him so that he stood there like a statue, still as stone; and Miranda in terror prayed her father to have mercy on her lover.

But he harshly refused her, and made Ferdinand follow him to his cell. There he set the prince to work, making him remove thousands of heavy logs of timber and pile them up; and Ferdinand patiently obeyed, and thought his toil all too well repaid by the sympathy of the sweet Miranda.

She in very pity would have helped him in his hard work, but he would not let her, yet he could not keep from her the secret of his love, and she, hearing it, rejoiced and promised to be his wife.

Then Prospero released him from his servitude, and glad at heart, he gave his consent to their marriage.

"Take her," he said, "she is thine own."

In the meantime, Antonio and Sebastian in another part of the island were plotting the murder of Alonso, the King of Naples, for Ferdinand being dead, as they thought, Sebastian would succeed to the throne on Alonso's death. And they would have carried out their wicked purpose while their victim was asleep, but that Ariel woke him in good time.

Many tricks did Ariel play them. Once he set a banquet before them, and just as they were going to fall to, he appeared to them amid thunder and lightning in the form of a harpy, and immediately the banquet disappeared. Then Ariel upbraided them with their sins and vanished too.

Prospero by his enchantments drew them all to the grove without his cell, where they waited, trembling and afraid, and now at last bitterly repenting them of their sins.

Prospero determined to make one last use of his magic power, "And then," said he, "I'll break my staff and deeper than did ever plummet sound I'll drown my book."

So he made heavenly music to sound in the air, and appeared to them in his proper shape as the Duke of Milan. Because they repented, he forgave them and told them the story of his life since they had cruelly committed him and his baby daughter to the mercy of wind and waves. Alonso, who seemed sorriest of them all for his past crimes, lamented the loss of his heir. But Prospero drew back a curtain and showed them Ferdinand and Miranda playing at chess.

Great was Alonso's joy to greet his loved son again, and when he heard that the fair maid with whom Ferdinand was playing was Prospero's daughter, and that the young folks had plighted their troth, he said—

"Give me your hands, let grief and sorrow still embrace his heart that doth not wish you joy."

So all ended happily. The ship was safe in the harbor, and next day they all set sail for Naples, where Ferdinand and Miranda were to be married. Ariel gave them calm seas and auspicious gales; and many were the rejoicings at the wedding.

Then Prospero, after many years of absence, went back to his own dukedom, where he was welcomed with great joy by his faithful subjects. He practiced the arts of magic no more, but his life was happy, and not only because he had found his own again, but chiefly because, when his bitterest foes who had done him deadly wrong lay at his mercy, he took no vengeance on them, but nobly forgave them.

As for Ariel, Prospero made him free as air, so that he could wander where he would, and sing with a light heart his sweet song—

"Where the bee sucks, there suck I: In a cowslip's bell I lie; There I couch when owls do cry. On the bat's back I do fly After summer, merrily: Merrily, merrily, shall I live now, Under the blossom that hangs on the bough."

AS YOU LIKE IT

Retold by E. Nesbit

There was once a wicked duke named Frederick, who took the dukedom that should have belonged to his brother, sending him into exile. His brother went into the Forest of Arden, where he lived the life of a bold forester, as Robin Hood did in Sherwood Forest in merry England.

The banished duke's daughter, Rosalind, remained with Celia, Frederick's daughter, and the two loved each other more than most sisters. One day there was a wrestling match at court, and Rosalind and Celia went to see it. Charles, a celebrated wrestler, was there, who had killed many men in contests of this kind. Orlando, the young man he was to wrestle with, was so slender and youthful, that Rosalind and Celia thought he would surely be killed, as others had been; so they spoke to him, and asked him not to attempt so dangerous an adventure; but the only effect of their words was to make him wish more to come off well in the encounter, so as to win praise from such sweet ladies.

Orlando, like Rosalind's father, was being kept out of his inheritance by his brother, and was so sad at his brother's unkindness that, until he saw Rosalind, he did not care much whether he lived or died. But now the sight of the fair Rosalind gave him strength and courage, so that he did marvelously, and at last, threw Charles to such a tune, that the wrestler had to be carried off the ground. Duke Frederick was pleased with his courage, and asked his name.

"My name is Orlando, and I am the youngest son of Sir Rowland de Boys," said the young man.

Now Sir Rowland de Boys, when he was alive, had been a good friend to the banished duke, so that Frederick heard with regret whose son Orlando was, and would not befriend him. But Rosalind was delighted to hear that this handsome young stranger was the son of her father's old friend, and as they were going away, she turned back more than once to say another kind word to the brave young man.

"Gentleman," she said, giving him a chain from her neck, "wear this for me. I could give more, but that my hand lacks means."

Rosalind and Celia, when they were alone, began to talk about the handsome wrestler, and Rosalind confessed that she loved him at first sight.

"Come, come," said Celia, "wrestle with thy affections."

"Oh," answered Rosalind, "they take the part of a better wrestler than myself. Look, here comes the duke."

"With his eyes full of anger," said Celia.

"You must leave the court at once," he said to Rosalind. "Why?" she asked.

"Never mind why," answered the duke, "you are banished. If within ten days you are found within twenty miles of my court, you die."

So Rosalind set out to seek her father, the banished duke, in the Forest of Arden. Celia loved her too much to let her go alone, and as it was rather a dangerous journey, Rosalind, being the taller, dressed up as a young countryman, and her cousin as a country girl, and Rosalind said that she would be called Ganymede, and Celia, Aliena. They were very tired when at last they came to the Forest of Arden, and as they were sitting on the grass a countryman passed that way, and Ganymede asked him if he could get them food. He did so, and told them that a shepherd's flocks and house were to be sold. They bought these and settled down as shepherd and shepherdess in the forest.

In the meantime, Oliver, having sought to take his brother Orlando's life, Orlando also wandered into the forest, and there met with the rightful duke, and being kindly received, stayed with him. Now, Orlando could think of nothing but Rosalind, and he went about the forest carving her name on trees, and writing love sonnets and hanging them on the bushes, and there Rosalind and Celia found them. One day Orlando met them, but he did not know Rosalind in her boy's clothes, though he liked the pretty shepherd youth, because he fancied a likeness in him to her he loved.

"There is a foolish lover," said Rosalind, "who haunts these woods and hangs sonnets on the trees. If I could find him, I would soon cure him of his folly."

Orlando confessed that he was the foolish lover, and Rosalind said—"If you will come and see me every day, I will pretend to be Rosalind, and I will take her part, and be wayward and contrary, as is the way of women, till I make you ashamed of your folly in loving her."

And so every day he went to her house, and took a pleasure in saying to her all the pretty things he would have said to Rosalind; and she had the fine and secret joy of knowing that all his love-words came to the right ears. Thus many days passed pleasantly away.

One morning, as Orlando was going to visit Ganymede, he saw a man asleep on the ground, and that there was a lioness crouching near, waiting for the man who was asleep to wake: for they say that lions will not prey on anything that is dead or sleeping. Then Orlando looked at the man, and saw that it was his wicked brother, Oliver, who had tried to take his life. He fought with the lioness and killed her, and saved his brother's life.

While Orlando was fighting the lioness, Oliver woke to see his brother, whom he had treated so badly, saving him from a wild beast at the risk of his own life. This made him repent of his wickedness, and he begged Orlando's pardon, and from thenceforth they were dear brothers. The lioness had wounded Orlando's arm so much, that he could not go on to see the shepherd, so he sent his brother to ask Ganymede to come to him.

Oliver went and told the whole story to Ganymede and Aliena, and Aliena was so charmed with his manly ways of confessing his faults, that she fell in love with him at once.

But when Ganymede heard of the danger Orlando had been in she fainted; and when she came to herself, said truly enough, "I should have been a woman by right."

Oliver went back to his brother and told him all this, saying, "I love Aliena so well that I will give up my estates to you and marry her, and live here as a shepherd."

"Let your wedding be to-morrow," said Orlando, "and I will ask the duke and his friends."

When Orlando told Ganymede how his brother was to be married on the morrow, he added: "Oh, how bitter a thing it is to look into happiness through another man's eyes."

Then answered Rosalind, still in Ganymede's dress and speaking with his voice — "If you do love Rosalind so near the heart, then when your brother marries Aliena, shall you marry her."

Now the next day the duke and his followers, and Orlando, and Oliver, and Aliena, were all gathered together for the wedding.

Then Ganymede came in and said to the duke, "If I bring in your daughter Rosalind, will you give her to Orlando here?" "That I would," said the duke, "if I had all kingdoms to give with her."

"And you say you will have her when I bring her?" she said to Orlando. "That would I," he answered, "were I king of all kingdoms."

Then Rosalind and Celia went out, and Rosalind put on her pretty woman's clothes again, and after a while came back.

She turned to her father—"I give myself to you, for I am yours." "If there be truth in sight," he said, "you are my daughter."

Then she said to Orlando, "I give myself to you, for I am yours." "If there be truth in sight," he said, "you are my Rosalind."

"I will have no father if you be not he," she said to the duke, and to Orlando, "I will have no husband if you be not he."

So Orlando and Rosalind were married, and Oliver and Celia, and they lived happy ever after, returning with the duke to the kingdom. For Frederick had been shown by a holy hermit the wickedness of his ways, and so gave back the dukedom of his brother, and himself went into a monastery to pray for forgiveness.

The wedding was a merry one, in the mossy glades of the forest. A shepherd and shepherdess who had been friends with Rosalind, when she was herself disguised as a shepherd, were married on the same day, and all with such pretty feastings and merry-makings as could be nowhere within four walls, but only in the beautiful green wood.

THE MERCHANT OF VENICE

Retold by E. Nesbit

Antonio was a rich and prosperous merchant of Venice. His ships were on nearly every sea, and he traded with Portugal, with Mexico, with England, and with India. Although proud of his riches, he was very generous with them, and delighted to use them in relieving the wants of his friends, among whom his relation, Bassanio, held the first place.

Now Bassanio, like many another gay and gallant gentleman, was reckless and extravagant, and finding that he had not only come to the end of his fortune, but was also unable to pay his creditors, he went to Antonio for further help.

"To you, Antonio," he said, "I owe the most in money and in love: and I have thought of a plan to pay everything I owe if you will but help, me."

"Say what I can do, and it shall be done," answered his friend.

Then said Bassanio, "In Belmont is a lady richly left, and from all quarters of the globe renowned suitors come to woo her, not only because she is rich, but because she is beautiful and good as well. She looked on me with such favor when last we met, that I feel sure that I should win her away from all rivals for her love had I but the means to go to Belmont, where she lives."

"All my fortunes," said Antonio, "are at sea, and so I have no ready money; but luckily my credit is good in Venice, and I will borrow for you what you need."

There was living in Venice at this time a rich money-lender, named Shylock. Antonio despised and disliked this man very much, and treated him with the greatest harshness and scorn. He would thrust him, like a cur, over his threshold, and would even spit on him. Shylock submitted to all these indignities with a patient shrug; but deep in his heart he cherished a desire for revenge on the rich, smug merchant. For Antonio both hurt his pride and injured his business. "But for him," thought Shylock, "I should be richer by half a million ducats. On the market place, and wherever he can, he denounces the rate of interest I charge, and—worse than that—he lends out money freely."

So when Bassanio came to him to ask for a loan of three thousand ducats to Antonio for three months, Shylock hid his hatred, and turning to Antonio, said—"Harshly as you have treated me, I would be friends with you and have your love. So I will lend you the money and charge you no interest. But, just for fun, you shall sign a bond in which it shall be agreed that if you do not repay me in three months' time, then I shall have the right to a pound of your flesh, to be cut from what part of your body I choose."

"No," cried Bassanio to his friend, "you shall run no such risk for me."

"Why, fear not," said Antonio, "my ships will be home a month before the time, I will sign the bond."

Thus Bassanio was furnished with the means to go to Belmont, there to woo the lovely Portia. The very night he started, the money-lender's pretty daughter, Jessica, ran away from her father's house with her lover, and she took with her from her father's hoards some bags of ducats and precious stones. Shylock's grief and anger were terrible to see. His love for her changed to hate. "I would she were dead at my feet and the jewels in her ear," he cried. His only comfort now was in hearing of the serious losses which had befallen Antonio, some of whose ships were wrecked. "Let him look to his bond," said Shylock, "let him look to his bond."

Meanwhile Bassanio had reached Belmont, and had visited the fair Portia. He found, as he had told Antonio, that the rumor of her wealth and beauty had drawn to her suitors from far and near. But to all of them Portia had but one reply. She would only accept that suitor who would pledge himself to abide by the terms of her father's will. These were conditions that frightened away many an ardent wooer. For he who would win Portia's heart and hand, had to guess which of three caskets held her portrait. If he guessed aright, then Portia would be his bride; if wrong, then he was bound by oath never to reveal which casket he chose, never to marry, and to go away at once.

The caskets were of gold, silver, and lead. The gold one bore this inscription:—"Who chooseth me shall gain what many men desire"; the silver one had this:—"Who chooseth me shall get as much as he deserves"; while on the lead one were these words:—"Who chooseth me must give and hazard all he hath." The Prince of Morocco, as brave as he was black, was among the first to submit to this test. He chose the gold casket, for he said neither base lead nor silver could contain her picture. So he chose the gold casket, and found inside the likeness of what many men desire—death.

After him came the haughty Prince of Arragon, and saying, "Let me have what I deserve—surely I deserve the lady," he chose the silver one, and found inside a fool's head. "Did I deserve no more than a fool's head?" he cried.

Then at last came Bassanio, and Portia would have delayed him from making his choice from very fear of his choosing wrong. For she loved him dearly, even as he loved her. "But," said Bassanio, "let me choose at once, for, as I am, I live upon the rack."

Then Portia bade her servants to bring music and play while her gallant lover made his choice. And Bassanio took the oath and walked up to the caskets—the musicians playing softly the while. "Mere outward show," he said, "is to be despised. The world is still deceived with ornament, and so no gaudy gold or shining silver for me. I choose the lead casket; joy be the consequence!" And opening it, he found fair Portia's portrait inside, and he turned to her and asked if it were true that she was his.

"Yes," said Portia, "I am yours, and this house is yours, and with them I give you this ring, from which you must never part."

And Bassanio, saying that he could hardly

speak for joy, found words to swear that he would
never part with the ring while he lived.

Then suddenly all his happiness was dashed with sorrow, for messengers came from Venice to tell him that Antonio was ruined, and that Shylock demanded from the Duke of Venice the fulfilment of the bond, under which he was entitled to a pound of the merchant's flesh. Portia was as grieved as Bassanio to hear of the danger which threatened his friend.

"First," she said, "take me to church and make me your wife, and then go to Venice at once to help your friend. You shall take with you money enough to pay his debt twenty times over."

But when her newly-made husband had gone, Portia went after him, and arrived in Venice disguised as a lawyer, and with an introduction from a celebrated lawyer Bellario, whom the Duke of Venice had called in to decide the legal questions raised by Shylock's claim to a pound of Antonio's flesh. When the court met, Bassanio offered Shylock twice the money borrowed, if he would withdraw his claim. But the money-lender's only answer was—

"If every ducat in six thousand ducats Were in six parts, and every part a ducat, I would not draw them,—I would have my bond"

It was then that Portia arrived in her disguise, and not even her own husband knew her. The duke gave her welcome on account of the great Bellario's introduction, and left the settlement of the case to her. Then in noble words she bade Shylock have mercy. But he was deaf to her entreaties. "I will have the pound of flesh," was his reply.

"What have you to say?" asked Portia of the merchant.

"But little," he answered; "I am armed and well prepared."

"The court awards you a pound of Antonio's flesh," said Portia to the money-lender.

"Most righteous judge!" cried Shylock. "A sentence: come, prepare."

"Tarry a little. This bond gives you no right to Antonio's blood, only to his flesh. If, then, you spill a drop of his blood, all your property will be forfeited to the state. Such is the law."

And Shylock, in his fear, said, "Then I will take Bassanio's offer."

"No," said Portia sternly, "you shall have nothing but your bond. Take your pound of flesh, but remember, that if you take more or less, even by the weight of a hair, you will lose your property and your life."

Shylock now grew very much frightened. "Give me my three thousand ducats that I lent him, and let him go."

Bassanio would have paid it to him, but said Portia, "No! He shall have nothing but his bond."

"You, a foreigner," she added, "have sought to take the life of a Venetian citizen, and thus by the Venetian law, your life and goods are forfeited. Down, therefore, and beg mercy of the duke."

Thus were the tables turned, and no mercy would have been shown to Shylock, had it not been for Antonio. As it was, the money-lender forfeited half his fortune to the state, and he had to settle the other half on his daughter's husband, and with this he had to be content.

Bassanio, in his gratitude to the clever lawyer, was induced to part with the ring his wife had given him, and with which he had promised never to part, and when on his return to Belmont he confessed as much to Portia, she seemed very angry, and vowed she would not be friends with him until she had her ring again. But at last she told him that it was she who, in the disguise of the lawyer, had saved his friend's life, and got the ring from him. So Bassanio was forgiven, and made happier than ever, to know how rich a prize he had drawn in the lottery of the caskets.

PILGRIM'S PROGRESS _John Bunyan, the son of a man who mended broken kettles and pans, a tinker, was born in England in 1628. Though a wild lad, with little education, he married a splendid wife who changed the evil course of his life and interested him in religion.

This earnest, powerful, fighting Puritan preacher aroused his congregation so much and so often that the authorities put him in jail. Eight years before Bunyan's birth 74 Puritan men and 28 women, members of Dr. Robinson's church, escaped persecution by sailing in the Mayflower and landing at

Plymouth Rock. For twelve years Bunyan was locked up in the little jail at the end of the bridge at Bedford. He made laces to support his family, and read the Bible and Fox's Book of Martyrs. Though an ignorant man, he became deeply religious.

Except the Bible, and possibly Shakespeare, probably no other book in the English language has been read by more people.

In the version here given the story has been condensed by omitting the less dramatic passages, but the author's text remains otherwise unchanged._

CHRISTIAN STARTS ON HIS JOURNEY

By John Bunyan

As I walk'd through the wilderness of this world, I lighted on a certain place where was a Den, and I laid me down in that place to sleep; and as I slept, I dreamed a Dream. I dreamed, and behold I saw a Man cloathed with Rags, standing in a certain place, with his face from his own house, a Book in his hand, and a great Burden upon his back.

I looked, and saw him open the Book, and read therein; and as he read, he wept and trembled; and not being able longer to contain, he brake out with a lamentable cry, saying, What shall I do?

I saw also that he looked this way and that way, as if he would run; yet he stood still, because, as I perceived, he could not tell which way to go. I looked then, and saw a man named Evangelist, coming to him, and asked, Wherefore dost thou cry?

He answered, Sir, I perceive by the Book in my hand, that I am condemned to die, and after that to come to Judgment, and I find that I am not willing to do the first, nor able to do the second.

Then said Evangelist, If this be thy condition, why standest thou still? He answered, Because I know not whither to go. Then he gave him a *Parchment-roll*, and there was written within, *Fly from the wrath to come*.

The Man therefore read it, and looking upon *Evangelist* very carefully, said, Whither must I fly?

Then said *Evangelist*, pointing with his finger over a very wide field, Do you see yonder _Wicket-gate? The Man said, No. Then sad the other, Do you see yonder shining Light? He said, I think I do. then said *Evangelist*, Keep that Light in your eye, and go up directly thereto: so shalt thou see the Gate; at which, when thou knockest, it shall be told thee what thou shalt do.

So I saw in my Dream that the Man began to run.

Now he had not run far from his own door, but his Wife and Children, perceiving it, began to cry after him to return; but the

Man put his fingers in his ears, and ran on, crying, *Life!*
Life! Eternal Life! So he looked not behind him, but fled
towards the middle of the Plain.

The Neighbors also came out to see him run; and as he ran, some mocked, others threatened, and some cried after him to return; and among those that did so, there were two that resolved to fetch him back by force. The name of the one was *Obstinate*, and the name of the other was *Pliable*. Now by this time the Man was got a good distance from them; but however they were resolved to pursue him, which they did, and in a little time they overtook him. Then said the Man, Neighbors, wherefore are you come? They said, To persuade you to go back with us. But he said, That can by no means be; be content, good Neighbors, and go along with me.

OBST. What, said *Obstinate*, and leave our friends and our comforts behind us!

CHR. Yes, said *Christian*, for that was his name, because that *all* which you shall forsake is not worthy to be compared with a *little* of that that I am seeking to enjoy; and if you will go along with me and hold it, you shall fare as I myself; for there where I go, is enough and to spare: Come away, and prove my words. Read it so, if you will, in my Book.

OBST. Tush, said *Obstinate*, away with your Book; will you go back with us or no?

CHR. No, not I, said the other, because I have laid my hand to the Plow.

OBST. Come then, Neighbor *Pliable*, let us turn again, and go home without him.

PLI. Well, Neighbor *Obstinate*, said *Pliable*, I intend to go along with this good man, and to cast in my lot with him.

Now I saw in my Dream, that when *Obstinate* was gone
back, *Christian* and *Pliable* went talking over the Plain.

They drew near to a very miry *Slough*, that was in the midst of the plain; and they, being heedless, did both fall suddenly into the bog. The name of the slough was *Dispond*. Here they wallowed for a time, being grievously bedaubed with the dirt; and *Christian*, because of the Burden that was on his back, began to sink in the mire.

PLI. Then said *Pliable*, Ah Neighbor *Christian*, where are you now?

CHR. Truly, said Christian, I do not know.

PLI. At that Pliable began to be offended, and angerly said to his fellow, Is this the happiness you have told me all this while of? If we have such ill luck at our first setting out, what may we expect 'twixt this and our Journey's end? May I get out again with my life, you shall possess the Country alone.

And with that he gave a desperate struggle or two, and got out of the mire on that side of the Slough which was next to his own house: so away he went, and Christian saw him no more.

Wherefore Christian was left to tumble in the Slough of Dispond alone; he endeavoured to struggle to the side of the Slough, but could not get out, because of the Burden that was upon his back: But I beheld in my Dream, that a man came to him, whose name was Help, who said, Give me thy hand: so he gave him his hand, and he drew him out, and set him upon sound ground, and bid him go on his way.

EVAN. What doest thou here, Christian? Art not thou the man that I found crying without the walls of the City of Destruction?

CHR. Yes, dear Sir, I am the man.

EVAN. Did not I direct thee the way to the little Wicket-gate?

CHR. Yes, dear Sir, said Christian.

EVAN. How is it then that thou art so quickly turned aside? for thou art now out of the way.

CHR. I met with a Gentleman so soon as I had got over the Slough of Dispond, who persuaded me that I might, in the village before me, find a man that could take off my Burden.

EVAN. What was he?

CHR. He looked like a Gentleman, and talked much to me, and got me at last to yield; so I came hither: but when I beheld this Hill, and how it hangs over the way, I suddenly made a stand, lest it should fall on my head.

EVAN. From this little Wicket-gate, and from the way thereto, hath this wicked man turned thee, to the bringing of thee almost to destruction; hate therefore his turning thee out of the way, and abhor thyself for hearkening to him.

CHR. Sir, what think you? Is there hopes? May I now go back and go up to the Wicket-gate? Shall I not be abandoned for this, and sent back from thence ashamed? I am sorry I have hearkened to this man's counsel: But may my sin be forgiven?

EVAN. Then said *Evangelist* to him, Thy sin is very great, yet will the man at the Gate receive thee, for he has good-will for men. So *Christian* went on with haste, neither spake he to any man by the way; and in process of time he got up to the Gate. Now over the Gate there was written, *Knock and it shall be opened unto you.*

He knocked therefore more than once or twice, and at last there came a grave person to the gate named *Good-will*, who asked Who was there? and whence he came? and what he would have?

CHR. I come from the City of *Destruction*, but am going to Mount *Zion*, that I may be delivered from the wrath to come. I would therefore, Sir, since I am informed that by this Gate is the way thither, know if you are willing to let me in.

GOOD-WILL. I am willing with all my heart, said he; and with that he opened the Gate. But how is it that you came alone?

CHR. Because none of my Neighbors saw their danger, as I saw mine.

GOOD-WILL. Did any of them know of your coming?

CHR. Yes, my Wife and Children saw me at the first, and called after me to turn again; also some of my Neighbors stood crying and calling after me to return; but I put my fingers in my ears, and so came on my way.

GOOD-WILL. But did none of them follow you, to persuade you to go back?

CHR. Yes, both *Obstinate* and *Pliable*; but when they saw that they could not prevail, *Obstinate* went railing back, but *Pliable* came with me a little way.

GOOD-WILL. But why did he not come through?

CHR. We indeed came both together, until we came to the Slough of *Dispond*, into the which we also suddenly fell. And then was my Neighbor Pliable discouraged, and would not adventure further. Wherefore getting out again on that side next to his own house, he told me I should possess the brave country alone for him; so he went *his* way, and I came *mine*: he after *Obstinate*, and I to this Gate.

Christian began to gird up his loins, and to address himself to his Journey. So the other told him, that some distance from the Gate, he would come to the house of the *Interpreter*, at whose door he should knock, and he would shew him excellent things. Then *Christian* took his leave of his Friend, and he again bid him God speed.

THE INTERPRETER SHOWS CHRISTIAN MANY EXCELLENT THINGS

By John Bunyan

Christian went on till he came to the house of the *Interpreter*, where he knocked over and over; at last one came to the door, and asked Who was there?

CHR. Sir, here is a Traveller, who was bid by an acquaintance of the good man of this house to call here for my profit; I would therefore speak with the Master of the house. So he called for the Master of the house, who after a little time came to *Christian*, and asked him what he would have?

CHR. Sir, said Christian, I am a man that am come from the City of *Destruction*, and am going to the Mount *Zion*; and I was told by the Man that stands at the Gate at the head of this way, that if I called here, you would shew me excellent things, such as would be a help to me in my Journey.

INTER. Then said the Interpreter, Come in, I will shew thee that which will be profitable to thee.

I saw moreover in my Dream, that the *Interpreter* took him by the hand, and had him into a little room, where sat two little Children, each one in his chair. The name of the eldest was *Passion*, and the name of the other *Patience*. *Passion* seemed to be much discontent; but *Patience* was very quiet. Then *Christian* asked, What is the reason of the discontent of *Passion*? The *Interpreter* answered, The Governor of them would have him stay for his best things till the beginning of the next year; but he will have all now; but *Patience* is willing to wait.

Then I saw that one came to *Passion*, and brought him a bag of treasure, and poured it down at his feet, the which he took up and rejoiced therein; and withal, laughed *Patience* to scorn. But I beheld but a while, and he had lavished all away, and had nothing left but Rags.

CHR. Then said *Christian* to the *Interpreter*, Expound this matter more fully to me.

INTER. So he said, These two Lads are figures: *Passion*, of the men of *this* world; and *Patience*, of the men of *that* which is to come; for as here thou seest, *Passion* will have all now this year, that is to say, in this world; so are the men of this world: they must have all their good things now, they cannot stay till next year, that is, until the next world, for their portion of good. That proverb, *A Bird in the Hand is worth two in the Bush*, is of more authority with them than are all the Divine testimonies of the good of the world to come. But as thou sawest that he had quickly lavished all away, and had presently left him nothing but Rags; so will it be with all such men at the end of this world.

CHR. Then said *Christian*, Now I see that *Patience* has the best wisdom, and that upon many accounts. 1. Because he stays for the best things. 2. And also because he will have the Glory of his, when the other has nothing but Rags.

INTER. Nay, you may add another, to wit, the glory of the *next* world will never wear out; but *these* are suddenly gone, Therefore *Passion* had not so much reason to laugh at *Patience*, because he had his good things first, as *Patience* will have to laugh at *Passion*, because he had his best things last; for *first* must give place to *last*, because *last* must have his time to come; but last gives place to nothing; for there is not another to succeed, He therefore that hath his portion *first*, must needs have a time to spend it; but he that hath his portion *last*, must have it lastingly; therefore it is said of Dives, *In thy lifetime thou receivedst thy good things, and likewise* Lazartis *evil things; but now he is comforted, and thou art tormented.*

CHR. Then I perceive 'tis not best to covet things that are now, but to wait for things to come.

INTER. You say truth: *For the things which are seen are* Temporal; *but the things that are not seen are* Eternal. But though this be so, yet since things present and our fleshly appetite are such near neighbors one to another; and, again, because things to come and carnal sense are such strangers one to another; therefore it is that the first of these so suddenly fell into *amity*, and that *distance* is so continued between the second.

Then I saw in my Dream that the *Interpreter* took *Christian* by the hand, and led him into a place where was a Fire burning against a wall, and one standing by it, always casting much Water upon it, to quench it; yet did the Fire burn higher and hotter.

Then said *Christian*, What means this?

The *Interpreter answered*, This Fire is the work of Grace that is wrought in the heart; he that casts Water upon it, to extinguish and put it out, is the *Devil*; but in that thou seest the Fire notwithstanding burn higher and hotter, thou shalt also see the reason of that. So he had him about to the backside of the wall, where he saw a man with a Vessel of Oil in his hand, of the which he did also continually cast (but secretly) into the Fire.

Then said *Christian,* What means this?

The *Interpreter answered,* This is Christ, who continually, with the Oil of his Grace, maintains the work already begun in the heart: by the means of which notwithstanding what the Devil can do, the souls of his people prove gracious still. And in that thou sawest that the man stood behind the wall to maintain the Fire, that is to teach thee that it is hard for the tempted to see how this work of Grace is maintained in the soul.

I saw also that the *Interpreter* took him again by the hand, and led him into a pleasant place, where was builded a stately Palace, beautiful to behold; at the sight of which *Christian* was greatly delighted: He saw also upon the top thereof, certain persons walking, who were cloathed all in gold.

Then said *Christian,* May we go in thither?

Then the *Interpreter* took him, and led him up toward the door of the Palace; and behold, at the door stood a great company of men, as desirous to go in, but durst not. There also sat a man at a little distance from the door, at a table-side, with a Book and his Inkhorn before him, to take the name of him that should enter therein; He saw also, that in the door-way stood many men in armour to keep it, being resolved to do the men that would enter what hurt and mischief they could. Now was *Christian* somewhat in a maze. At last, when every man started back for fear of the armed men, *Christian* saw a man of a very stout countenance come up to the man that sat there to write, saying, *Set down my name, Sir:* the which when he had done, he saw the man draw his Sword, and put an Helmet upon his head, and rush toward the door upon the armed men, who laid upon him with deadly force; but the man, not at all discouraged, fell to cutting and hacking most fiercely. So after, he had received and given many wounds to those that attempted to keep him out, he cut his way through them all, and pressed forward into the Palace, at which there was a pleasant voice heard from those that were within, even of those that walked upon the top of the Palace, saying,

Come in, Come in; Eternal Glory thou shalt win.

So he went in, and was cloathed with such garments as they. Then *Christian* smiled, and said, I think verily I know the meaning of this.

Now, said *Christian,* let me go hence. Nay, stay, said the *Interpreter,* till I have shewed thee a little more, and after that thou shalt go on thy way. So he took him by the hand again, and led him into a very dark room, where there sat a man in an Iron Cage.

Now the Man, to look on, seemed very sad; he sat with his eyes looking down to the ground, his hands folded together; and he sighed as if he would break his heart. Then said *Christian, What means this?* At which the *Interpreter* bid him talk with the Man.

Then said *Christian* to the Man, *What art thou?* The Man answered, *I am what I was not once.*

CHR. What wast thou once?

MAN. The Man said, I was once a fair and flourishing Professor, both in mine own eyes, and also in the eyes of others; I once was, as I thought, fair for the Coelestial City, and had then even joy at the thoughts that I should get thither.

CHR. Well, but what art thou now?

MAN. I am now a man of *Despair*, and am shut up in it, as in this Iron Cage. I cannot get out; O *now* I cannot.

CHR. But how camest thou in this condition?

MAN. I left off to watch and be sober; I laid the reins upon the neck of my lusts; I sinned against the light of the Word and the goodness of God; I have grieved the Spirit, and he is gone; I tempted the Devil, and he is come to me; I have provoked God to anger, and he has left me; I have so hardened my heart, that I *cannot* repent.

Then said *Christian* to the *Interpreter*, But are there no hopes for such a man as this? Ask him, said the *Interpreter*.

CHR. Then said *Christian*, Is there no hope, but you must be kept in the Iron Cage of Despair?

MAN. No, none at all.

CHR. Why? The Son of the Blessed is very pitiful.

MAN. I have crucified him to myself afresh, I have despised his Person, I have despised his Righteousness, I have counted his Blood an unholy thing; I have done despite to the Spirit of Grace: Therefore I have shut myself out of all the Promises, and there now remains to me nothing but threatnings, dreadful threatnings, fearful threatnings of certain Judgment and fiery Indignation, which shall devour me as an Adversary.

CHR. For what did you bring yourself into this condition?

MAN. For the Lusts, Pleasures, and Profits of this World; in the enjoyment of which I did then promise myself much delight; but now every one of those things also bite me, and gnaw me like a burning worm.

CHR. But canst thou not now repent and turn?

MAN. God hath denied me repentance: his Word gives me no encouragement to believe; yea, himself hath shut me up in this Iron Cage; nor can all the men in the world let me out. O Eternity! Eternity! how shall I grapple with the misery that I must meet with in Eternity!

INTER. Then said the *Interpreter* to *Christian*, Let this man's misery be remembered by thee, and be an everlasting caution to thee.

CHR. Well, said *Christian*, this is fearful; God help me to watch and be sober, and to pray that I may shun the cause of this man's misery. Sir, is it not time for me to go on my way now?

INTER. Tarry till I shall shew thee one thing more, and then thou shalt go thy way.

So he took *Christian* by the hand again, and led him into a Chamber, where there was one rising out of bed; and as he put on his raiment, he shook and trembled. Then said *Christian*, Why doth this man thus tremble? The *Interpreter* then bid him tell to *Christian* the reason of his so doing. So he began and said, This night, as I was in my sleep, I dreamed, and behold the Heavens grew exceeding black; also it thundred and lightned in most fearful wise, that it put me into an agony; so I looked up in my Dream, and saw the Clouds rack at an unusual rate, upon which I heard a great sound of a Trumpet, and saw also a Man sit upon a Cloud, attended with the thousands of Heaven; they were all in flaming fire, also the Heavens were in a burning flame. I heard then a Voice saying, *Arise ye dead, and come to Judgment*; and with that the Rocks rent, the Graves opened, and the Dead that were therein came forth. Some of them were exceeding glad, and looked upward; and some sought to hide themselves under the Mountains. Then I saw the Man that sat upon the Cloud open the Book, and bid the World draw near. Yet there was, by reason of a fierce flame which issued out and came from before him, a convenient distance betwixt him and them, as betwixt the Judge and the Prisoners at the bar. I heard it also proclaimed to them that attended on the Man that sat on the Cloud, *Gather together the Tares, the Chaff, and Stubble, and cast them into the burning Lake*. And with that, the bottomless pit opened, just whereabout I stood; out of the mouth of which there came in an abundant manner, smoke and coals of fire, with hideous noises. It was also said to the same persons, *Gather my Wheat into the Garner*. And with that I saw many catch'd up and carried away into the Clouds, but I was left behind. I also sought to hide myselfs but I could not, for the Man that sat upon the Cloud still kept his eye upon me: my sins also came into my mind; and my Conscience did accuse me on every side. Upon this I awaked from my sleep.

CHR. But what was it that made you so afraid of this sight?

MAN. Why, I thought that the day of Judgment was come, and that I was not ready for it: but this frighted me most, that the Angels gathered up several, and left me behind; also the pit of Hell opened her mouth just where I stood: my Conscience too afflicted me; and as I thought, the Judge had always his eye upon me, shewing indignation in his countenance.

Then said the *Interpreter* to *Christian, Hast thou considered all these things?*

CHR. Yes, and they put me in *hope* and *fear*.

INTER. Well, keep all things so in thy mind that they may be as a Goad in thy sides, to prick thee forward in the way thou must go. Then *Christian* began to gird up his loins, and address himself to his Journey. Then said the *Interpreter*, The Comforter be always with thee, good *Christian*, to guide thee in the way that leads to the City. So *Christian* went on his way.

CHRISTIAN'S FIGHT WITH THE MONSTER APOLLYON

By John Bunyan

In the Valley of *Humiliation*, poor *Christian* was hard put to it; for he had gone but a little way, before he espied a foul *Fiend* coming over the field to meet him; his name is *Apollyon*. Then did *Christian* begin to be afraid, and to cast in his mind whether to go back or to stand his ground: But he considered again that he had no Armour for his back, and therefore thought that to turn the back to him might give him the greater advantage with ease to pierce him with his Darts. Therefore he resolved to venture and stand his ground; For, thought he, had I no more in mine eye than the saving of my life, 'twould be the best way to stand.

So he went on, and *Apollyon* met him. Now the Monster was hideous to behold; he was cloathed with scales like a Fish (and they are his pride); he had wings like a Dragon, feet like a Bear, and out of his belly came Fire and Smoke; and his mouth was as the mouth of a Lion. When he was come up to *Christian*, he beheld him with a disdainful countenance, and thus began to question with him.

APOL. Whence come you? and whither are you bound?

CHR. I am come from the City of *Destruction*, which is the place of all evil, and am going to the City of *Zion*.

APOL. By this I perceive thou art one of my Subjects, for all that country is mine, and I am the Prince and God of it. How is it then that thou hast run away from the King? Were it not that I hope thou mayest do me more service, I would strike thee now at one blow to the ground.

CHR. I was born indeed in your dominions, but your service was hard, and your wages such as a man could not live on, *for the wages of sin is death*; therefore when I was come to years, I did as other considerate persons do, look out, if perhaps I might find something better.

APOL. There is no Prince that will thus lightly lose his Subjects, neither will I as yet lose thee: but since thou complainest of thy service and wages, be content to go back; what our country will afford, I do here promise to give thee.

CHR. But I have let myself to another, even to the King of Princes, and how can I with fairness go back with thee?

APOL. Thou hast done in this, according to the Proverb, changed a bad for a worse; but it is ordinary for those that have professed themselves his Servants, after a while to give him the slip, and return again to me: Do thou so too, and all shall be well.

CHR. I have given him my faith, and sworn my allegiance to him; how then can I go back from this, and not be hanged as a Traitor?

APOL. Thou didst the same to me, and yet I am willing to pass by all, if now thou wilt yet turn again and go back.

CHR. What I promised thee was in my non-age; and besides, I count that the Prince under whose Banner now I stand is able to absolve me; yea, and to pardon also what I did as to my compliance with thee; and besides, O thou destroying *Apollyon*, to speak truth, I like his Service, his Wages, his Servants, his Government, his Company and Country, better than thine; and therefore leave off to persuade me further; I am his Servant, and I will follow him.

APOL. Consider again when thou art in cool blood, what thou art like to meet with in the way that thou goest. Thou knowest that for the most part, his Servants come to an ill end, because they are transgressors against me and my ways: How many of them have been put to shameful deaths; and besides, thou countest his service better than mine, whereas he never came yet from the place where he is to deliver any that served him out of our hands; but as for me, how many times, as all the World very well knows, have I delivered, either by power or fraud, those that have faithfully served me, from him and his, though taken by them; and so I will deliver thee.

CHR. His forbearing at present to deliver them is on purpose to try their love, whether they will cleave to him to the end; and as for the ill end thou sayest they come to, that is most glorious in their account; for present deliverance, they do not much expect it, for they stay for their Glory, and then they shall have it, when their Prince comes in his and the Glory of the Angels.

APOL. Thou hast already been unfaithful in thy service to him, and how dost thou think to receive wages of him?

CHR. Wherein, O *Apollyon*, have I been unfaithful to him?

APOL. Thou didst faint at first setting out, when thou wast almost choked in the Gulf of *Dispond*; thou didst attempt wrong ways to be rid of thy Burden, whereas thou shouldest have stayed till thy Prince had taken it off; thou didst sinfully sleep and lose thy choice thing; thou wast also almost persuaded to go back, at the sight of the Lions; and when thou talkest of thy Journey, and of what thou hast heard and seen, thou art inwardly desirous of vain-glory in all that thou sayest or doest.

CHR. All this is true, and much more which thou hast left out; but the Prince whom I serve and honor is merciful, and ready to forgive; but besides, these infirmities possessed me in thy Country, for there I sucked them in, and I have groaned under them, been sorry for them, and have obtained Pardon of my Prince.

APOL. Then *Apollyon* broke out into a grievous rage, saying, I am an enemy to this Prince; I hate his Person, his Laws, and People; I am come out on purpose to withstand thee.

CHR. *Apollyon*, beware what you do, for I am in the King's High-way, the way of Holiness, therefore take heed to yourself.

APOL. Then *Apollyon* straddled quite over the whole breadth of the way, and said, I am void of fear in this matter; prepare thyself to die; for I swear by my infernal Den, that thou shalt go no further; here will I spill thy soul.

And with that he threw a flaming Dart at his breast, but *Christian* had a Shield in his hand, with which he caught it, and so prevented the danger of that.

Then did *Christian* draw, for he saw 'twas time to bestir him: and *Apollyon* as fast made at him, throwing Darts as thick as Hail; by the which, notwithstanding all that *Christian* could do to avoid it, *Apollyon* wounded him in his *head,* his *hand,* and *foot*: This made *Christian* give a little back; *Apollyon* therefore followed his work amain, and *Christian* again took courage, and resisted as manfully as he could. This sore Combat lasted for above half a day, even till *Christian* was almost quite spent; for you must know that *Christian,* by reason of his wounds, must needs grow weaker and weaker.

Then *Apollyon* espying his opportunity, began to gather up close to *Christian,* and wrestling with him, gave him a dreadful fall; and with that *Christian's* Sword flew out of his hand. Then said *Apollyon, I am sure of thee now:* and with that he had almost pressed him to death, so that *Christian* began to despair of life: but as God would have it, while *Apollyon* was fetching of his last blow, thereby to make a full end of this good man, *Christian* nimbly stretched out his hand for his Sword, and caught it, saying, *Rejoice not against me, O mine Enemy! when I fall I shall arise;* and with that gave him a deadly thrust, which made him give back, as one that had received his mortal wound: *Christian,* perceiving that, made at him again, saying, *Nay, in all these things we are more than Conquerors through him that loved us*. And with that *Apollyon* spread forth his Dragon's wings, and sped him away, that *Christian* for a season saw him no more.

In this Combat no man can imagine, unless he had seen and heard as I did, what yelling and hideous roaring *Apollyon* made all the time of the fight, he spake like a Dragon; and on the other side, what sighs and groans burst from *Christian's* heart. I never saw him all the while give so much as one pleasant look, till he perceived he had wounded *Apollyon* with his two- edged Sword; then indeed he did smile, and look upward; but 'twas the dreadfullest sight that ever I saw.

So when the Battle was over, *Christian* said, I will here give thanks to him that hath delivered me out of the mouth of the Lion, to him that did help me against *Apollyon*. And so he did, saying, Great *Beelzebub*, the Captain of this Fiend, Design'd my ruin; therefore to this end He sent him harness'd out: and he with rage That hellish was, did fiercely me engage: But blessed *Michael* helped me, and I By dint of Sword did quickly make him fly. Therefore to him let me give lasting praise, And thank and bless his holy name always. Then there came to him a hand, with some of the leaves of the Tree of Life, the which *Christian* took, and applied to the wounds that he had received in the Battle, and was healed immediately. He also sat down in that place to eat Bread, and to drink of the Bottle that was given him a little before; so being refreshed, he addressed himself to his Journey, with his Sword drawn in his hand; for he said, I know not but some other Enemy may be at hand. But he met with no other affront from *Apollyon* quite through this Valley.

CHRISTIAN AND HOPEFUL ARE CAPTIVES IN DOUBTING CASTLE

By John Bunyan

I saw then that they went on their way to a pleasant River, which *David* the King called the *River of God*, but *John, the River of the Water of Life*. Now their way lay just upon the bank of the River; here therefore *Christian* and his Companion walked with great delight; they drank also of the water of the River, which was pleasant and enlivening to their weary spirits; besides, on the banks of this River on either side were *green Trees*, that bore all manner of Fruit; and the Leaves of the Trees were good for Medicine; with the Fruit of these Trees they were also much delighted; and the Leaves they ate to prevent Surfeits, and other Diseases that are incident to those that heat their blood by Travels. On either side of the River was also a Meadow, curiously beautified with Lilies; and it was green all the year long. In this Meadow they lay down and slept, for here they might *lie down safely*. When they awoke, they gathered again of the Fruit of the Trees, and drank again of the water of the River, and then lay down again to sleep. Thus they did several days and nights, and when they were disposed to go on they eat and drank, and departed.

Now I beheld in my Dream, that they had not journeyed far, but the River and the way for a time parted; at which they were not a little sorry, yet they durst not go out of the way. Now the way from the River was rough, and their feet tender by reason of their Travels; *so the soul of the Pilgrims was much discouraged because of the way*. Now a little before them, there was on the left hand of the road a *Meadow*, and a Stile to go over into it, and that Meadow is called *By-path-Meadow*. Then said *Christian* to his fellow, If this Meadow lieth along by our way-side, let's go over into it. Then he went to the Stile to see, and behold a Path lay along by the way on the other side of the fence. 'Tis according to my wish, said *Christian*, here is the easiest going; come good Hopeful, and let us go over.

HOPE. But how if this Path should lead us out of the way?

CHR. That's not like, said the other; look, doth it not go along by the way-side? So *Hopeful*, being persuaded by his fellow, went after him over the Stile. When they were gone over, and were got into the Path, they found it very easy for their feet: and withal, they looking before them, espied a man walking as they did, (and his name was *Vain-confidence*) so they called after him, and asked him whither that way led? He said, To the Coelestial Gate. Look, said *Christian*, did I not tell you so? by this you may see we are right. So they followed, and he went before them. But behold the night came on, and it grew very dark, so that they that were behind lost the sight of him that went before.

He therefore that went before (*Vain-confidence* by name) not seeing the way before him, fell into a deep Pit, which was on purpose there made by the Prince of those grounds, to catch *vain-glorious* fools withal, and was dashed in pieces with his fall.

Now *Christian* and his fellow heard him fall. So they called to know the matter, but there was none to answer, only they heard a groaning. Then said *Hopeful*, Where are we now? Then was his fellow silent, as mistrusting that he had led him out of the way; and now it began to rain, and thunder, and lighten in a very dreadful manner, and the water rose amain.

Then *Hopeful* groaned in himself, saying, *Oh that I had kept on my way!*

CHR. Who could have thought that this Path should have led us out of the way?

HOPE. I was afraid on't at the very first, and therefore gave you that gentle caution. I would have spoken plainer, but that you are older than I.

CHR. Good Brother be not offended; I am sorry I have brought thee out of the way, and that I have put thee into such imminent danger; pray my Brother forgive me, I did not do it of an evil intent.

HOPE. Be comforted my brother, for I forgive thee; and believe too that this shall be for our good,

CHR. I am glad I have with me a merciful Brother; but we must not stand thus, let's try to go back again.

HOPE. But good Brother let me go before.

CHE. No, if you please, let me go first, that if there be any danger, I may be first therein, because by my means we are both gone out of the way.

HOPE. No, said Hopeful, you shall not go first; for your mind being troubled may lead you out of the way again. Then for their encouragement, they heard the voice of one saying, *Let thine heart be towards the High-way, even the way that thou wentest, turn again.* But by this time the waters were greatly risen; by reason of which the way of going back was very dangerous. (Then

I thought that it is easier going out of the way when we are in, than going in when we are out.) Yet they adventured to go back; but it was so dark, and the flood was so high, that in their going back they had like to have been drowned nine or ten times.

Neither could they, with all the skill they had, get again to the Stile that night. Wherefore at last, lighting under a little shelter, they sat down there till the day brake; but being weary, they fell asleep. Now there was not far from the place where they lay, a Castle called *Doubting Castle*, the owner whereof was Giant *Despair*, and it was in his grounds they were now sleeping: wherefore he, getting up in the morning early, and walking up and down in his fields, caught *Christian* and *Hopeful* asleep in his grounds. Then with a *grim* and *surly* voice he bid them awake, and asked them whence they were? and what they did in his grounds? They told him they were Pilgrims, and that they had lost their way. Then said the Giant, You have this night trespassed on me, by trampling in and lying on my grounds, and therefore you must go along with me. So they were forced to go, because he was stronger than they. They also had but little to say, for they knew themselves in a fault. The Giant therefore drove them before him, and put them into his Castle, into a very dark Dungeon, nasty and stinking to the spirits of these two men. Here then they lay from *Wednesday* morning till *Saturday* night, without one bit of bread, or drop of drink, or light, or any to ask how they did; they were therefore here in evil case, and were far from friends and acquaintance. Now in this place *Christian* had double sorrow, because 'twas through his unadvised haste that they were brought into this distress.

Now Giant *Despair* had a Wife, and her name was *Diffidence*. So when he was gone to bed, he told his Wife what he had done, to wit, that he had taken a couple of Prisoners and cast them into his Dungeon, for trespassing on his grounds. Then he asked her also what he had best do further to them. So she asked him what they were, whence they came, and whither they were bound; and he told her. Then she counselled him that when he arose in the morning he should beat them without any mercy. So when he arose, he getteth him a grievous Crab-tree Cudgel, and goes down into the Dungeon to them, and there first falls to rating of them, as if they were dogs, although they gave him never a word of distaste. Then he falls upon them, and beats them fearfully, in such sort, that they were not able to help themselves, or to turn them upon the floor. This done, he withdraws and leaves them, there to condole their misery, and to mourn under their distress: so all that day they spent the time in nothing but sighs and bitter lamentations. The next night she talking with her Husband about them further, and understanding that they were yet alive, did advise him to counsel them to make away themselves. So when morning was come, he goes to them in a surly manner as before, and perceiving them to be very sore with the stripes that he had given them the day before, he told them, that since they were never like to come out of that place, their only way would be forthwith to make an end of themselves, either with Knife, Halter, or Poison; For why, said he, should you chuse life, seeing it is attended with so much bitterness? But they desired him to let them go. With that he looked ugly upon them, and rushing to them had doubtless made an end of them himself, but that he fell into one of his Fits, (for he sometimes in Sun-shine weather fell into Fits) and lost for a time the use of his hand; wherefore he withdrew, and left them as before, to consider what to do. Then did the Prisoners consult between themselves, whether 'twas best to take his counsel or no; and thus they began to discourse:

CHR. Brother, said *Christian*, what shall we do? The life that we now live is miserable: for my part I know not whether is best, to live thus, or to die out of hand. *My soul chuseth strangling rather than life,* and the Grave is more easy for me than this Dungeon. Shall we be ruled by the Giant?

HOPE. Indeed our present condition is dreadful, and death would be far more welcome to me than *thus* for ever to abide; but yet let us consider, the Lord of the Country to which we are going hath said, Thou shalt do no murder, no not to another man's person; much more then are we forbidden to take his counsel to kill ourselves. And let us consider again, that all the Law is not in the hand of Giant *Despair*. Others, so far as I can understand, have been taken by him as well as we, and yet have escaped out of his hand. Who knows but that God that made the world may cause that Giant *Despair* may die? or that at some time or other he may forget to lock us in? or but he may in short time have another of his Fits before us, and may lose the use of his limbs? and if ever that should come to pass again, for my part I am resolved to pluck up the heart of a man, and to try my utmost to get from under his hand. I was a fool that I did not try to do it before; but however, my Brother, let's be patient, and endure a while; the time may come that may give us a happy release; but let us not be our own murderers. With these words *Hopeful* at present did moderate the mind of his Brother; so they continued together (in the dark) that day, in their sad and doleful condition.

Well, towards evening the Giant goes down into the Dungeon again, to see if his prisoners had taken his counsel; but when he came there he found them alive, and truly, alive was all; for now, what for want of Bread and Water, and by reason of the Wounds they received when he beat them, they could do little but breathe: But, I say, he found them alive; at which he fell into a grievous rage, and told them that seeing they disobeyed his counsel, it should be worse with them than if they had never been born.

At this they trembled greatly, and I think that *Christian* fell into a Swoon; but coming a little to himself again, they renewed their discourse about the Giant's counsel, and whether yet they had best to take it or no. Now *Christian* again seemed to be for doing it, but *Hopeful* made his second reply as followeth:

HOPE. My Brother, said he, rememberest thou not how valiant thou hast been heretofore? *Apollyon* could not crush thee, nor could all that thou didst hear, or see, or feel in the Valley of the *Shadow of Death*. What hardship, terror, and amazement hast thou already gone through, and art thou now nothing but fear? Thou seest that I am in the Dungeon with thee, a far weaker man by nature than thou art; also this Giant has wounded me as well as thee, and hath also cut off the Bread and Water from my mouth; and with thee I mourn without the light. But let's exercise a little more patience, remember how thou playedst the man at Vanity Fair, and wast neither afraid of the Chain, nor Cage, nor yet of bloody Death: wherefore let us (at least to avoid the shame that becomes not a Christian to be found in) bear up with patience as well as we can.

Now night being come again, and the Giant and his Wife being in bed, she asked him concerning the Prisoners, and if they had taken his counsel: To which he replied, They are sturdy Rogues, they chuse rather to bear all hardship, than to make away themselves. Then said she, Take them into the Castle-yard to-morrow, and shew them the Bones and Skulls of those that thou hast already dispatch'd, and make them believe, e'er a week comes to an end, thou also wilt tear them in pieces, as thou hast done their fellows before them.

So when the morning was come, the Giant goes to them again, and takes them into the Castle-yard and shews them as his Wife had bidden him. These, said he, were Pilgrims as you are, once, and they trespassed in my grounds, as you have done; and when I thought fit, I tore them in pieces, and so within ten days I will do you. Go get you down to your Den again; and with that he beat them all the way thither. They lay therefore all day on *Saturday* in a lamentable case, as before. Now when night was come, and when Mrs. Diffidence and her Husband the Giant were got to bed, they began to renew their discourse of their Prisoners; and withal the old Giant wondered, that he could neither by his blows nor counsel bring them to an end. And with that his Wife replied, I fear, said she, that they live in hope that some will come to relieve them, or that they have pick-locks about them, by the means of which they hope to escape. And sayest thou so, my dear? said the Giant, I will therefore search them in the morning.

Well on *Saturday* about midnight they began to *pray*, and continued in Prayer till almost break of day.

Now a little before it was day, good *Christian*, as one half amazed, brake out in passionate speech: *What a fool*, quoth he, *am I, thus to lie in a stinking*

Dungeon, when I may as well walk at liberty. I have a Key in my bosom called Promise, that will, I am persuaded, open any Lock in *Doubting* Castle. Then said *Hopeful*, That's good news; good Brother, pluck it out of thy bosom and try.

Then *Christian* pulled it out of his bosom, and began to try at the Dungeon door, whose bolt (as he turned the Key) gave back, and the door flew open with ease, and *Christian* and *Hopeful* both came out. Then he went to the outward door that leads into the Castle-yard, and with his Key opened that door also. After he went to the iron Gate, for that must be opened too, but that Lock went damnable hard, yet the Key did open it. Then they thrust open the Gate to make their escape with speed; but that Gate as it opened made such a creaking, that it waked Giant *Despair*, who hastily rising to pursue his Prisoners, felt his limbs to fail, for his Fits took him again, so that he could by no means go after them. Then they went on, and came to the King's High-way again, and so were safe, because they were out of his jurisdiction.

Now when they were gone over the Stile, they began to contrive with themselves what they should do at that Stile, to prevent those that should come after from falling into the hands of Giant *Despair*. So they consented to erect there a Pillar, and to engrave upon the side thereof this sentence, *Over this Stile is the way to* Doubting *Castle, which is kept by Giant* Despair, *who despiseth the King of the Coelestial Country, and seeks to destroy his holy Pilgrims.* Many therefore that followed after read what was written, and escaped the danger. This done, they sang as follows:

Out of the way we went, and then we found
What 'twas to tread upon forbidden ground;
And let them that come after have a care,
Lest heedlessness makes them, as we, to fare.
Lest they for trespassing his prisoners are,
Whose Castle's *Doubting, and whose name's Despair.*

CHRISTIAN AND HOPEFUL ARRIVE AT THE CAELESTIAL CITY

By John Bunyan

I saw that as they went on, there met them two men, in Raiment that shone like Gold, also their faces shone as the light.

These men asked the Pilgrims whence they came? and they told them. They also asked them where they had lodged, what difficulties and dangers, what comforts and pleasures they had met in the way? and they told them. Then said the men that met them, You have but two difficulties more to meet with, and then you are in the City.

And I slept, and Dreamed again, and saw the same two Pilgrims going down the Mountains along the High-way towards the City.

Now you must note that the City stood upon a mighty Hill, but the Pilgrims went up that Hill with ease because they had these two men to lead them up by the arms; also they had left their *mortal Garments* behind them in the River. They therefore went up here with much agility and speed, though the foundation upon which the City was framed was higher than the Clouds. They therefore went up through the Regions of the Air, sweetly talking as they went, being comforted, because they safely got over the River, and had such glorious Companions to attend them.

The talk that they had with the Shining Ones was about the glory of the place, who told them that the beauty and glory of it was inexpressible. There, said they, is the Mount *Sion*, the heavenly *Jerusalem*, the innumerable company of Angels, and the Spirits of just men made perfect. You are going now, said they, to the Paradise of God, wherein you shall see the Tree of Life, and eat of the never-fading fruits thereof; and when you come there, you shall have white Robes given you, and your walk and talk shall be every day with the King, even all the days of Eternity. There you shall not see again such things as you saw when you were in the lower Region upon the earth, to wit, sorrow, sickness, affliction, and health, *for the former things are passed away.* You are now going to *Abraham,* to *Isaac,* and *Jacob,* and to the Prophets, men that God hath taken away from the evil to come, and that are now resting upon their beds, each one walking in his righteousness. The men then asked, What must we do in the holy place? To whom it was answered, You must there receive the comfort of all your toil, and have joy for all your sorrow; you must reap what you have sown, even the fruit of all your Prayers and Tears, and sufferings for the King by the way. In that place you must wear Crowns of Gold, and enjoy the perpetual sight and vision of the Holy One, *for there you shall see him as he is.* There also you shall serve him continually with praise, with shouting, and thanksgiving, whom you desired to serve in the World, though with much difficulty, because of the infirmity of your flesh. There your eyes shall be delighted with seeing, and your ears with hearing the pleasant voice of the Mighty One. There you shall enjoy your friends again, that are gone thither before you; and there you shall with joy receive even every one that follows into the holy place after you. There also shall you be cloathed with Glory and Majesty, and put into an equipage fit to ride out with the King of Glory. When he shall come with sound of Trumpet in the Clouds, as upon the wings of the Wind, you shall come with him; and when he shall sit upon the Throne of Judgment, you shall sit by him; yea, and when he shall pass sentence upon all the workers of iniquity, let them be Angels or Men, you also shall have a voice in that Judgment, because they were his and your Enemies. Also when he shall again return to the City, you shall go too, with sound of Trumpet, and be ever with him.

Now while they were thus drawing towards the Gate, behold a company of the Heavenly Host came out to meet them; to whom it was said by the other two Shining Ones, These are the men that have loved our Lord when they were in the World, and that have left all for his Holy Name, and he hath sent us to fetch them, and we have brought them thus far on their desired Journey, that they may go in and look their Redeemer in the face with joy. Then the Heavenly Host gave a great shout, saying, *Blessed are they that are called to the Marriage Supper of the Lamb.* There came out also at this time to meet them, several of the King's Trumpeters, cloathed in white and shining Raiment, who with melodious noises and loud, made even the Heavens to echo with their sound. These Trumpeters saluted *Christian* and his fellow with ten thousand welcomes from the World, and this they did with shouting and sound of Trumpet.

This done, they compassed them round on every side; some went before, some behind, and some on the right hand, some on the left, (as 'twere to guard them through the upper Regions) continually sounding as they went with melodious noise, in notes on high: so that the very sight was to them that could behold it, as if Heaven itself was come down to meet them. Thus therefore they walked on together; and as they walked, ever and anon these

Trumpeters, even with joyful sound, would, by mixing their musick with looks and gestures, still signify to *Christian* and his Brother, how welcome they were into their company, and with what gladness they came to meet them; and now were these two men as 'twere in Heaven before they came at it, being swallowed up with the sight of Angels, and with hearing of their melodious notes. Here also they had the City itself in view, and they thought they heard all the Bells therein ring to welcome them thereto. But above all, the warm and joyful thoughts that they had about their own dwelling there, with such company, and that for ever and ever. Oh, by what tongue or pen can their glorious joy be expressed! And thus they came up to the Gate.

Now when they were come up to the Gate, there was written over it in Letters of Gold, *Blessed are they that do his Commandments, that they may have right to the Tree of Life, and may enter in through the Gates into the City.*

Then I saw in my Dream, that the Shining Men bid them call at the Gate; the which when they did, some from above looked over the Gate, to wit, *Enoch, Moses,* and *Elijah, &c.*, to whom it was said, These Pilgrims are come from the City of *Destruction* for the love that they bear to the King of this place; and then the Pilgrims gave in unto them each man his Certificate, which they had received in the beginning; those therefore were carried in to the King, who when he had read them, said, Where are the men? To whom it was answered, They are standing without the Gate. The King then commanded to open the Gate, *That the righteous nation,* saith he, *that keepeth Truth may enter in.*

Now I saw in my Dream that these two men went in at the Gate: and lo, as they entered, they were transfigured, and they had Raiment put on that shone like Gold. There was also that met them with Harps and Crowns, and gave them to them, the Harps to praise withal, and the Crowns in token of honour. Then I heard in my Dream that all the Bells in the City rang again for joy, and that it was said unto them, *Enter ye into the joy of your Lord.* I also heard the men themselves, that they sang with a loud voice, saying, *Blessing, Honour, Glory, and Power, be to him that sitteth upon the Throne, and to the Lamb for ever and ever.*

Now just as the Gates were opened to let in the men, I looked in after them, and behold, the City shone like the Sun; the Streets also were paved with Gold, and in them walked many men, with Crowns on their heads, Palms in their hands, and golden Harps to sing praises withal.

There were also of them that had wings, and they answered one another without intermission, saying, *Holy, Holy, Holy, is the Lord.* And after that they shut up the Gates. Which when I had seen, I wished myself among them.

Now while I was gazing upon all these things, I turned my head to look back, and saw Ignorance come up to the River-side; but he soon got over, and that without half that difficulty which the other two men met with. For it happened that there was then in that place one Vain-hope a Ferry-man, that with his Boat helped him over; so he, as the other I saw, did ascend the Hill to come up to the Gate, only he came alone; neither did any man meet him with the least encouragement. When he was come up to the Gate, he looked up to the writing that was above, and then began to knock, supposing that entrance should have been quickly administered to him; but he was asked by the men that looked over the top of the Gate, Whence came you? and what would you have? He answered, I have eat and drank in the presence of the King, and he has taught in our Streets. Then they asked him for his Certificate, that they might go in and shew it to the King. So he fumbled in his bosom for one, and found none. Then said they, Have you none? But the man answered never a word. So they told the King, but he would not come down to see him, but commanded the two Shining Ones that conducted *Christian* and *Hopeful* to the City, to go out and take *Ignorance*, and bind him hand and foot, and have him away. Then they took him up, and carried him through the air to the door that I saw in the side of the Hill, and put him in there. Then I saw that there was a way to Hell even from the Gates of Heaven, as well as from the City of *Destruction*. So I awoke, and behold it was a Dream.

IVANHOE AND GUY MANNERING

_Before we have reached the second page of what Anthony Trollope called "the most favorite novel in the English language," the Commander of the Knights Templars and his followers have reined up their horses outside the old hall of Rotherwood, and a loud blast from the horn convinces us that they won't wait very long for an invitation to enter. And there is Rowena, for whom the Disinherited Knight shall fight against all comers. We hold our breaths as he rides full-tilt at the Norman Knight and strikes him full on the visor of his helmet, throwing horse and rider to the ground. Here are Isaac the Jew and Rebecca his beautiful daughter; and Wamba the jester, disguised as a monk, is rescuing Cedric—

Does any boy or girl need to know more of what Ivanhoe is about?

No one who begins to read Guy Mannering will wish to put it down until he has finished it._

IVANHOE

Retold by Sir Edward Sullivan

At the time when King Richard, of the Lion Heart, was absent from his country, and a prisoner in the power of the perfidious and cruel Duke of Austria, there lived in England a highborn Saxon, named Cedric. He was one of the few native princes who still continued to occupy the home of his fathers; but, like many more of the conquered English people, he had felt the tyranny and oppressive insolence of the haughty Norman barons. He was a man of great personal strength, possessed of a hasty and choleric temper, but he had shrewdly refrained from showing any open hostility to the successors of the Conqueror; and so contrived to maintain his ancient state in his mansion at Rotherwood, while many others in a similar situation had been compelled to give up their homes and properties to the supporters of the Norman invader.

He had an only son, Wilfred by name, with whom he had quarrelled; and the young man, finding himself disinherited, had adopted the profession of a champion of the Cross, and sailed away to Palestine with the army of the Crusaders.

One evening, in the autumn of the year, Cedric was about to sit down to supper in the old hall at Rotherwood, when the blast of a horn was heard at his gate. In a few minutes after, a warder announced that the Prior Aymer, of Jorvaulx, and the good knight Brian de Bois-Guilbert, commander of the valiant order of Knights Templars, with a small retinue, requested hospitality and lodging for the night, being on their way to a tournament which was to be held not far from Ashby-de-la-Zouche.

"Normans both," muttered Cedric; "but they are welcome to the hospitality of Rotherwood. Admit them."

The noble guests were ushered in shortly after, accompanied by their attendants, and Cedric bade them welcome to his hall.

When the repast was about to begin, the steward, suddenly raising his wand, said aloud: "Forbear! Place for the Lady Rowena." As he spoke a side-door at the upper end of the hall opened, and Rowena, the fair and stately ward of Cedric, followed by four female attendants, entered the apartment. All stood up to receive her, and replying to their courtesy by a mute gesture of salutation, she moved gracefully forward to assume her place at the board, while the eyes of Brian de Bois-Guilbert seemed to be riveted by the striking beauty of her face.

As the banquet went on, conversation was interrupted by the entrance of a page, who announced that there was a stranger at the gate imploring admittance and hospitality.

"Admit him," said Cedric, "be he who or what he may."

The page retired; and returning shortly after, whispered into the ear of his master:

"It is a Jew, who calls himself Isaac of York."

"St. Mary!" said the abbot, crossing himself, "an unbelieving Jew, and admitted into this presence!"

"A dog Jew," echoed the Templar, "to approach a defender of the Holy Sepulchre!"

"Peace, my worthy guests," said Cedric; "my hospitality must not be bounded by your dislikes. Let him have a board and a morsel apart."

Introduced with little ceremony, and advancing with fear and hesitation, and many a bow of deep humility, a tall thin old man, with an aquiline nose and piercing black eyes, approached the lower end of the board. Cedric nodded coldly in answer to his repeated salutations, and signed to him to take a place at the lower end of the table, where, however, no one offered to make room for him.

A pilgrim, at length, who sat by the chimney, took compassion upon him, and resigned his seat, saying briefly, "Old man, my garments are dried, my hunger is appeased, thou art both wet and fasting." And, so saying, he placed some food before the Jew on the small table at which he had himself supped, and, without waiting for the old man's thanks, went to the other side of the hall.

As the feast proceeded, a discussion arose amongst the banqueters as to which knights had borne them best in Palestine among the champions of the Cross. De Bois-Guilbert seemed to speak slightingly of the English warriors, while giving the place of honour to the Knights of the Temple.

"The English chivalry were second to NONE" said the pilgrim, who had listened to this conversation with marked impatience. "SECOND to NONE, I say, who ever drew sword in defence of the Holy Land. I say, besides, for I saw it, that King Richard himself and five of his knights held a tournament after the taking of St. John-de- Acre, as challengers, and proved themselves superior to all comers."

The swarthy countenance of the Templar grew darker with a bitter scowl of rage as he listened to these words; but his angry confusion became only more marked as the pilgrim went on to give the names of the English knights who had so distinguished themselves. He paused as he came to the name of the sixth.

"His name dwells not in my memory," he said; "but he was a young knight of lesser renown and lower rank."

"Sir palmer," said Brian de Bois-Guilbert scornfully, "this assumed forgetfulness, after so much has been remembered, comes too late to serve your purpose. I will myself tell the name of the knight before whose lance I fell: it was the Knight of Ivanhoe; nor was there one of the six that, for his years, had more renown in arms. Yet this will I say, and loudly, that, were he in England, I would gladly meet him in this week's tournament, mounted and armed as I now am."

"If Ivanhoe ever returns from Palestine I will be his surety that he meets you," replied the palmer.

Not long after, the grace-cup was served round, and the guests, after making deep obeisance to their landlord and the Lady Rowena, arose, and retired with their attendants for the night.

As the palmer was being guided to his chamber he was met by the waiting-maid of Rowena, who informed him that her mistress desired to speak with him.

A short passage and an ascent of some steps led him to the lady's apartment.

As the pilgrim entered she ordered her attendants, excepting only one, to retire.

"Pilgrim," said the lady, after a moment's pause, during which she seemed uncertain how to address him, "you this night mentioned a name—I mean the name of Ivanhoe—I would gladly hear news of him. Where and in what condition did you leave him?"

"I know little of the Knight of Ivanhoe," answered the palmer with a troubled voice. "He hath, I believe, surmounted the persecution of his enemies in Palestine, and is on the eve of returning to England."

The Lady Rowena sighed deeply.

"Would to God," she then said, "he were here safely arrived, and able to bear arms in the approaching tourney. Should Athelstane of Coningsburgh obtain the prize, Ivanhoe is like to hear evil tidings when he reaches England."

Finding that there was no further information to be obtained about the knight, in whose fate she seemed to take so deep an interest, she bade her maidens to offer the sleeping-cup to the holy man, and having presented him with a piece of gold, wished him good- night.

As the palmer was being conducted to his room he inquired of his attendant where Isaac the Jew was sleeping, and learned that he occupied the room next to his own.

As soon as it was dawn the pilgrim entered the small apartment where the Jew was still asleep. Stirring him with his pilgrim's staff, he told him that he should rise without delay, and leave the mansion. "When the Templar crossed the hall yesternight," he continued, "I heard him speak to his Mussulman slaves in the Saracen language, which I well understand, and he charged them to watch the journey of the Jew, to seize upon him when at a convenient distance from the mansion, and to conduct him to the castle of Philip de Malvoisin, or to that of Reginald Front-de- Boeuf."

It is impossible to describe the extremity of terror which seized upon the Jew at this information. He knew only too well of the relentless persecution to which his kindred were subjected at this period, and how, upon the slightest and most unreasonable pretences, their persons and their property were exposed to every turn of popular fury.

He rose, accordingly, in haste.

It was not, however, such an easy matter to make their exit from the mansion. Gurth, the swineherd, a servant of much importance at that time, when appealed to open the gate, refused to let the visitors out at such an unseasonable hour.

"Nevertheless," said the pilgrim, "you will not, I think, refuse *me* that favour."

So saying, he whispered something in his ear in Saxon. Gurth started as if electrified, and hastened at once to procure their mules for the travellers, and to open the postern gate to let them out.

As the pilgrim mounted, he reached his hand to Gurth, who kissed it with the utmost possible veneration. The two travellers were soon lost under the boughs of the forest path.

They continued their journey at great speed; and the Jew noticed with amazement that the palmer appeared to be familiar with every path and outlet of the wood. When they had travelled some distance from Rotherwood, and were approaching the town of Sheffield, the Jew expressed a wish to recompense the palmer for the interest he had taken in his affairs.

"I desire no recompense," answered his fellow traveller.

"Yet I can tell thee something thou lackest," said Isaac, "and, it may be, supply it too. Thy wish even now is for a horse and armour."

The palmer started.

"What fiend prompted that guess?" said he hastily.

"Under that palmer's gown," replied the Jew, "is hidden a knight's chain and spurs of gold. I saw them as you stooped over my bed this morning."

Without waiting to hear his companion's reply, he wrote some words in Hebrew on a piece of paper, and handed it to the pilgrim, saying:

"In the town of Leicester all men know the rich Jew, Kirjath Jairam of Lombardy; give him this scroll, and he will give thee everything that can furnish thee forth for the tournament; when it is over thou wilt return them safely. But hark thee, good youth, thrust thyself not too forward in this vain hurly-burly. I speak not for endangering the steed and coat of armour, but for the sake of thine own life and limbs."

"Gramercy for thy caution," said the palmer, smiling; "I will use thy courtesy frankly — and it will go hard with me but I will requite it."

They then parted, and took different roads for the town of Sheffield.

When the morning of the tournament arrived the field of contest at Ashby-de-la-Zouche presented a brilliant and romantic scene. On the verge of a wood was an extensive meadow, of the finest and most beautiful green turf, surrounded on one side by the forest, and fringed on the other by straggling oak-trees. The ground, as if fashioned on purpose for the martial display which was intended, sloped gradually down on all sides to a level bottom, which was enclosed for the lists with strong palisades. At each end of the enclosure two heralds were stationed, and a strong body of men-at-arms, for maintaining order and ascertaining the quality of the knights who proposed to engage in the contest.

On a platform beyond the southern entrance were pitched five magnificent pavilions, adorned with pennons of russet and black— the chosen colours of the five knights challengers. That in the centre, as the place of honour, had been assigned to Brian de Bois-Guilbert, whose renown in all games of chivalry had occasioned him to be adopted as the chief and leader of the challengers.

Outside the lists were galleries, spread with tapestry and carpets, for the convenience of the ladies and nobles who were expected to attend the tournament. Another gallery raised higher than the rest, and opposite to the spot where the shock of combat was to take place, was decorated with much magnificence, and graced by a sort of throne and canopy, on which the royal arms were emblazoned. Squires, pages, and yeomen, in rich liveries, waited around the place of honour, which was designed for Prince John, the brother of the absent king, and his attendants. Opposite to this royal gallery was another, even more gaily decorated, reserved as the seat of honour for the Queen of Beauty and of Love. But who was to fill the place on the present occasion no one was prepared to guess.

Gradually the galleries became filled with knights, nobles and ladies, while the lower space was crowded with yeomen and burghers.

Amongst the latter was Isaac the Jew, richly and magnificently dressed, and accompanied by his daughter, the beautiful Rebecca, whose exquisite form, shown to advantage by a becoming Eastern dress, did not escape the quick eye of the prince himself, as he rode by at the head of his numerous and gaily-dressed train.

As the prince assumed his throne, he gave signal to the heralds to proclaim the laws of the tournament, which were briefly as follows:

First: The five challengers were to undertake all comers.

Secondly: Any knight might select any antagonist for combat by touching his shield. If he did so with the reverse of his lance, the trial of skill was made with what were called the arms of courtesy, that is, with lances at whose extremity a piece of round flat board was fixed, so that no danger was encountered, save from the shock of the horses and riders. But if the shield was touched with the sharp end of the lance, the knights were to fight as in actual battle.

Thirdly: The knight whom the prince should declare to be the victor was to receive as prize a war-horse of exquisite beauty and matchless strength, and in addition to this reward, he should have the peculiar honour of naming the Queen of Love and Beauty.

When the proclamation was made the heralds retired, and through the open barriers five knights advanced slowly into the arena. Approaching the challengers, each touched slightly, and with the reverse of his lance, the shield of the antagonist to whom he wished to oppose himself, and then retreated to the extremity of the lists, where all remained drawn up in a line.

At the flourish of clarions and trumpets they started out against each other at full gallop; and such was the superior skill or good fortune of the challengers, that those opposed to Bois-Guilbert, Malvoisin, and Front-de-Boeuf rolled on the ground. The antagonist of Grantmesnil broke his spear; while the fifth knight alone maintained the honour of his party.

A second and third party of knights took the field, and although they had various success, yet, upon the whole, the advantage decidedly remained with the challengers, not one of whom lost his seat. A fourth combat followed; and here, too, the challengers came off victorious.

Prince John now began to talk of awarding the prize to Brian de Bois-Guilbert, who had proved himself to be the best of the Norman knights; but his attention, and that of the other spectators, was arrested by the sound of a solitary trumpet, which breathed a note of defiance from the northern end of the enclosure.

All eyes were turned to see the new champion, and no sooner were the barriers opened than he paced into the lists. His suit of armour was formed of steel, richly inlaid with gold, and the device on his shield was a young oak-tree pulled up by the roots, with the word "Disinherited" inscribed upon it. Riding straight up to Brian de Bois-Guilbert, he struck with the sharp end of his spear the shield of the victorious Norman until it rang again. All stood astonished at his presumption, but none more than the redoubted knight whom he had thus defied to mortal combat.

When the two champions stood opposed to each other at the two extremities of the lists the public expectation was strained to highest pitch.

The trumpets had no sooner given the signal than the combatants vanished from their posts with the speed of lightning, and closed in the centre of the lists with the shock of a thunderbolt. The lances burst into shivers, both the knights being almost unhorsed. Retiring to the extremity of the lists, each received a fresh lance from the attendants; and again, amidst a breathless silence, they sprung from their stations, and closed in the centre of the open space, with the same speed, the same dexterity, the same violence, but not the same equal fortune, as before.

The Norman's spear, striking the centre of his antagonist's shield, went to shivers, and the Disinherited Knight reeled in his saddle. On the other hand, the unknown champion had aimed his spear's point at the helmet of his opponent. Fair and true he hit the Norman on the visor, and saddle, horse, and man rolled on the ground under a cloud of dust.

"We shall meet again, I trust," said the defeated champion, as he extricated himself from the stirrups and fallen steed.

"If we do not," said the Disinherited Knight, "the fault will not be mine. On foot or horseback, with spear, with axe, or with sword, I am alike ready to encounter thee."

Without alighting from his horse, the conqueror called for a bowl of wine, and, opening the beaver of his helmet, announced that he quaffed it "To all true English hearts, and to the confusion of foreign tyrants."

He then desired a herald to proclaim that he was willing to encounter the rest of the challengers in the order in which they pleased to advance against him.

The gigantic Front-de-Boeuf, armed in sable armour, was the first who took the field. But he was soon defeated.

Sir Philip Malvoisin next advanced; and against him the stranger was equally successful. De Grantmesnil soon after avowed himself vanquished; and Ralph de Vipont summed up the list of the stranger's triumphs, being hurled to the ground with such force that he was borne senseless from the lists.

The acclamations of thousands applauded the award of the prince, announcing that day's honours to the Disinherited Knight.

The marshal of the field now approached the victor, praying him to suffer his helmet to be unlaced, ere they conducted him to receive the prize of the day's tourney from the hands of Prince John. But the Disinherited Knight, with all courtesy, declined their request. The prince himself made many inquiries of those in his company about the unknown stranger; but none could guess who he might be. Someone suggested that it might, perhaps, be King Richard himself; and John turned deadly pale as he heard the words, for he had been plotting to seize the throne during his brother's absence.

The victorious knight received his prize, speaking not a word in reply to the complimentary expressions of the prince, which he only acknowledged with a low bow. Leaping into the saddle of the richly-accoutred steed which had been presented to him, he rode up to where the Lady Rowena was seated, and, heedless of the many Norman beauties who graced the contest with their presence, gracefully sinking the point of his lance he deposited the coronet which it supported at the feet of the fair Saxon. The trumpets instantly sounded, while the heralds proclaimed the Lady Rowena the Queen of Beauty and of Love for the ensuing day.

Soon after the vast multitude had retired from the deserted field and lights began to glimmer through the twilight, announcing the toil of the armourers, which was to continue through the whole night in order to repair or alter the suits of armour to be used again on the morrow.

The next day dawned in unclouded splendour, and at ten o'clock the whole plain was crowded with horsemen, horsewomen, and foot- passengers, hastening to the tournament; and shortly after a grand flourish of trumpets announced the arrival of Prince John and his gorgeous retinue.

About the same time arrived Cedric the Saxon with the Lady Rowena. He had been accompanied on the previous day by another noble Saxon,

Athelstane, Lord of Coningsburgh, a suitor for the hand of Rowena, and one who considered his union with that lady as a matter already fixed beyond doubt, by the assent of Cedric and her other friends. Rowena herself, however, had never given her consent to such an alliance; and entertained but a poor opinion of her would-be lover, whose pretensions for her hand she had received with marked disdain. Her Saxon lover was not one of her party at the tourney on the second day. He had observed with displeasure that Rowena was selected by the victor on the preceding day as the object of that honour which it became his privilege to confer, and Athelstane, confident of his own strength and skill, had himself donned his armour with a determination to make his rival feel the weight of his battle-axe.

The combat on the second day of the tournament was on a much more extended scale than that of the previous one; and when the signal for battle was given some fifty knights, at the same moment, charged wildly at each other in the lists. The champions encountered each other with the utmost fury, and with alternate success; the tide of battle seeming to flow now toward the southern, now toward the northern extremity of the lists as the one or the other party prevailed. The clang of the blows, and the shouts of the combatants, mixed fearfully with the sound of the trumpets, and drowned the groans of those who fell, and lay rolling beneath the feet of the horses. The splendid armour of the knights was now defaced with dust and blood, and gave way at every stroke of the sword and battle-axe; while the gay plumage, shorn from the crests, drifted upon the breeze like snowflakes.

In the thick of the press and turmoil of the fight Bois-Guilbert and the Disinherited Knight repeatedly endeavoured to single out each other, spurred by mutual animosity. Such, however, was the crowd and confusion that, during the earlier part of the conflict, their efforts to meet were unavailing. But when the field became thin, by the numbers on either side who had yielded themselves vanquished or had been rendered incapable of continuing the strife, the Templar and the unknown knight at length encountered, hand to hand, with all the fury that mortal animosity, joined to rivalry of honour, could inspire. Such was the skill of each in parrying and striking that the spectators broke forth into a unanimous and involuntary shout of delight and admiration.

But at this moment the party of the Disinherited Knight had the worst. Front-de-Boeuf and Athelstane, having defeated those immediately opposed to them, were now free to come to the aid of their friend the Templar; and, turning their horses at the same moment, the two spurred against the Disinherited Knight.

This champion, exposed as he was to the furious assaults of three opponents each of whom was almost a match for him single-handed, must now have soon been overpowered when an unexpected incident changed the fortunes of the day.

Amongst the ranks of the Disinherited Knight was a champion in black armour, mounted on a black horse, whose shield bore no device of any kind. He had engaged with some few combatants, and had easily defeated them during the earlier stages of the contest, but seemed to take no further interest in the event of the fight, acting the part rather of a spectator than of a party in the tournament.

The moment, however, he saw his leader so hard bestead he seemed to throw aside his apathy, and setting spurs to his horse he came to his assistance like a thunderbolt, exclaiming, in a voice like a trumpet call, "Disinherited to the rescue!"

Under the fury of his first stroke, Front-de-Boeuf, horse and all, rolled stunned to the ground. He then turned his steed upon Athelstane, and, wrenching from the hand of the bulky Saxon the battle-axe which he wielded, bestowed him such a blow upon the crest, that the Lord of Coningsburgh also lay senseless on the field. Having achieved this double feat, he returned calmly to the extremity of the lists, leaving his leader to cope as best he could with Brian de Bois-Guilbert. This was no longer matter of so much difficulty as formerly. The Templar's horse had bled much, and gave way under the shock of the Disinherited Knight's charge. As Bois-Guilbert rolled on the field, his antagonist sprung from horseback, and was in the act of commanding his adversary to yield or die, when Prince John gave the signal that the conflict was at an end.

It being now the duty of the prince to name the knight who had done best, he determined, although contrary to the advice of those about him, that the honour of the day remained with the Black Knight.

To the surprise of all present, however, the knight thus preferred was nowhere to be found. He had left the lists immediately when the conflict ceased, and had been observed by some spectators to move slowly down one of the forest glades. After he had been summoned twice by sound of trumpet, it became necessary to name another; and the Disinherited Knight was for the second time named champion of the day.

As the victor was led towards the throne of the Lady Rowena, it was observed that he tottered. Rowena was about to place the chaplet which she held in her hand upon the helmet of the champion who kneeled before her, when the marshals exclaimed, "It must not be thus, his head must be bare;" and at once removed his helmet. The features which were exposed were those of a young man of twenty-five; but his countenance was as pale as death, and marked in one or two places with streaks of blood.

Rowena had no sooner beheld him than she uttered a faint shriek; but at once summoning up all her energies, she placed upon the drooping head of the victor the splendid chaplet which was the destined reward of the day.

The knight bent low, and kissed the hand of the lovely Sovereign by whom his valour had been rewarded; and then, sinking yet farther forward, lay prostrate at her feet.

There was a general consternation. Cedric, who had been struck mute by the sudden appearance of his banished son, now rushed forward, as if to separate him from Rowena. But this had been already accomplished by the marshals of the field, who, guessing the cause of Ivanhoe's swoon, had hastened to undo his armour, and found that the head of a lance had penetrated his breast-plate and inflicted a wound in his side.

The name of Ivanhoe was no sooner pronounced than it flew from mouth to mouth throughout the vast assembly. It was not long ere it reached the circle of the prince, whose brow darkened as he heard the news. He knew that Ivanhoe had been a close attendant on his brother King Richard in the Holy Land; and as such he looked upon him as his own enemy. He was about to give the signal for retiring from the lists, when a small billet was put into his hand. He broke the seal with apparent agitation, and read the words, "Take heed to yourself, for the devil is unchained."

He turned as pale as death; and taking two of his courtiers aside, he put the billet into their hands. "It means," he said in a faltering voice, "that my brother Richard has obtained his freedom."

"It is time, then," said Fitzurse, his confidential attendant, "to draw our party to a head, and prepare our forces to meet him."

In sullen ill-humour the prince left the place of tournament to hold high festival at the Castle of Ashby; but it was more than his courtiers could do to rouse him from the overpowering gloom which seemed to agitate his mind throughout the evening. On the next day it was settled that the prince and all those who were ready to support him should attend a meeting at York for the purpose of making general arrangements for placing the crown upon the head of the usurper, and ousting King Richard from his sovereign rights.

Meanwhile, Cedric the Saxon, when he saw his son drop down senseless in the lists at Ashby, had given orders, half in pity, half in anger, to his attendants to convey Ivanhoe to a place where his wound might be dressed as soon as the crowd had dispersed. The attendants were, however, anticipated in this good office. The crowd dispersed, indeed, but the knight was nowhere to be seen. The only information which could be collected from the bystanders was, that he had been raised with care by certain well- attired grooms, and placed in a litter belonging to a lady among the spectators, in which he had immediately been transported out of the press.

Cedric and his friends, having seen the last of the tournament and the festivities which followed it, now set out on their return to Rotherwood. Their way lay through a thickly-wooded country, which was at the time held to be dangerous to travellers from the number of outlaws whom oppression and poverty had driven to despair, and who occupied the forests in large bands. From these rovers, however, Cedric and Athelstane accounted themselves secure, as they had in attendance ten servants. They knew, besides, that the outlaws were chiefly peasants and yeomen of Saxon descent, and were generally supposed to respect the persons and property of their countrymen.

As the travellers journeyed on their way, they were alarmed by repeated cries for assistance; and when they rode up to the place from whence they came, they were surprised to find a horse-litter placed upon the ground, beside which sat a young woman, richly dressed in the Jewish fashion, while an old man, whose yellow cap proclaimed him to belong to the same nation, walked up and down, wringing his hands, as if affected by some strange disaster.

It was some time before Isaac of York, for it was he, could explain the nature of his trouble. When at length he began to come to himself out of his agony of terror, he said that he had hired a body-guard of six men at Ashby, together with mules for carrying the litter of a sick friend; but that they all had fled away from him, having heard that there was a strong band of outlaws lying in wait in the woods before them. When he implored permission to continue his journey under the protection of Cedric and his party, Athelstane was strongly opposed to allowing the "dog of a Jew," as he called him, to travel in their company. The Lady Rowena, however, had at the same time been approached by the old man's daughter, who, kissing the hem of her garment, implored her to have compassion on them. "It is not for myself that I pray this favour," said Rebecca; "nor is it even for that poor old man; but it is in the name of one dear to many, and dear even to you, that I beseech you to let this sick person be transported with care and tenderness under your protection."

So noble and solemn was the air with which Rebecca made this appeal, that on the intercession of Rowena Cedric readily consented to allow the Jew and his daughter, together with their sick friend, to attach themselves to his party.

Twilight was already coming on as the company proceeded on their journey. The path upon which the party travelled was now so narrow as not to admit above two riders abreast. They accordingly quickened their pace, in order to get as rapidly as possible out of the dangerous neighborhood which they were traversing. They had just crossed a' brook, whose banks were broken, swampy, and overgrown with dwarf willows, when they were assailed in front, flank and rear by a large body of men in the dress of outlaws, and with an impetuosity to which, in their confused and ill-prepared condition, it was impossible to offer effectual resistance. Both the Saxon chiefs were made prisoners at the same moment, while the attendants, embarrassed with baggage, surprised and terrified at the fate of their masters, fell an easy prey to the assailants; and the Lady Rowena, the Jew and his daughter experienced the same misfortune. Wamba, the jester, alone escaped, showing upon the occasion much more courage than those who pretended to greater sense. As he wandered through the forest, a dog, which he recognised, jumped up and fawned upon him, and Gurth, the swineherd, shortly after made his appearance. He was horrified to hear from his fellow-servant of the misfortune which had befallen their master and his party; and the two were about to hasten away for the purpose of procuring aid, when a third person suddenly appeared, and commanded them both to halt. Notwithstanding the twilight, and although his dress and arms showed him to be an outlaw, Wamba recognised him to be Locksley, the yeoman, a man who had carried off the prize for archery at the tournament a day or two before.

"What is the meaning of all this," he said; "or who is it that rifle and ransom and make prisoners in these forests?"

The yeoman then left, bidding Gurth and Wamba, on the peril of their lives, not to stir until he returned.

He was not long away, and on returning said that he had found out who the attacking party were and whither they were bound.

"Cedric the Saxon," he said, "the friend of the rights of Englishmen, shall not want English hands to help him in this extremity. Come, then, with me, until I gather more aid."

So saying, he walked through the wood at a great pace, followed by the jester and the swineherd.

It was after three hours' good walking that the servants of Cedric, with their mysterious guide, arrived at a small opening in the forest. Beneath an enormous oak-tree several yeomen lay stretched on the ground, while another, as sentinel, walked to and fro in the moonlight shade. Locksley, on being recognised, was welcomed with every token of respect and attachment; and he at once gave orders to collect what force they could.

"A set of gallants," he said, "who have been masquerading in such guise as our own, are carrying a band of prisoners to Torquilstone, the castle of Front-de-Boeuf. Our honour is concerned to punish them, and we will find means to do so."

In the meantime Cedric and the other prisoners had been hurried along by Bois-Guilbert and De Bracy, and safely lodged in the strong and ancient castle of Reginald Front-de-Boeuf. Once within the castle, the prisoners were separated. Cedric and Athelstane were confined in one apartment, the Lady Rowena in another, while the poor Jew was hastily thrust into a dungeon-vault, the floor of which was deep beneath the level of the ground, and his daughter Rebecca was locked into a cell in a distant and sequestered turret.

The dungeon occupied by Isaac of York was dark and damp. Chains and shackles, which had been the portion of former captives, hung rusted on the gloomy walls, and in the rings of one of those sets of fetters there remained the mouldering bones of some unhappy prisoner who had been left to perish there in other days. At one end of this ghastly apartment was a large fire-grate, over the top of which were stretched some transverse bars of iron, half devoured with rust.

For nearly three hours the wretched Jew remained sitting in a corner of his dungeon, when steps were heard on the stair by which it was approached. The bolts were withdrawn, the hinges creaked as the wicket opened, and Reginald Front-de-Boeuf, followed by two Saracen slaves of the Templar, entered the prison.

"Most cursed dog of an accursed race!" he said to Isaac, "see'st thou these scales? In these shalt thou weigh me out a thousand silver pounds."

"Holy Abraham!" returned the Jew, "heard man ever such a demand? Not within the walls of York, ransack my house and that of all my tribe, wilt thou find the tithe of that huge sum of silver."

"Prepare, then," said the Norman, "for a long and lingering death."

And he ordered the slave to make ready the fire.

"See'st thou, Isaac," he said, "the range of bars above that glowing charcoal? On that warm couch shalt thou lie, stripped of thy clothes. One of these slaves shall maintain the fire beneath thee, while another shall anoint thy wretched limbs with oil, lest the roast should burn. Now, choose between such a scorching bed and the payment of a thousand pounds of silver; for, by the head of my father, thou hast no other option."

"So may Abraham, Jacob, and all the fathers of our people assist me," said Isaac; "I cannot make the choice, because I have not the means of satisfying your exorbitant demand."

"Seize him, and strip him, slaves!" said the knight, "and let the fathers of his race assist him if they can."

The assistants stepped forward, and laying hands on the unfortunate man, waited the hardhearted baron's further signal.

The unhappy Jew eyed their savage countenances and that of Front-de-Boeuf, in hope of discovering some symptoms of relenting; and as he looked again at the glowing furnace his resolution at length gave way.

"I will pay!" he said. "That is," he added, after a moment's pause, "I will pay it with the help of my brethren. Let my daughter Rebecca go forth to York, and she will bring the treasure here."

"Thy daughter!" said Front-de-Boeuf, as if surprised. "By heavens! Isaac, I would I had known of this; I gave the black-browed girl to be a handmaiden to Sir Brian de Bois-Guilbert, to do as it might please him with her. My word is passed to my comrade in arms; nor would I break it for ten Jews and Jewesses to boot."

The yell which Isaac raised at this unfeeling communication made the vault ring.

"Robber and villain!" he exclaimed, "I will pay thee nothing—not one silver penny will I pay thee—unless my daughter is delivered to me in safety and honour. Do thy worst. Take my life if thou wilt, and say the Jew, amidst his tortures, knew how to disappoint the Christian."

"Strip him, slaves! and chain him down upon the bars," said Front-de-Boeuf.

The Saracens, in obedience to this savage order, had already torn from the feeble and struggling old man his upper garment, and were proceeding totally to disrobe him, when the sound of a bugle, twice winded without the castle, penetrated even to the recesses of the dungeon; and immediately after, loud voices were heard calling for Sir Reginald Front-de-Boeuf. Unwilling to be found engaged in his hellish occupation, the savage baron gave the slaves a signal to restore Isaac's garment, and hastily quitted the dungeon with his attendants.

During the time the unhappy Jew was undergoing his terrible ordeal in the gloomy dungeon, his daughter Rebecca, in her lonely turret, had been exposed to attentions no less unpleasant.

On being left in the secluded cell, she found herself in the presence of an old hag, who kept murmuring to herself a Saxon rhyme, as if to beat time to the spindle at which she was engaged. As soon as they were alone the old woman addressed the Jewess, telling her that she was once as young and fair as herself, when Front-de-Boeuf, the father of the man who now lorded it in the castle, attacked the place and slew her father and his seven sons, and she became the prey and scorn of the conqueror.

"Is there no help? Are there no means of escape?" said Rebecca. "Richly, richly would I requite thine aid."

"Think not of it," said the hag, "from hence there is no escape but through the gates of death; and it is late, late," she added shaking her gray head, "ere these open to us. Fare thee well, Jewess!—thou hast to do with them that have neither scruple nor pity." And so saying she left the room, locking the door behind her.

Before long a step was heard on the stair, and the door of the turret-chamber slowly opened, and Brian de Bois-Guilbert entered the room. He commenced to address the Jewess with flattering speeches, saying that he loved her, and that she must now be his. But Rebecca rejected his proffered love with scorn, protesting that she would proclaim his villainy from one end of Europe to the other. "At least," she said, "those who tremble not at thy crime will hold thee accursed for having so far dishonoured the cross thou wearest as to follow a daughter of my people."

"Thou art keen-witted, Jewess," replied the Templar, well aware of the truth of what she spoke; "but loud must be thy voice of complaint, if it is heard beyond the iron walls of this castle. One thing only can save thee, Rebecca. Submit to thy fate, embrace our religion, and thou shalt go forth in such state that many a Norman lady shall envy thee thy lot."

"Submit to my fate!" said Rebecca, "and, sacred Heaven! to what fate? Embrace thy religion, and what religion can it be that harbours such a villain? Craven knight! forsworn priest! I spit at thee and I defy thee. The God of Abraham's promise hath opened an escape to His daughter, even from this abyss of infamy!"

As she spoke she threw open the latticed window, and in an instant after stood on the very verge of the parapet outside, with not the slightest screen between her and the tremendous depth below. Unprepared for such a desperate effort, Bois-Guilbert had time neither to intercept nor to stop her. As he offered to advance, she exclaimed, "Remain where thou art, proud Templar, or at thy choice advance! One foot nearer, and I plunge myself from the precipice; my body shall be crushed out of the very form of humanity upon the stones below ere it become the victim of thy brutality!"

The Templar hesitated, and a resolution which would have never yielded to pity or distress gave way to his admiration for her fortitude. "Come down," he said, "rash girl! I swear by earth, and sea, and sky, I will offer thee no offence. Many a law, many a commandment have I broken, but my word never."

"Thus far," said Rebecca, "I will trust thee;" and she descended from the verge of the battlement, but remained standing close by one of the embrasures. "Here," she said, "I take my stand. If thou shalt attempt to diminish by one step the distance now between us, thou shalt see that the Jewish maiden will rather trust her soul with God than her honour to the Templar."

As she spoke, the bugle was heard to sound, announcing that the presence of the knight was required in another part of the castle; and as he instantly obeyed the summons, Rebecca found herself once more alone.

When the Templar reached the hall of the castle, he found De Bracy there already. They were soon after joined by Front-de-Boeuf.

"Let us see the cause of this cursed clamour," said Front-de-Boeuf. "Here is a letter, and if I mistake not, it is in Saxon."

The Templar took the paper from his hand and read it. It was a demand to surrender the prisoners within one hour, failing which the castle would be instantly besieged; and it was signed at the end by Wamba and Gurth, by the Black Knight and Locksley.

The answer which was returned from the castle to this missive announced that the prisoners would not be given up; but that permission would be given to a man of religion to come to receive their dying confession, as it had been determined to execute them before noon.

When this reply was brought back to the party of the Black Knight, a hurried consultation was held as to what they should do. There being no churchman amongst them, and as no one else seemed willing to undertake the risk of trusting himself within the castle, Wamba, the jester, was selected for the office. He was soon muffled in his religious disguise; and imitating the solemn and stately deportment of a friar, he departed to execute his mission.

As he approached the castle gate, he was at once admitted, and shortly after was ushered into the apartment where Cedric and Athelstane were confined; and the three were left alone. It was not long before Cedric recognised the voice of his jester. The faithful servant at once suggested that his master should change garments with him, and so make his escape. But it required the strong pressure of both Wamba and Athelstane before Cedric would consent. At length he yielded, and the exchange of dress was accomplished. He left the apartment saying that he would rescue his friends, or return and die along with them.

In a low-arched and dusky passage by which Cedric endeavoured to work his way to the hall, he was met by Urfried, the old crone of the tower.

"Come this way, father," she said to him; "thou art a stranger, and canst not leave the castle without a guide. Come hither, for I would speak with thee."

So saying, she proceeded to conduct the unwilling Cedric into a small apartment, the door of which she heedfully secured. "Thou art a Saxon, father," she said to him; "the sounds of my native language are sweet to mine ears, though seldom heard for many years."

She then told him the story of her unhappy and degraded life, and how she was once the daughter of the noble thane of Torquilstone.

"Thou the daughter of Torquil Wolfganger!" said Cedric; "thou — thou, the daughter of my father's friend and companion in arms!"

"Thy father's friend!" echoed Urfried; "then Cedric, called the Saxon, stands before me. But why this religious dress?"

"It matters not who I am," said Cedric; "proceed, unhappy woman, unhappy Ulrica, I should say, for thou canst be none other, with thy tale of horror and guilt. Wretched woman!" he exclaimed, as she concluded her miserable history, "so thou hast lived, when all believed thee murdered; hast lived to merit our hate and execration; lived to unite thyself with the vile tyrant who slew thy nearest and dearest!"

"I hated him with all my soul," replied Ulrica; "I also have had my hours of vengeance; I have fomented the quarrels of our foes; I have seen their blood flow, and heard their dying groans; I have seen my oppressor fall at his own board by the hand of his own son. Yet here I dwelt, till age, premature age, has stamped its ghastly features on my countenance, scorned and insulted where I was once obeyed. Thou art the first I have seen for twenty years by whom God was feared or man regarded; and dost thou bid me despair?"

"I bid thee repent," said Cedric; "but I cannot, I will not, longer abide with thee."

"Stay yet a moment!" said Ulrica. "Revenge henceforth shall possess me wholly, and thou thyself shalt say that, whatever was the life of Ulrica, her death well became the daughter of the noble Torquil. Hasten to lead your forces to the attack, and when thou shalt see a red flag wave from the eastern turret, press the Normans hard; they will have enough to do within. Begone, I pray thee; follow thine own fate, and leave me to mine."

As she spoke she vanished through a private door, and Front-de-Boeuf entered the apartment.

"Thy penitents, father," he said, "have made a long shrift; but come, follow me through this passage, that I may dismiss thee by the postern."

As Cedric was leaving the castle, the Norman gave him a note to carry to Philip de Malvoisin, begging him to send assistance with all the speed he could. He promised the friar a large reward for doing the errand, and as they parted at the postern door he thrust into Cedric's reluctant hand a piece of gold, adding, "Remember, I will flay off thy cowl and skin if thou failest in thy purpose."

When Front-de-Boeuf rejoined his friends and found out the trick which had been played upon him, and that Cedric had escaped, his rage was unbounded, and it was only on De Bracy interceding for him that he consented to spare the life of the poor jester.

Before long the inmates of the castle had other things to occupy them. The enemy was announced to be under their very walls; and each knight repaired hastily to his post, and at the head of the few followers whom they were able to muster they awaited with calm determination the threatened assault.

When at length the attack upon the castle was commenced all was at once bustle and clamour within its gloomy walls. The heavy step of men-at-arms traversed the battlements, or resounded on the narrow and winding passages and the stairs which led to the various bartizans and points of defence. The voices of the knights were heard animating their followers, or directing means of defence; while their commands were often drowned in the clashing of armour or the clamourous shouts of those whom they addressed. The shrill bugle without was answered by a flourish of Norman trumpets from the battlements, while the cries of both parties augmented the fearful din. Showers of well-directed arrows came pouring against each embrasure and opening in the parapets, as well as every window where a defender might be suspected to be stationed; and these were answered by a furious discharge of whizzing shafts and missiles from the walls.

And so for some time the fight went on; many combatants falling on either side. But soon the conflict became even more desperate when the Black Knight, at the head of a body of his followers, led an attack upon the outer barrier of the barbican. Down came the piles and palisades before their irresistible onslaught; but their headlong rush through the broken barriers was met by Front-de- Boeuf himself and a number of the defenders.

The two leaders came face to face, and fought hand to hand on the breach amid the roar of their followers who watched the progress of the strife. Hot and fierce was the combat that ensued between them; but ere many minutes had passed the giant form of Front-de- Boeuf tottered like an oak under the steel of the woodman, and dropped to the ground.

His followers rushed forward to where he lay, and their united force compelling the Black Knight to pause, they dragged their wounded leader within the walls.

An interval of quiet now succeeded, the besiegers remaining in possession of the outer defences of the castle, and the besieged retiring for the time within the walls of the fortress.

During the confusion which reigned amongst the followers of Front- de- Boeuf when the attack had commenced, Rebecca had been allowed to take the place of the old crone, Ulrica, who was in close attendance on the wounded man who had been brought into the castle in company with Isaac of York and the other captives. The sufferer was Ivanhoe himself, who had so mysteriously disappeared on the conclusion of the tournament, when his father, Cedric, had sent his servants to attend him to a place of safety. The gallant young warrior, who, as he fell fainting to the ground, seemed to be abandoned by all the world, had been transported from the lists at the entreaty of Rebecca, to the house at Ashby then occupied by Isaac of York, where his wounds were dressed and tended by the Jewish maiden herself. So great was her skill and knowledge of medicine, that she undertook to restore the injured knight to health in eight days' time; but she informed him of the necessity they were under of removing to York, and of her father's resolution to transport him thither, and tend him in his own house until his wound should be healed. It was on their journey to that town that they were overtaken on the road by Cedric and his party, in whose company they were afterwards carried captive to the Castle of Torquilstone.

But to return to the assault. When Front-de-Boeuf, deeply wounded, was rescued by his followers from the fury of the Black Knight, he was conveyed to his chamber. As he lay upon his bed, racked with pain and mental agony, and filled with the fear of rapidly approaching death, he heard a voice address him.

"Think on thy sins," it said, "Reginald Front-de-Boeuf; on rebellion, on rapine, on murder."

"Who is there? What art thou?" he exclaimed in terror. "Depart, and haunt my couch no more; let me die in peace."

"In peace thou shalt NOT die," repeated the voice; "even in death shalt thou think on the groans which this castle has echoed, on the blood that is engrained in its floors."

"Go, leave me, fiend!" replied the wounded Norman. "Leave me and seek the Saxon witch, Ulrica, who was my temptress; let her, as well as I, taste the tortures which anticipate hell."

"She already tastes them," said Ulrica, stepping before the couch of Front-de-Boeuf; "she hath long drunken of this cup, and its bitterness is now sweetened to see that thou dost partake it."

"Detestable fury!" exclaimed the Norman. "Ho! Giles, Clement, Eustace, seize this witch, and hurl her from the battlements; she has betrayed us to the Saxon."

"Call on them again, valiant baron," said the hag, with a smile of grisly mockery; "but know, mighty chief, thou shalt have neither answer nor aid. Listen to these horrid sounds," for the din of the recommenced assault and defence now rung fearfully loud from the battlements of the castle; "in that war-cry is the downfall of thy house. And know, too, even now, the doom which all thy power and strength is unable to avoid, though it is prepared for thee by this feeble hand. Markest thou the smouldering and suffocating vapour which already eddies in sable folds through the chamber? Rememberest thou the magazine of fuel that is stored beneath these apartments?"

"Woman!" exclaimed the wounded man with fury, "thou hast not set fire to it? By heaven thou hast, and the castle is in flames!"

"They are fast rising, at least," said Ulrica; "and a signal shall soon wave to warn the besiegers to press hard upon those who would extinguish them. Farewell, Front-de-Boeuf; farewell for ever."

So saying, she left the apartment; and Front-de-Boeuf could hear the crash of the ponderous key, as she locked and double-locked the door behind her.

Meanwhile, the Black Knight had led his forces again to the attack; and so vigorous was their assault, that before long the gate of the castle alone separated them from those within. At this moment the besiegers caught sight of the red flag upon the tower which Ulrica had described to Cedric; and, as she had bade them do, the assailants at once redoubled their efforts to break in the postern gate.

The defenders, finding the castle to be on fire, now determined to sell their lives as dearly as they could; and, headed by De Bracy, they threw open the gate, and were at once involved in a terrific conflict with those outside. The Black Knight, with portentous strength, forced his way inward in despite of De Bracy and his followers. Two of the foremost instantly fell, and the rest gave way, notwithstanding all their leaders' efforts to stop them. The Black Knight was soon engaged in desperate combat with the Norman chief, and the vaulted roof of the hall rung with their furious blows. At length De Bracy fell.

"Yield thee, De Bracy," said the Black Champion, stooping over him, and holding against the bars of his helmet the fatal poniard with which the knights despatched their enemies. "Yield thee, rescue or no rescue, or thou art but a dead man."

"I will not yield," replied the Norman faintly, "to an unknown conqueror. Tell me thy name, or work thy pleasure on me."

The Black Knight whispered something into the ear of the vanquished.

"I yield me to be true prisoner, rescue or no rescue," then answered De Bracy, in a tone of sullen submission.

"Go to the barbican," said the victor in a tone of authority, "and wait there my further orders."

"Yet first let me say," said De Bracy, "what it imports thee to know. Wilfred of Ivanhoe is wounded and a prisoner, and will perish in the burning castle without present help."

"Wilfred of Ivanhoe!" exclaimed the Black Knight—"prisoner, and perish! The life of every man in the castle shall answer it if a hair of his head be singed. Show me his chamber!"

When the Black Knight reached the room, Ivanhoe was alone. Rebecca, who had remained with him until a few moments before, had just been carried off forcibly by Bois-Guilbert. Raising the wounded man with ease, the Black Knight rushed with him to the postern gate, and having there delivered his burden to the care of two yeomen, he again entered the castle to assist in the rescue of the other prisoners.

One turret was now in bright flames, which flashed out furiously from window and shot-hole. But in other parts the besiegers pursued the defenders of the castle from chamber to chamber, and satiated in their blood the vengeance which had long animated them against the soldiers of the tyrant, Front-de Boeuf. Most of the garrison resisted to the uttermost; few of them asked quarter, none received it.

As the fire commenced to spread rapidly through all parts of the castle, Ulrica appeared on one of the turrets. Her long dishevelled gray hair flew back from her uncovered head, while the delight of gratified vengeance contended in her eyes with the fire of insanity. Before long the towering flames had surmounted every obstruction, and rose to the evening skies one huge and burning beacon, seen far and wide through the adjacent country; tower after tower crashed down, with blazing roof and rafter. The vanquished, of whom very few remained, scattered and escaped into the neighbouring wood. The maniac figure of Ulrica was for a long time visible on the lofty stand she had chosen, tossing her arms abroad with wild exultation. At length, with a terrific crash, the whole turret gave way, and she perished in the flames which had consumed her tyrant.

When day dawned the outlaws and their rescued prisoners assembled around the trysting-tree in the oak forest, beside the now ruined castle. Two only of Front-de-Boeuf's captives were missing: Athelstane and the Jewish maiden, the former being reported as amongst the slain, and Rebecca having been carried off by Bois- Guilbert before her friends could effect her rescue.

When the outlaws had divided the spoils which they had taken from the Castle of Torquilstone, Cedric prepared to take his departure. He left the gallant band of foresters sorrowing deeply for his lost friend, the Lord of Coningsburgh; and he and his followers had scarce departed, when a procession moved slowly from under the greenwood branches in the direction which he had taken, in the centre of which was the car in which the body of Athelstane was laid.

When the funeral train had passed out of sight, Locksley addressed the Black Knight, and asked him if he had any request to make, as his reward for the gallantry he had displayed.

"I accept the offer," said the knight; "and I ask permission to dispose of Sir Maurice de Bracy at my own pleasure."

"He is already thine," said Locksley, "and well for him!"

"De Bracy," said the knight, "thou art free; depart. He whose prisoner thou art scorns to take mean revenge for what is past. But beware of the future, lest a worse thing befall thee. Maurice de Bracy, I say, BEWARE!" De Bracy bowed low and in silence, threw himself upon a horse, and galloped off through the wood.

"Noble knight," then said Locksley, "I would fain beg your acceptance of another gift. Here is a bugle, which an English yeoman has once worn; I pray you to keep it as a memorial of your gallant bearing. If ye should chance to be hard bestead in any forest between Trent and Tees, wind three notes upon it, and ye shall find helpers and rescue."

"Gramercy for the gift, bold yeoman," said the knight; "and better help than thine and thy rangers would I never seek, were it at my utmost need."

So saying, he mounted his strong war-horse, and rode off through the forest.

During all this time Isaac of York sat mournfully apart, grieving for the loss of his dearly-loved daughter Rebecca. He was assured that she was still alive, but that there was no hope of rescuing her from the clutches of Bois-Guilbert, except by the payment of a ransom of six hundred crowns. On consenting to pay this amount to the Prior of Jorvaulx, who had just then joined the party in the wood, the Jew was given a letter, written by the prior himself, directed to Bois-Guilbert at the Preceptory of Templestowe, whither the maiden had been carried off, commanding that Rebecca should be set at liberty. And with this epistle the unhappy old man set out to procure his daughter's liberation.

Meanwhile there was brave feasting in the Castle of York to which Prince John had invited those nobles, prelates, and leaders by whose assistance he hoped to carry through his ambitious projects upon his brother's throne. Deep was the prince's disappointment when he learnt of the fall of Torquilstone, and the defeat of the knights who failed to defend it, and on whose support he strongly relied. The rumoured intelligence had scarcely reached him, when De Bracy was ushered into his presence, his armour still bearing the marks of the late fray, and covered with clay and dust from crest to spur.

"The Templar is fled," said De Bracy, in answer to the prince's eager questions; "Front-de-Boeuf you will never see more; and," he added in a low and emphatic tone, "Richard is in England; I have seen him and spoken with him."

Prince John turned pale, tottered, and caught at the back of an oaken bench to support himself.

On awakening from the stupor into which he had been thrown by the unexpected intelligence, he determined to endeavour to seize his brother, and hold him a prisoner. He appealed to De Bracy to assist him in this project, and became at once deeply suspicious of the knight's loyalty towards him when he declined to lift hand against the man who had spared his own life.

Driven almost to desperation, and with bitter complaints against those who had promised to support him, John now treacherously directed Waldemar Fitzurse, one of his most intimate attendants, to depart at once, with a chosen band of followers, for the purpose of overtaking King Richard, and, if possible, securing him as a prisoner.

In the meantime, Isaac of York, though suffering much from the ill-treatment he had received at Torquilstone, made his way to the Preceptory of Templestowe, for the purpose of negotiating his daughter's redemption. Before reaching his destination he was told that Lucas de Beaumanoir, the Grand Master of the Order of the Templars, was then on visit to the preceptory. He had come, the Jew was informed, for the purpose of correcting and punishing many of the members of the body whose conduct had of late been open to severe censure; and he was recognised, besides, as the most tyrannical oppressor of the Jewish people.

In spite of this ominous intelligence, Isaac pursued his way, and on arriving at Templestowe was at once shown into the presence of the Grand Master himself. With fear and trembling he produced the letter of the Prior of Jorvaulx to Bois-Guilbert. Beaumanoir tore open the seal and perused the letter in haste, with an expression of surprise and horror. He had not until then been informed of the presence of the Jewish maiden in the abode of the Templars, and great was his fury and indignation on learning that she was amongst them. He denounced Rebecca as a witch, by whose enchantment Bois-Guilbert had been led to offend against the rules of the Holy Order, and in tones of passion and scorn he refused to listen to Isaac's protestations of her innocence.

"Spurn this Jew from the gate," he said to one of his attendants, "and shoot him dead if he oppose or turn again. With his daughter we will deal as the Christian law and our own high office warrant."

Poor Isaac was hurried off accordingly, and expelled from the preceptory, all his entreaties, and even his offers, unheard and disregarded. He had hitherto feared for his daughter's honour; he was now to tremble for her life.

Orders were at once given by the Grand Master to prepare the great hall of the preceptory for the trial of Rebecca as a sorceress; and even the president of the establishment did not hesitate to aid in procuring false evidence against the unfortunate Jewess, for the purpose of ingratiating himself with Beaumanoir, from whom he had kept secret the presence of Rebecca in the holy precincts.

When the ponderous castle bell had tolled the point of noon, the Jewess was led from her secluded chamber into the great hall in which the Grand Master had for the time established his court of justice. As she passed through the crowd of squires and yeomen, who already filled the lower end of the vast apartment, a scrap of paper was thrust into her hand, which she received almost unconsciously, and continued to hold without examining its contents. The assurance that she possessed some friend in this awful assembly gave her courage to look around, and to mark into whose presence she had been conducted. She gazed accordingly upon a scene which might well have struck terror into a bolder heart than hers.

On an elevated seat at the upper end of the great hall, directly before the accused, sat the Grand Master of the Temple, in full and ample robes of flowing white, holding in his hand the mystic staff, which bore the symbol of the Order. At his feet was placed a table, occupied by two scribes, whose duty it was to record the proceedings of the day. Their chairs were black and formed a marked contrast to the warlike appearance of the knights who attended the solemn gathering. The preceptors, of whom there were four present, occupied seats behind their superiors; and behind them stood the esquires of the Order, robed in white.

The whole assembly wore an aspect of the most profound gravity — the reflection, as it were, of the sombre countenance of the austere and relentless Grand Master. The lower part of the hall was filled with guards and others whom curiosity had drawn together to witness the important and impressive ceremony.

The Grand Master himself, in a short speech, announced the charge against the Jewess; and, on its conclusion, several witnesses were called to prove the risks to which Bois-Guilbert exposed himself in endeavouring to save Rebecca from the blazing castle; while other witnesses testified to the apparent madness of the Templar in bringing the Jewess to the preceptory. A poor Saxon peasant was next dragged forward to the bar, who had been cured of a palsy by the accused. Most unwilling was his testimony, and given with many tears; but he admitted that two years since he had been unable to stir from his bed until the remedies applied by Rebecca's directions had in some degree restored the use of his limbs. With a trembling hand he produced from his bosom a small box of ointment, bearing some Hebrew characters upon the lid, which was, with most of the audience, a sure proof that the devil had stood apothecary.

Witnesses skilled in medicine were then brought forward to prove that they knew nothing of the materials of which the unguent was compounded, and who suggested that it must have been manufactured by means both unlawful and magical. Other witnesses came forward to prove that Rebecca's cures were accomplished by means of mutterings in an unknown tongue, and songs of a sweet, strange sound, which made the ears of the hearer tingle and his heart throb, adding that her garments were of a strange and mystic form, and that she had rings impressed with cabalistic devices, all which were, in those ignorant and superstitious times, easily credited as proofs of guilt.

On the conclusion of this weighty evidence the Grand Master in a solemn tone demanded of Rebecca what she had to say against the sentence of condemnation which he was about to pronounce.

"To invoke your pity," said the lovely Jewess, with a voice somewhat tremulous with emotion, "would, I am aware, be as useless as I should hold it mean. To state that to relieve the sick and wounded of another religion cannot be displeasing to God were also unavailing; to plead that many things which these men (whom may Heaven pardon!) have spoken against me are impossible would avail me but little, since you believe in their possibility, and still less would it advantage me to explain that the peculiarities of my dress, language, and manners are those of my people. I am friendless, defenceless, and the prisoner of my accuser there. He is of your own faith; his lightest word would weigh down the most solemn protestations of the distressed Jewess, and yet to himself, yes, Brian de Bois-Guilbert, to thyself I appeal, whether these accusations are not false?"

There was a pause; all eyes turned to the Templar. He was silent.

"Speak," she said, "if thou art a man; if thou art a Christian, speak! I conjure thee, by the habit which thou dost wear, by the name thou dost inherit, by the honour of thy mother, I conjure thee to say, are these things true?"

"Answer her, brother," said the Grand Master.

"The scroll, the scroll!" was all that Bois-Guilbert uttered in reply, looking to Rebecca.

The Jewess instantly remembered the slip of paper which she continued to hold in her hand, and, looking at it without being observed, she read the words, *"Demand a champion!"*

"Rebecca," said the Grand Master, who believed the words of Bois-Guilbert had reference to some other writing, "hast thou aught else to say?"

"There is yet one chance of life left to me," said the Jewess, "even by your own fierce laws. I deny this charge; I maintain my innocence. I challenge the privilege of trial by combat, and will appear by my champion. There lies my gage."

She took her embroidered glove from her hand and flung it down before the Grand Master, with an air of mingled simplicity and dignity which excited universal surprise and admiration.

A short consultation then took place between Beaumanoir and the preceptors, in which it was decided that Brian de Bois-Guilbert was the fittest knight to do battle for the Holy Order. To him, accordingly, the glove of Rebecca was handed; and the Jewess was commanded to find a champion by the third day following. It was further intimated to her that should she fail to do so, or if her champion should be discomfited, she should die the death of a sorceress, according to doom.

Being granted permission to communicate with her father, she hastily wrote a few lines in Hebrew to him, imploring him to seek out Wilfred, the son of Cedric, and let him know that she was in sore need of a champion. As it fortuned, the messenger who did her errand had not far to go before he met Isaac of York.

The poor old man, on learning his daughter's terrible condition, was quite overcome; but, cheered in some measure by the kindly words of a rabbi who was with him, he determined, weak and feverish though he was, to make a last effort for the child he loved so dearly. And having said farewell the two Jews parted, Isaac to seek out Ivanhoe, and the rabbi to go to York to look for other assistance.

In the twilight of the day of her trial, if it could be called such, a low knock was heard at the door of Rebecca's prison- chamber; and shortly after Brian de Bois-Guilbert entered the apartment.

She drew back in terror at the sight of the man who had been the cause of all her misfortunes; but he bade her not to be afraid. He had come, he said, to tell her that he was prepared to refuse to do battle for the Templars against her and sacrifice his name and honour as a member of the Holy Order, and that he would leave the preceptory, appear in three days in disguise, and himself be her champion against any knight who should confront him, on one condition: that she should accept him as a lover.

Rebecca listened to his words, and then with scorn refused his offer.

"So be it then, proud damsel," said Bois-Guilbert; "thou hast thyself decided thine own fate. I shall appear in the lists against thy champion, and know that there lives not the knight who may cope with me alone save Richard Coeur-de-Lion and his minion Ivanhoe. Ivanhoe, as thou well knowest, is unable to bear his corslet, and Richard is in a foreign prison. Farewell." And so saying the Templar left the apartment.

Pending this time, so full of terror and anxiety for poor Rebecca, the Black Knight, having left the company of the generous outlaw, held his way to a neighbouring religious house to which the wounded Ivanhoe had been removed when the castle was taken. Here he remained for the night; and the following day he set out for Coningsburgh to attend the obsequies of the deceased Athelstane, Wamba alone being his companion.

They had ridden together for some distance when the quick eye of the jester caught sight of some men in armour concealed in a brake not far from where they were.

Almost immediately after three arrows were discharged from the suspected spot, one of which glanced off the visor of the Black Knight.

"Let us close with them," said the knight, and he rode straight to the thicket. He was met by six or seven men-at-arms, who ran against him with their lances at full career. Three of the weapons struck against him, and splintered with as little effect as if they had been driven against a tower of steel.

The attacking party then drew their swords and assailed him on every side. But many as they were to one they had met their match; and a man reeled and fell at every blow delivered by the Black Knight. His opponents, desperate as they were, now bore back from his deadly blows, and it seemed as if the terror of his single strength was about to gain the battle against such odds when a knight in blue armour, who had kept himself behind the other assailants, spurred forward with his lance, and taking aim, not at the rider but at the steed, wounded the noble animal mortally.

"That was a felon stroke!" exclaimed the Black Knight, as the horse fell to the earth bearing his rider along with him.

At this moment Wamba winded the outlaw's bugle, which he had been given to carry. The sudden sound made the murderers bear back once more, and Wamba did not hesitate to rush in and assist his knight to rise.

"Shame on ye, false cowards!" exclaimed he in the blue harness; "do ye fly from the empty blast of a horn blown by a jester?"

Animated by his words, they attacked the Black Knight anew, whose best refuge was now to place his back against an oak, and defend himself with his sword. The felon knight, who had taken another spear, watching the moment when his formidable antagonist was most closely pressed, galloped against him in hopes to nail him with his lance against the tree; but Wamba, springing forward in good time, checked the fatal career of the Blue Knight, by hamstringing his horse with a stroke of his sword; and horse and man went heavily to the ground. Almost immediately after, a band of yeomen, headed by Locksley, broke forth from the glade, who, joining manfully in the fray, soon disposed of the ruffians, all of whom lay on the spot dead, or mortally wounded.

The visor of the Blue Knight, who still lay entangled under his wounded steed, was now opened, and the features of Waldemar Fitzurse were disclosed.

"Stand back, my masters," said the Black Knight to those about him; "I would speak with this man alone. And now, Waldemar Fitzurse, say me the truth: confess who set thee on this traitorous deed."

"Richard," answered the fallen knight, "it was thy father's son."

Richard's eyes sparkled with indignation, but his better nature overcame it. "Take thy life unasked," he said; "but, on this condition, that in three days thou shalt leave England, and that thou wilt never mention the name of John of Anjou as connected with thy felony." Then, turning to where the yeomen stood apart, he said, "Let this knight have a steed, Locksley, and let him depart unharmed. Thou bearest an English heart, and must needs obey me. I am Richard of England!"

At these words the yeomen kneeled down before him, tendering their allegiance, while they implored pardon for their offences.

"Rise, my friends," said Richard. "Your misdemeanours have been atoned by the loyal services you rendered my distressed subjects before the walls of Torquilstone, and the rescue you have this day afforded your sovereign. Arise, my liegemen, and be good subjects in future. And thou, brave Locksley—"

"Call me no longer Locksley, my liege," said the outlaw; "I am Robin Hood of Sherwood Forest."

Before many more minutes had gone a sylvan repast was hastily prepared beneath a huge oak-tree for the King of England. Amongst those who partook of the forest hospitality of the outlaws were Ivanhoe and Gurth, who just then came on the scene, the former now all but cured of his wound, thanks to the healing balsam with which he had been provided by Rebecca the Jewess.

When the feast was concluded, the king, attended by Ivanhoe, Wamba, and Gurth, proceeded on his way to Coningsburgh. As the travellers approached the ancient Saxon fortress, they could see the huge black banner floating from the top of the tower, which announced that the obsequies of the late owner were still in the act of being solemnized. All around the castle was a scene of busy commotion, the whole countryside being gathered from far and near to partake of the funeral banquet. Cooks and mendicants, strolling soldiers from Palestine, pedlars, mechanics, wandering palmers, hedge-priests, Saxon minstrels and Welsh bards, together with jesters and jugglers, formed a motley and hungry gathering, such as could only be seen on the occasion which now brought them together; and through this riotous crowd Richard and his followers with difficulty made their way.

As they entered the apartment where Cedric sat, Ivanhoe muffled his face in his mantle. Upon the entrance of Richard, the Saxon arose gravely to bid him welcome. Having greeted him and his friends with the mournful ceremony suited to the occasion, Cedric led his knightly guest to another apartment, where he was about to leave him, when the Black Knight took his hand.

"I crave to remind you, noble thane," he said, "that when we last parted you promised to grant me a boon."

"It is granted ere named, noble knight," said Cedric, still unaware that he was speaking to the king.

"Know me, then, from henceforth," said the Black Knight, "as Richard Plantagenet; the boon I crave is that thou wilt forgive and receive to thy paternal affection this good knight here, Wilfred of Ivanhoe."

"And this is Wilfred!" said Cedric, pointing to his son.

"My father! my father!" said Ivanhoe, prostrating himself at Cedric's feet, "grant me thy forgiveness!"

"Thou hast it, my son," said Cedric, raising him up. But he had scarce uttered the words when the door flew open, and Athelstane, arrayed in the garments of the grave, stood before them, pale, haggard, and like something arisen from the dead.

The effect of this apparition on the persons present was utterly appalling. Cedric started back in amazement. Ivanhoe crossed himself, repeating prayers in Saxon, Latin, and Norman-French, while Richard alternately said "*Benedicite*" and swore, "*Mort de ma vie!*"

"In the name of God," said Cedric, starting back, "if thou art mortal, speak! Living or dead, noble Athelstane, speak to Cedric!"

"I will," said the spectre, "when I have collected breath. Alive, saidst thou? I am as much alive as he can be who has fed on bread and water for three days. I went down under the Templar's sword, stunned, indeed, but unwounded, for the blade struck me flatlings, being averted by the good mace with which I warded the blow. Others, of both sides, were beaten down and slaughtered above me, so that I never recovered my senses until I found myself in a coffin—an open one, by good luck—placed before the altar in church."

Having concluded his story, still breathless with excitement, he looked about him. He had caught a glimpse of Ivanhoe as he first came into the apartment, but had lost sight of him owing to the crowd of eager listeners by which the room was now thronged. Filled with a spirit of generosity to his rival, he took the hand of Rowena, who stood beside him, and was about to place it in that of Ivanhoe, when it was found that Wilfred had vanished from the room.

It was at length discovered that a Jew had been to seek the knight, and that, after a very brief conference, he had called for Gurth and his armour, and had left the castle. King Richard was also gone, and no one knew whither.

Meanwhile, the tiltyard of the Preceptory of Templestowe was prepared for the combat which should decide the life or death of Rebecca. As the hour approached which was to determine the fate of the unfortunate Jewess, a vast multitude had gathered to witness a spectacle even in that age but seldom seen.

At one end of the lists arose the throne of the Grand Master, surrounded with seats for the preceptors and the knights of the Order, over which floated the sacred standard of the Templars.

At the opposite end was a pile of faggots, so arranged around a stake, deeply fixed in the ground, as to leave a space for the victim whom they were destined to consume. Close by stood four black slaves, whose colour and African features, then so little known in England, appalled the multitude, who gazed on them as demons.

Soon the slow and sullen sounds of the great church bell chilled with awe the hearts of the assembled crowd; and before long the Grand Master, preceded by a stately retinue, approached his throne. Behind him came Brian de Bois-Guilbert, armed cap-a-pie in bright armour, but looking ghastly pale. A long procession followed, and next a guard of warders on foot, in sable livery, amidst whom might be seen the pale form of the accused maiden. All her ornaments had been removed, and a coarse white dress, of the simplest form, had been substituted for her Oriental garments; yet there was such an exquisite mixture of courage and resignation in her look that even in this garb, and with no other ornament than her long black tresses, each eye wept that looked upon her.

The unfortunate Jewess was conducted to a black chair placed near the pile; and soon after a loud and long flourish of trumpets announced that the court were seated for judgment.

There was a dead pause of many minutes.

"No champion appears for the appellant," said the Grand Master.

Another pause succeeded; and then the knights whispered to each other that it was time to declare the pledge of Rebecca forfeited. At this instant a knight, urging his horse to speed, appeared on the plain advancing towards the lists. A hundred voices exclaimed, "A champion! A champion!" and amidst a ringing cheer the knight rode into the tilt-yard, although his horse appeared to reel from fatigue.

To the summons of the herald, who demanded his rank, his name, and purpose, the stranger answered, raising his helmet as he spoke, "I am Wilfred of Ivanhoe."

"I will not fight with thee at present," said Bois-Guilbert. "Get thy wounds healed."

"Ha! proud Templar," said Ivanhoe, "hast thou forgotten that twice didst thou fall before this lance? I will proclaim thee a coward in every court in Europe unless thou do battle without farther delay."

"Dog of a Saxon!" said the Templar, "take thy lance, and prepare for the death thou hast drawn upon thee!"

At once each champion took his place, the trumpets sounded, and the knights charged each other in full career. The wearied horse of Ivanhoe, and its no less exhausted rider, went down, as all had expected, before the well-aimed lance and vigorous steed of the Templar. But although the spear of Ivanhoe did but touch the shield of Bois-Guilbert, that champion, to the astonishment of all who beheld it, reeled in his saddle, lost his stirrups, and fell in the lists.

Ivanhoe was soon on foot, hastening to mend his fortune with his sword; but his antagonist arose not. Wilfred, placing his foot on his breast, and the sword's point to his throat, commanded him to yield him, or die on the spot. Bois-Guilbert returned no answer.

"Slay him not, sir knight," cried the Grand Master. "We allow him vanquished."

He descended into the lists, and commanded them to unhelm the conquered champion. His eyes were closed; the dark red flush was still on his brow. As they looked on him in astonishment the eyes opened, but they were fixed and glazed. The flush passed from his brow, and gave way to the pallid hue of death.

Unscathed by the lance of his enemy, he had died a victim to the violence of his own contending passions.

"This is indeed the judgment of God," said the Grand Master, looking upwards; "Thy will be done!"

Turning then to Wilfred of Ivanhoe, he said, "I pronounce the maiden free and guiltless. The arms and the body of the deceased knight are at the will of the victor."

His further speech was interrupted by a clattering of horses' feet, and the Black Knight, followed by a numerous band of men- at-arms, galloped into the lists.

At a glance he saw how matters stood. "Bohun," he said, addressing one of his attendant knights, "do thine office."

The officer stepped forward, and, laying his hand on the shoulder of Albert de Malvoisin, said, "I arrest thee of high treason."

"Who dares to arrest a Knight of the Temple in my presence?" said the Grand Master; "and by whose authority is this bold outrage offered?"

"By my authority," said the king, raising his visor, "and by the order of Richard Plantagenet who stands before you."

While he spoke the royal standard of England was seen to float over the towers of the preceptory instead of the Temple banner; and before long the followers of the king were in complete possession of the entire castle.

Meanwhile Rebecca, giddy and almost senseless at the rapid change of circumstances, was locked in the arms of her aged father; and shortly after the two retreated hurriedly from the lists.

Not many days passed before the nuptials of Wilfred and the fair Rowena were celebrated in the noble minster of York, attended by the king in person.

On the second morning after this happy bridal Rebecca was shown into the apartment of the Lady of Ivanhoe. She had come, she said, to pay the debt of gratitude which she owed to Wilfred, and to ask his wife to transmit to him her grateful farewell. She prayed that God might bless their union, and, as she rose to leave, she handed Rowena a casket filled with most precious jewels. "Accept them, lady," she said; "to me they are valueless; I will never wear jewels more. My father and I, we are going to a far country where at least we shall dwell in liberty. He to whom I dedicate my future life will be my Comforter if I do His will. Say this to thy lord should he chance to inquire after the fate of her whose life he saved." She then hastened to bid Rowena adieu, and glided from the apartment.

Wilfred lived long and happily with his bride, for they were attached to each other by the bonds of early affection, and they loved each other the more from the recollection of the obstacles which had so long impeded their union.

GUY MANNERING

Retold by Sir Edward Sullivan

The Castle of Ellangowan was an old and massive structure, situated by the seashore in the southwestern part of Scotland. It had been for many years the dwelling-place of a family named Bertram, each of whom had in succession borne the title of the Laird of Ellangowan. They had once been people of wealth and importance in the neighbourhood; but through lack of prudence and other misfortunes, they had, one after another, lost much of the greatness and prosperity which had belonged to them in better days. One of their number became at last so poor that he could no longer maintain the old family residence; so he contented himself with occupying a much smaller house which he had himself built, from the windows of which he could still look out on the ancient abode of his forefathers, as it dwindled year by year to the condition of a neglected ruin.

At the time that our story commences, one Godfrey Bertram was the Laird of Ellangowan, and the owner of the now diminished estates. He was a good-tempered, easy-going kind of man, and became, in consequence, very popular with all the poorer people of the district, and especially with the gipsies, a large number of whom were at all times to be found in the neighbourhood.

His wife had brought him a little money when he married; and he and she continued to lead a quiet and not unhappy life in their new home. Amongst Mr. Bertram's most intimate companions in his retirement was one Abel Sampson, a tall and awkward-looking man, with a harsh voice and huge feet, who was known to the people around as "the dominie." He was a man who spoke but little, and generally used very long words when he did; but he had a kindly and good-natured heart. He was for a time the parish schoolmaster at the village of Kippletringan, which was close to Ellangowan, and was employed now and then as a kind of clerk by the laird.

The village of Kippletringan was situated a little distance from the sea; and although the neighbourhood was dignified by the possession of a customhouse, the place was still the favourite haunt of a large body of desperate and determined smugglers, who, it was supposed, were assisted by many of the small shopkeepers of the locality in disposing of the contraband goods which were surreptitiously brought from foreign parts.

One cloudy November evening, a young traveller, Guy Mannering by name, just come from the University of Oxford, was making his way with difficulty over the wild and lonely moorland which extended for many miles on the outskirts of the village. He had lost the road to Kippletringan, whither he was bound, but was lucky enough to find a guide to conduct him there before he had gone completely astray; and late at night he arrived at Godfrey Bertram's house, where he was hospitably welcomed by the owner. Supper was got ready, a good bottle of wine was opened, and the laird and the dominic and Guy Mannering were enjoying themselves comfortably, when the conversation was interrupted by the shrill voice of someone coming upstairs.

"It's Meg Merrilies, the gipsy, as sure as I'm a sinner," said Mr. Bertram; and, as the door opened, a tall woman, full six feet high, with weather-beaten features and hair as black as midnight, stepped into the room.

Her appearance was altogether of so strange a kind, that it made Mannering start. After some conversation with the laird, the gipsy woman informed him that she had come to tell the fortune of his little son, who was born that night, and asked to be told the exact hour of his birth.

Now Guy Mannering himself, amongst other accomplishments, possessed a knowledge of the stars; and on learning the time at which young Bertram was born, he went outside to study the heavens, with a view to foretelling what the future of the child would be.

The sky had become beautifully clear, for the rising wind had swept away the clouds with which it had been previously overcast, and the observer was enabled to note carefully the positions of the principal planets, from which he made out that three periods of the infant's life would be attended by great danger to him, namely, his fifth, his tenth, and his twenty-first year.

On the morning following, Mannering strolled out towards the old castle, thinking to himself whether he should tell Mr. Bertram what he had learned from the stars respecting his young son's future life. The castle was merely a ruin at this time, and as he wandered amidst the gloomy remnants of the ancient structure, his attention was arrested by the voice of the gipsy whom he had seen the night before. He soon found an opening in one of the walls through which he could observe Meg Merrilies without himself being seen.

She was sitting on a broken stone, in a strange, wild dress, and engaged in spinning a thread drawn from wool of three different colours. She was at the same time half singing and half muttering a kind of charm, which seemed to have reference to the child which had been born the night before; and as she finished, Mannering heard her murmur something about the thread of life being three times broken and three times mended, and distinctly heard her say: "He'll be a lucky lad an he win through wi't." [Footnote: "He will be a lucky lad if he lives through it."]

He was about to speak to the gipsy, when he heard a hoarse voice calling to her in angry tones from outside, and in a moment after, a man, who was apparently a sea-captain, came in to where Meg Merrilies was seated.

He was short in height, but prodigiously muscular, strong, and thick-set, with a surly and savage scowl upon his unpleasant features. He spoke with a foreign accent, and upbraided the gipsy for keeping him waiting so long, ordering her, with a curse, to come and bless his ship before it set out on its voyage. While still addressing the gipsy, he caught sight of Guy Mannering, and was about to draw a weapon against him, when she told him that he was a friend of Mr. Bertram's. He then introduced himself to Mannering, and said his name was Dirck Hatteraick, the captain of the vessel that was lying off the shore. Mannering wished him good-day shortly after, and as he saw him embarking in a small boat, he was convinced, from his conversation and appearance, that the captain was a smuggler.

On returning to the new house at Ellangowan, Mannering learned from Mr. Bertram that this Dirck Hatteraick was the terror of all the excise and custom-house cruisers, with which he had had many a fierce fight.

Before Guy Mannering took his departure from Ellangowan, Mr. Bertram asked him the result of his studying the stars on the preceding night, and, in reply, was handed a paper by Mannering, which he was told he should keep in a sealed envelope for five whole years.

When the visitor had gone, Mrs. Bertram, the mother of the baby boy, was very anxious to read the paper, for she was a superstitious lady; but after a struggle with her curiosity, she contented herself with making a small velvet bag, into which she sewed the paper, and the whole was then hung as a charm round the neck of her young child.

Time rolled on, and when little Harry Bertram grew to be four years old, he was already a great favourite with Dominie Sampson, who had acted as his tutor and was his constant companion. But just about this time the Laird of Ellangowan was appointed one of the magistrates of the county; and shortly after his appointment he began, little by little, to become very unpopular with the gipsies, with whom he had before been such a favourite. He thought it his duty now to punish and exterminate all amongst them who were poachers and trespassers, and caused even the poor beggars at his door to be sent to the workhouse.

One tribe of these gipsies, amongst whom Meg Merrilies was a kind of queen, had lived for a long time unmolested in a few huts in a glen upon the estate of Ellangowan, at a place called Derncleugh. It was a miserable and squalid village, but for all that Mr. Bertram was determined to evict them and all their poor belongings. He was no doubt doing as the law directed him, but, as far as concerned the inhabitants of Derncleugh, he was acting with great harshness, for Meg Merrilies had all along shown a strong affection for his boy, little Harry Bertram.

The day of eviction came at length, and a large body of men under the direction of Frank Kennedy, a custom-house officer, made their way to the miserable village, and on the gipsies refusing to leave peaceably, proceeded to unroof their cottages and pull down the wretched doors and windows. There was no resistance, and when the work was ended, the now homeless tribe gathered together the remnants of their property, and set forth with sullen and revengeful thoughts to look for a new settlement.

Mr. Bertram had been some distance from home on the day of the eviction; but on returning in the evening he met the troop of gipsies. Some of the men muttered angry remarks as he passed them on the road, but he thought it best to make no answer. Meg Merrilies had, however, lagged behind the rest, and was standing alone on a high bank above the road as the laird went by. Her dress was even stranger than usual, and her black hair hung loose about her, while her dark eyes flashed angrily. She had a light sapling in her hand, and as the laird looked up to where she stood, she said to him:

"Ride your ways, Laird of Ellangowan! ride your ways, Godfrey Bertram! This day have ye quenched seven smoking hearths — see if your own fire burn the blither for that. Ye have riven the roof off seven cottar houses — look if your own roof-tree stand the faster. Ride your ways, Godfrey Bertram! what do ye glower after our folk for? There's thirty hearts there that would have spent their life-blood ere ye had scratched your finger. Yes, there's thirty yonder, from the old wife of an hundred to the babe that was born last week, that ye have turned out o' their houses, to sleep with the black-cock in the moors! Ride your ways, Ellan- gowan! Our bairns are hanging at our weary backs; look that your braw cradle at home be the fairer spread up. Not that I am wishing ill to little Harry, God forbid! So ride your way, for these are the last words ye'll ever hear Meg Merrilies speak, and this is the last twig that I'll ever cut in the bonny woods of Ellangowan."

And having uttered this dark and threatening speech, she turned contemptuously from him, to join her comrades in misfortune.

Meanwhile, the smugglers under their captain, Dirck Hatteraick, had been carrying on their lawless trade as usual, and the Laird of Ellangowan was as determined to put them down as he had been to get rid of the gipsies. He was actively assisted in his endeavours against them by the same Frank Kennedy who had carried out the eviction of Meg Merrilies and her companions, and the smugglers had sworn to be revenged upon their enemy.

On the day that young Harry Bertram was five years old, Dirck Hatteraick's ship was in the bay outside the village of Kippletringan. A sloop of war in the king's service was pursuing it in order to seize the smuggled goods which were on board, when Frank Kennedy, looking out, saw that Hatteraick was likely to escape, as he had got his vessel round a headland called Warroch Point, where it was concealed from the sloop, unless someone went down to the Point and made a signal to the pursuers.

He accordingly mounted his horse and galloped off. On his way he happened to meet little Bertram, who was walking with the dominie, and as he had often promised to give the child a ride, he took him up on his nag, and rode off towards the Point.

Shortly afterwards the discharges of several cannon were heard, and after an interval a still louder explosion, as of a vessel blown up.

As evening came on, Mr. and Mrs. Bertram were expecting little Harry to come home, and as he did not return, became very uneasy about him. After waiting for him in anxiety for some time, the news came in that Kennedy's horse had come back riderless to its stable.

All was now bustle at Ellangowan. The laird and his servants rushed away to the wood of Warroch; but they searched long and in vain for any trace of Kennedy or the boy. It was already growing dark, when a shrill and piercing shout was heard from the sea-shore under the wood, and on hurrying to the place, Mr. Bertram was horrified to see the dead body of Frank Kennedy lying on the beach, right under a high precipice of rocks.

In his wild dismay and terror for his child, and remembering the words of Meg Merrilies, the laird hurried away to Derncleugh, hoping to get some news of him from any of the gipsies who might still be lingering round the place. He wandered amongst the ruins of the cottages, where he found no one, although he noticed the remains of a fire in one of the huts. After a little, one of his servants came running to him and told him to come home at once — that Mrs. Bertram was dying. Half stupefied, he went back; but only to find that his wife was dead, that a little daughter had been born to him, and that his boy was gone.

The sheriff of the county arrived next morning and opened an inquiry. The wood was again searched, with the result that traces of a struggle were found near the top of the cliff, over the place where Kennedy's body was found lying. Footprints of men and of a small boy were seen here and there.

Witnesses who were examined said that they had seen the smuggler's ship grounding, and taking fire, and finally blowing up with a great explosion; but no one could say what had become of its crew. The gipsies were suspected, and Meg Merrilies was arrested; but when questioned she denied that she had been at the place. They found, however, a cut upon her arm; and on removing the handkerchief with which she had it bounda it was found to be marked with the name of Harry Bertram.

No further evidence could be procured of her guilt, and she was at length set free, under sentence of banishment from the county.

For many years after this Mr. Bertram continued to live a solitary and mournful life at Ellangowan. The poor dominie never ceased to blame himself for the loss of the boy, as Harry was in his charge on the day on which he had disappeared; but he still lived with the laird as before, and was chiefly employed in teaching Bertram's daughter, little Lucy, who was now growing up into a gentle and bonny girl.

The laird had been always a bad man of business, and after his wife's death he got into the hands of a scheming and dishonest attorney named Glossin, who in the end craftily succeeded in making himself rich at the expense of his employer.

The debts of the laird became at length so many that the property at Ellangowan had to be mortgaged, and things ultimately went so badly with the poor owner, that the men to whom he owed so much money determined to insist on the estate being sold, together with the house and all the furniture.

It was rumoured, too, amongst the country-folk that Glossin was the man, of all others, who was most eager to turn the Bertrams out of their house, in order that he might buy the property himself, and become the Laird of Ellangowan.

Now the property in Ellangowan had been what is called "settled" in such a way that it could not be sold if Mr. Bertram had a son living. It was therefore likely to be disposed of very cheap, as no one knew for certain that young Bertram was dead; while if he should happen to be alive, there was still a chance of his coming back and claiming the estates.

When Glossin, the attorney, found that there was no more to be got out of his client in the way of money, he commenced openly to show the wickedness of his bad and cruel nature; and the very sight of him became hateful to the unhappy Godfrey Bertram.

So things went on until Lucy Bertram was seventeen years old, and her father had become a weak and poor old man, and then Glossin determined to play his last card.

The estates of Ellangowan were advertised to be sold to the highest bidder, and a day was fixed for the auction.

Before describing how the sale took place, it will be necessary to tell something of Guy Mannering, who, as will be remembered, had left Ellangowan shortly after the day that young Harry Bertram was born.

He became a soldier; and having served for a long time in India, was appointed colonel of his regiment. His wife and daughter were with him there, and they had become very intimate with a young officer in the same regiment, called Vanbeest Brown, who, it was supposed, had came from Holland, where he had previously been engaged in trade of some kind. Colonel Mannering, for some reason, never cared for Brown, but chiefly because he had foolishly listened to the dishonourable suggestions of a friend, who, for reasons of his own, had secretly poisoned his mind against the young officer. The dislike ripened after some time into an open quarrel, followed by a duel between the colonel and his subaltern, in which, after exchanging shots, Mannering believed he killed his adversary. Mrs. Mannering died shortly after, and the colonel and his daughter returned to England.

Now it so happened that Colonel Mannering arrived at the village of Kippletringan a day or two before the time at which the sale of Ellangowan was to take place. He was much distressed at hearing the pitiable account that was given to him of his old friend, Godfrey Bertram; and the idea at once occurred to him that he would buy the property himself, and by doing so help the laird.

Accordingly, on the day of the auction, he made his way to Ellangowan House, where he was told, on inquiry, that the old laird was dangerously ill, and was to be found up at the ruined castle in company with his daughter. Thither Colonel Mannering went to look for him. He found old Mr. Bertram sitting in an easy- chair on the slope beside the castle with his feet wrapped in blankets, and beside him his daughter and the dominie, and a handsome young man whom he did not recognise, but who, he afterwards learned, was a gentleman called Charles Hazlewood, who was deeply in love with Miss Bertram.

Mannering was much affected when the old laird failed to remember him, for he had not forgotten his hospitable kindness many years before, on the night when little Harry was born. While he was engaged in conversation with Miss Bertram and her companion, a voice was heard close by, which Lucy at once recognised as that of her father's enemy, Glossin, and she sent the dominie to keep him away. The sound of the voice had, however, also reached the old man's ears. He started up on hearing it, and turning towards Glossin, he addressed him in tones of passion and indignation.

"Out of my sight, ye viper," he said; "ye frozen viper that I warmed till ye stung me! Are ye not afraid that the walls of my father's dwelling should fall and crush ye, limb and bone? Were ye not friendless, houseless, penniless, when I took ye by the hand; and are ye not expelling me—me, and that innocent girl— friendless, houseless, and penniless, from the house that has sheltered us and ours for a thousand years?"

A few moments after, the carriage was announced, in which Lucy Bertram and her father were to leave their home; but it was no longer necessary. The old Laird of Ellangowan was so exhausted by his last effort of indignant anger, that when he sunk upon his chair, he expired almost without a struggle or a groan.

The sale of the property was then postponed until after the funeral; and Colonel Mannering, having done what he could for Miss Bertram in her unhappy condition, left the neighbourhood with the intention of returning in time for the adjourned sale, for the purpose of buying the estate.

The appointed hour for the auction at length arrived, but Colonel Mannering had not come back. No one had even received a letter from him; and in his absence, as there was no other bidder, the infamous Glossin was declared to be the lawful purchaser, and a new Laird of Ellangowan.

At six o'clock that night a drunken post-boy reached the village with a letter from the colonel, containing instructions to buy the property. It had been delayed on its way, and was now no longer of any use.

Poor Lucy Bertram now found herself an orphan without house or home; but the kindness of some neighbours named Mac-Morlan, to some extent, assuaged the misery of her position. They insisted on her coming to live with them and Mr. Mac-Morlan even offered the dominie a clerkship in his establishment, where he might still be near his lady pupil, to whom, in spite of his strange and awkward ways, he was devotedly attached for her father's sake.

When Colonel Mannering, after the death of Mr. Bertram, left Ellangowan with the intention of coming back to buy the property, he travelled some distance, and after a while came to a post-town where he expected some letters. He received one letter, which displeased him very much, from a great friend of his who was living in the north of England, Mr. Mervyn by name, in whose care he had left his daughter, Julia Mannering, when he was starting for Kippletringan. This letter informed him that Miss Mannering was being serenaded at night from the lake beside the house by some unknown stranger, who had, however, disappeared before the letter was written.

On reading this intelligence the colonel hastened at once to Mr. Mervyn's residence, having first sent off the instructions in reference to the purchase of the Ellangowan estate which, as already said, arrived too late.

The lover who had been serenading Julia Mannering was in reality, the same Vanbeest Brown whom she had known in India, and with whom her father had fought the duel. Colonel Mannering had, however, no idea that Brown was still alive, and the daughter was afraid to tell her father that he was. Captain Brown, as he was now known, was a handsome and gallant young fellow; and, having returned to England with his regiment, and being still deeply devoted to Miss Mannering, he had lost no time in making his way to where she was staying in the house of Mr. Mervyn, her father's friend.

When Mannering arrived at Mr. Mervyn's, he said very little about the information which had been the cause of his return; but he told his daughter that he had taken a place near Kippletringan, called Woodbourne, where he meant to reside for some time. He also told her that she would have a pleasant companion in Lucy Bertram, the daughter of an old friend of his, who was going to stay with them in his new house.

Accordingly, as soon as Woodbourne was made ready to receive them, the colonel and his daughter Julia took up their residence there, and Lucy Bertram became their guest. Another inmate of the new house was the dominie, for whom Colonel Mannering had a liking, and who, he knew, could not bear to be parted altogether from Miss Bertram, whose tutor he had been from her earliest days. When the poor half-cracked dominie heard that he was to be employed as Colonel Mannering's librarian, his joy knew no bounds; and on seeing the large number of old books which were committed to his charge he became almost crazy with delight, and shouted his favourite word, "Pro-di-gi-ous!" till the roof rung to his raptures.

After a little time Lucy Bertram and Miss Mannering became fast friends, but the latter was careful never to say anything to her new companion about her lover, Captain Brown.

Now, Brown, when he found that Julia Mannering had gone to Woodbourne, determined to follow her, with the purpose of resuming his addresses, and he accordingly set out on foot towards the North.

It was a fine clear frosty winter's day when he found himself in the wilds of Cumberland on his way to his destination in Scotland. He had walked for some distance, when he stopped at a small public-house to procure refreshment. He here fell in with a farmer named Dandie Dinmont, a big, rollicking fellow, with an honest face and kindly ways, with whom he became friends in a very little time.

There was another person, however, in the inn on whom Brown could not avoid repeatedly fixing his eyes—a tall, witch-like woman. It was Meg Merrilies the gipsy; but time had grizzled her raven locks, and added many wrinkles to her wild features. As he looked at her, he could not help saying to himself: "Have I dreamed of such a figure?"

As he was asking himself the question, the gipsy suddenly made two strides towards him and seized his hand, at the same time saying to him:

"In God's name, young man, tell me your name, and whence you come!"

"My name is Brown, mother, and I come from the East Indies," he answered.

On hearing his answer she dropped his hand with a sigh, and said:

"It cannot be, then—it cannot be; but be what ye will, ye have a face and a tongue that puts me in mind of old times." As Brown took his departure on foot, the gipsy looked after him and muttered to herself: "I maun [Footnote: I must.] see that lad again."

The traveller had gone a considerable distance across the lonely moorland through which his road lay, when his little dog Wasp began to bark furiously at something in front of them. Brown quickened his pace, and soon caught sight of the subject of the terrier's alarm. In a hollow, a little below him, was his late companion Dandie Dinmont, engaged with two other men in a desperate struggle. In a moment Brown, who was both strong and active, came to the rescue; and, after a short fight, the two would-be murderers of the farmer were flying for their own lives across the heath, pursued by Wasp. Dinmont then took his friend upon his pony, and they succeeded after some time in reaching Charlie's Hope, the farmer's home, where they were welcomed by his wife and a large troop of children.

The next few days were spent salmon spearing, and hunting otters on the hills in the neighbourhood. One of the huntsmen, of whom there were a large number out, was a dark-featured man, resembling a gipsy in his appearance; and Brown noticed that whenever he approached him he endeavoured to hide his face. He could not remember, however, having ever seen the man before; but he learned, on asking about him, that he was a stranger in those parts, who had come from the south-west of Scotland, and that his name was Gabriel. Nothing further was known about him at Charlie's Hope.

Brown's visit to Dandie Dinmont was now at an end, and he again took the road for Woodbourne, the residence of Julia Mannering.

He had hired a chaise and horses, but had not gone far on the wild road to Kippletringan when night came on and the snow fell heavily; and shortly after, to make matters worse, the driver missed the way. When the horses were unable to proceed any further, Brown dismounted from the carriage in order to look for a house where he could ask the way; and as he wandered through the plantations which skirted the road, he saw a light in the distance amongst the trees. After traversing a deep and dangerous glen, he reached the house from which the light shone. It was an old and ruinous building. Before approaching the door, he peeped in through an aperture in the ruined wall, and saw in the room inside the figure of a man, stretched on a straw bed, with a blanket thrown over it. He could see that the man was dying. A woman clad in a long cloak was sitting by the bedside, and moistening at times the lips of the man with some liquid. She was singing a low monotonous strain.

She paused in her singing, and Brown heard a few deep groans come from the dying man.

"It will not be," she muttered to herself. "He cannot pass away with that on his mind; I must open the door."

Brown stood before her as she opened the door, and he at once recognised the same gipsy woman whom he had met in the inn a few days before. He noticed, too, that there was a roll of linen about the dying man's head, which was deeply stained with blood.

"Wretched woman, who has done this?" exclaimed Brown.

And the gipsy answered: "They that were permitted;" and she added after a few moments, "He's dead now."

Sounds of voices at a distance were now heard. "They are coming," said she to Brown; "you are a dead man." He was about to rush out, when the gipsy seized him with a strong grasp. "Here," she said, "here, be still, and you are safe; stir not, whatever you see or hear, and nothing shall befall you!"

She made him lie down among a parcel of straw, and covered him carefully; and then resumed her song.

Brown, though a soldier and a brave one, was terrified as he lay in his hiding-place. Peeping out through the straw, he saw five rough-looking men come in who seemed to be gipsies and sailors. They closed round the fire and commenced to drink, holding consultation together in a strange gibberish which he could not altogether understand. Whenever the gipsy woman addressed them, she spoke angrily to them; and more than once she called them murderers; they, however, did not seem to mind her.

They continued drinking and talking for a considerable time, but all that Brown could make out was that there was someone whom they were going to murder. They also referred to a murder committed some twenty years before, in which their dead companion had had a hand.

After some time spent in this way, one of the party went out and brought in a portmanteau, which Brown at once recognised as the one he had left in the chaise. They ripped it open, and after examining the contents, which included all the owner's ready money, with the exception of a trifling sum in his pocket, they divided the whole amongst them. Then they drank more; and it was not until morning that they left the building. When they left, they carried the dead body with them.

No sooner were they well outside, than Meg Merrilies got up from where she had been pretending to be asleep, and told Brown to follow her instantly. Brown obeyed with alacrity, feeling that he was already out of reach of danger when the villains had gone out; but before leaving he took up a cutlass belonging to one of the five, and brought it with him in the belief that he might yet have to fight with them for his life. The snow lay on the ground as he and the gipsy came out, and as he followed her he noticed that she chose the track the men had taken, so that her footprints might not be seen.

After a while, however, she turned from the track, and led the way up a steep and rugged path under the snow-laden trees, and on reaching a place some distance farther on, she pointed out the direction of Kippletringan, and told her companion to make what speed he could. Brown was entirely at a loss to make out the reason the gipsy had for taking such an interest in preserving his life from her comrades; and was even more puzzled by her conduct when she took an old purse from her pocket before parting, and gave it to him.

She said as she handed it to him: "Many's the alms your house has given Meg and hers." And Brown, as he thanked her for her kindness, asked her how he could repay the money she had given him.

"I have two boons to crave," answered the gipsy, speaking low and hastily: "one is that you will never speak of what you have seen this night; the other, that when I next call for you, be it in church or market, at wedding or at burial, meal-time or fasting, that ye leave everything else and come with me."

"That will do you little good, mother," answered Brown.

"But 'twill do yourself much good," replied Meg Merrilies. "I know what I am asking, and I know it has been the will of God to preserve you in strange dangers, and that I shall be the means to set you in your father's seat again. So give your promise, and mind that you owe your life to me this blessed night."

When Brown had promised, she parted from him, and was soon out of sight.

The young soldier could come to no other conclusion but that the woman was mad; and having in this way solved the mystery to his own satisfaction, he strode quickly on through the wood in search of the highroad to Kippletringan.

He reached the village at length, and engaged a room at the Gordon Arms, a comfortable inn kept by a Mrs. Mac-Candlish. On opening the purse which the gipsy had given him, he was astonished to find that it contained money and jewels worth about a hundred pounds. He accordingly entrusted it to the landlady of the inn for safe keeping.

The day after his arrival at the village of Kippletringan, he determined to see Miss Mannering; and learning that she was likely to be found with a party of skaters on a lake in the neighbourhood, he proceeded in that direction.

The skating party, of whom Julia Mannering was one, consisted of herself and Lucy Bertram, and young Charles Hazlewood, who, as before mentioned, was Miss Bertram's lover. Having spent some time upon the ice, they were returning to Woodbourne through the plantation. Hazlewood, who had a gun with him, had offered his arm to Miss Mannering, who was tired after skating, as they walked towards home. When they had proceeded some little distance in this way, Brown happened to meet them. He was wearing the rough suit in which he had spent the night in the gipsy's house, having been unable to procure a change on account of his portmanteau having been stolen.

Julia Mannering, who had had no intimation that her old lover was in the district, uttered a scream when she suddenly saw him standing before her; and Hazlewood, fancying from the rough appearance of the stranger that he was either a gipsy or a tramp, pointed his gun towards him, and ordered him to keep off.

Brown, in a fit of jealousy, and fearing that the gun might go off, rushed upon Hazlewood and seized the fowling-piece. But in the struggle which ensued between them it was discharged by accident, and young Hazlewood fell to the ground, wounded in the shoulder.

Brown, when he saw what had occurred, became frightened at the thought of the dangers of his position. He bounded over a hedge which divided the footpath from the plantation, and was not heard of again for a considerable time.

On the news of Hazlewood's being wounded getting abroad, the neighbourhood was thrown into a ferment of indignation. All the circumstances of the occurrence were exaggerated. It was universally believed that the attacking party was a smuggler or a gipsy, and that he had attempted in broad daylight to murder the young man. It was stated that the assailant had been seen earlier in the day wearing a smuggler's cutlass; and the purse which had been left at the inn was opened and found to contain property which had been previously stolen. Charles Hazlewood himself, however, continued to protest that the wounding was accidental; while the only person who could give any real account of the mysterious stranger, namely Julia

Mannering, for reasons best known to herself, never pretended that she had any idea who he was.

Amongst those who were most active in their endeavours to capture the missing Brown was Glossin, the new Laird of Ellangowan. It was plain, too, that he had some other motive for apprehending him than merely the desire to do his duty as a magistrate of the county, which he had now become.

On returning to his house one day, he was informed that Mac- Guffog, the thief-taker, had made a prisoner, and that he was waiting with him in the kitchen. When the prisoner was introduced to the magistrate's room, Glossin at once recognised that it was Dirck Hatteraick, the smuggler captain.

In the interview which took place between them, no one else being present, it transpired that Glossin had been a kind of partner with the smuggler at the time of Kennedy's murder and the disappearance of young Harry Bertram. Dirck Hatteraick told him, too, very plainly, that if he was to be condemned he would let the secret out and ruin Glossin. Glossin, who was much terrified at the thought of being discovered, then arranged, like a villain that he was, to imprison Hatteraick for that night in a room in the old castle of Ellangowan, and at the same time give him a small file with which he might rid himself of his handcuffs and escape. During the interview between them, Hatteraick also told the attorney that young Bertram was still alive, and at Kippletringan. Glossin's situation was therefore perilous in the extreme, for the schemes of a life of villainy seemed at once to be crumbling around and about him.

Hatteraick was accordingly then sent to his place of confinement in the old castle.

At midnight Glossin looked out from his bedroom towards the castle, and after watching for some time in an agony of guilty suspense, he saw the dark form of a man, whom he knew to be Hatteraick, drop from the prison window and make his way to the beach, where he succeeded in shoving out a boat which was lying there. In a few minutes after, he had hoisted the sail, and soon disappeared round the Point of Warroch.

Great was the alarm and confusion the next morning when it was discovered that the smuggler had escaped from prison. Constables were sent out in every direction to search for him, and Glossin took care to send them to places where they would be least likely to find him.

In the meantime he himself made his way to a cave by the seashore near the Point of Warroch, where he had arranged with Hatteraick to meet him the day after his escape.

Glossin had never been near this spot since the day on which the unfortunate Kennedy was murdered; and the terrible scene came back to his mind with all its accompaniments of horror as he stealthily approached the cavern. When he reached it and went in, he found Hatteraick in the dark and shivering with cold.

During the conversation that ensued between them he learned from the smuggler what had become of young Bertram after Kennedy's murder. He had been taken to Holland, Hatteraick said, and left with an old merchant named Vanbeest Brown, who took a fancy to the boy and called him by his own name. He had afterwards been sent to India; but the smuggler knew nothing of him from the time he went there. Bertram had, however, been seen, he said, a few days before, among the hills by a gipsy named Gabriel.

Glossin then discovered for the first time that it was young Bertram, in reality, who had wounded Hazlewood. In his terror at the thought of losing his property at Ellangowan if it came to be known that Harry Bertram was alive, yet at all times fertile in every kind of villainous device, Glossin now hit upon a new plan to get rid of the man who stood between him and his peace of mind. By making large promises to Hatteraick he induced the smuggler to agree to come by night, with a large body of his men, to the prison where Bertram would be confined for his attack on Hazlewood, and to break open the doors and carry him off. He said he would have the soldiers withdrawn on some pretence or other, so as to make the rescue more certain; and having completed the details of this desperate and lawless piece of villainy, he went back to Ellangowan.

But it is time to return to Brown, who was now a fugitive from justice in consequence of the unlucky accident of which his rashness had been the cause. He determined to make his way to England, and to wait there until he received letters from friends in his regiment establishing his identity, in possession of which he could again show himself at Kippletringan, and offer to young Hazlewood any explanation or satisfaction he might require. He accordingly took ship for Cumberland. He chanced on board to meet a man whose daughter was at the time in Colonel Mannering's service at Woodbourne and by his means contrived to get a letter delivered to Miss Mannering, in which he begged of her to forgive him for his rash conduct towards Hazlewood. Having landed on the English coast, he wrote to the colonel of his regiment for such testimony of his rank in the army as should place his character as a gentleman and an officer beyond question; and, as he was now reduced to great straits for want of funds, he wrote to his sturdy farmer friend, Dandie Dinmont, for the loan of a little money.

After a delay of some days, he received a short letter from Miss Mannering, in which she upbraided him for his thoughtless conduct, and bade him good-bye, telling him on no account to come back to Woodbourne.

On reading it over, he came somehow to the conclusion that Miss Mannering meant the opposite of all she had written, and in this belief he set sail at once for Kippletringan.

After a rough and dangerous voyage by night, he found himself in the morning off the Scottish coast. The weather had now cleared. A woody cape, that stretched into the sea, lay some little distance from the vessel; and, in answer to Brown's inquiries, the boatman told him that it was Warroch Point. Close beside it was the old castle of Ellangowan; and Brown felt a strange longing, as he looked at it, to be put ashore for the purpose of examining it more closely. The boatman readily acceded to his wishes, and landed him on the beach beneath the ruins.

And thus, in complete ignorance of his own real identity, surrounded by dangers, and without the assistance of a friend within the circle of several hundred miles, accused of a heavy crime, and almost penniless, did the weary wanderer, for the first time after an interval of many eventful years, approach the remains of the castle where his ancestors had once dwelt in lordly splendour.

It will have dawned upon the reader before now that the young soldier known to him as Brown was in reality no other than the Harry Bertram who had disappeared on the day when Kennedy was murdered. The name of Brown will consequently be dropped during the remainder of the story, and our hero will be called by his proper appellation—Bertram.

After wandering for some time through the ruined apartments of the castle, he stepped outside, and happened by chance to stand on the very spot where his father—the old Laird of Ellangowan—had died.

Glossin at that moment chanced to be engaged close by with a surveyor, in reference to some building plans connected with an intended addition to his house; and he was just saying to his companion that the whole ruin should be pulled down, when Bertram met him, and said:

"Would you destroy this fine old castle, sir?"

His face, person, and voice were so exactly like those of his father when alive, that Glossin almost believed that the grave had given up its dead.

But after a time he recovered his self-possession, and then set himself to discover if Bertram, whom he recognised, had any knowledge of his own identity. He was much terrified when he heard him repeat some lines of an old song, which he said he had learnt in his childhood:

"The dark shall be light, And the wrong made right,
When Bertram's right and Bertram's might
Shall meet on …;"

but, although he could not recall the end of the last line, Glossin thought he knew already a good deal too much about it.

A few of Glossin's men were now seen approaching up the slope, whereupon he immediately assumed a different attitude and tone towards Bertram.

"I believe your name is Brown, sir?" said Glossin.

"And what of that, sir?" replied Bertram.

"Why in that case," said Glossin, "you are my prisoner in the king's name."

After a slight resistance the prisoner was secured, and shortly after was brought before Sir Robert Hazlewood, one of the county magistrates, and accused of maliciously wounding Charles Hazlewood, his son.

In reply to the questions put to him, the prisoner said that he was a captain in a regiment of horse in his Majesty's service, and in a frank, manly way described how the wounding of Charles Hazlewood was merely an accident, for which he expressed a sincere sorrow. When required to give some proof of his rank in the army, he stated that his luggage had been stolen. When asked to say where he had spent the night on which it was taken, his promise to Meg Merrilies came to his mind, and he replied that he must refuse to answer the question. He was then pressed to account for his having worn a smuggler's cutlass; but he also declined to explain that matter. And his answers were equally unsatisfactory when questioned on the subject of the purse which the gipsy had given him.

Having failed to give any explanation of so many suspicious circumstances, the warrant for his committal to gaol was made out, although he stated that Colonel Mannering, whom he had known in India, could, if sent for, give evidence of his character and rank.

The colonel was, however, away from home at the time, and the friendless and unfortunate Bertram was removed to prison, pending Mannering's return.

"And now," said Glossin to himself, "to find Dirck Hatteraick and his people — to get the guard sent off — and then for the grand cast of the dice." And so saying he hastened away to complete with the smuggler captain the villainous plan on which they had previously agreed.

The prison in which Bertram now found himself was a building which adjoined the custom-house, and both were close beside the sea. Mac-Guffog, who has been already mentioned, was at the time the keeper; and a gruff and surly custodian he was, too. Bertram, however, succeeded in procuring from him the luxury of a separate room by promising the keeper a large sum of money. He was accordingly ushered into a small ill-furnished apartment, through the barred windows of which he could get a glimpse of the sea which was dashing sullenly against the outer walls.

As he was reflecting on his miserable situation, his attention was attracted by a loud knocking at the gate of the gaol; and shortly after his little dog Wasp, which he had left in the care of Dandie Dinmont, and Dinmont himself were shown into his room.

Bertram was delighted to have his old friend with him, and in answer to his eager inquiries as to how he came to be in prison, told him about the accident to young Hazlewood, and that he had been mistaken for a smuggler.

Dinmont, on his part, then related how he had come to know of Bertram's being locked up. Gabriel, the huntsman on the moors, he said, had informed him in a mysterious way that Bertram was in gaol, and that he was badly in need of a good friend to stay with him night and day for a day or two. Dinmont added that he had ridden sixty miles that day to come to his assistance.

They were interrupted in their conversation by Mac-Guffog, who told them that it was time for the visitor to leave; but by means of further promises he was induced to allow Dinmont to spend the night in the same room with his friend; and in no longtime after the two occupants of the wretched apartment were fast asleep.

Colonel Mannering, who had been from home for some days, returned to Woodbourne the night of the day on which Bertram had been sent to prison. The morning after his arrival, the dominie, who even after so many years continued to blame himself for the loss of little Harry, made his way, in a spirit of curiosity, to Warroch Point, a place he had never approached since the child had disappeared. As he wandered home again, filled with gloomy recollections of the day of Kennedy's murder, his steps bore him to the neighbourhood of Derncleugh, with its ruined remains of the old gipsy village. The place had for many years had the reputation of being haunted; more especially the tower, or Kaim, of Derncleugh. As he was passing by it, the door suddenly opened, and Meg Merrilies stepped out and stood before him. The dominie, believing she was some sorceress, addressed her in Latin, but the gipsy queen angrily interrupted him.

"Listen, ye fool, to what I tell ye," she said, "or ye'll rue it while there's a limb o' ye hangs together. Tell Colonel Mannering that I know he's seeking me. He knows, and I know, that the blood will be wiped out, and the lost will be found —

And Bertram's right, and Bertram's might,
Shall meet on Ellangowan height.

Give him this letter, don't fail, and tell him the time's coming now. Bid him to look at the stars as he looked at them before, and to do what I desire him in the letter."

She then led the frightened dominie by a short cut through the woods for about a quarter of a mile, and on reaching the common told him to stand still.

"Look," she said, "how the setting sun breaks through the cloud that's been darkening the sky all day. See the stream o' light that falls on the old tower of Ellangowan; that's not for nothing. Here I stood," she went on, stretching out her long sinewy arm and clenched hand — "here I stood when I told the last Laird of Ellangowan what was coming on his house, and did that fall to the ground? And here I stand again to bid God prosper the just heir of Ellangowan that will soon be brought to his own. I'll no live to see it, maybe; but there will be many a blithe eye see it though mine be closed. And now, Abel Sampson, as ever ye loved the house of Ellangowan, away with my message to the English colonel as if life and death were upon your haste."

So saying, she turned suddenly from the amazed dominie, who hurried back to Woodbourne, exclaiming as he went, "Prodigious! prodigious! pro-di-gi-ous!"

The kindly interest of Meg Merrilies in the fate of Bertram did not, however, end here.

Shortly after quitting the dominie she met young Hazlewood on the road, and told him, in a mysterious way, that the guard of soldiers had been drawn off from the custom-house, and brought to his father's house, in the expectation of an attack being made upon it that night.

"Nobody means to touch his house," she added; "so send the horsemen back to their post quietly. They will have work to-night; the guns will flash and the swords will glitter in the moonlight."

She then asked him if he bore any malice to the man that wounded him, and on Hazlewood assuring her that he had always thought it was an accident, she said: "Then do what I bid ye, for if he was left to his ill wishers he would be a bloody corpse ere morn." And she then disappeared into the wood.

Charles Hazlewood, who now felt certain some diabolical plot was on foot for the murder of the man who had accidentally wounded him, rode back at once to his father's house.

He found the place occupied with dragoons, and instantly endeavoured to persuade his father to send them back to the custom-house.

Glossin had, however, impressed the old man with a fixed idea of the impending danger to his house, and he refused to allow the soldiers to go. While his son was still arguing with him, the sheriff of the country came in hurriedly, and told him that he had had information that the removal of the troops from the custom-house was only part of a plan, and that they should at once return. Orders were accordingly given without delay, and the dragoons were shortly after on their way again to the place from which they came.

But we must return to Bertram and his companion in their unpleasant abode, in the prison.

Towards midnight Bertram woke after his first sleep. The air of the small apartment had become close and confined, and he got up for the purpose, if possible, of opening the window. His failure to open it reminded him painfully that he was now a prisoner. He was no longer inclined to sleep, so he continued for some time to gaze out on the troubled sea, as it rolled under the indistinct light of a hazy and often overclouded moon. As he looked he fancied he saw in the distance a boat being rowed towards the shore; and before long he found that he had not been mistaken. The boat, which was a large one, drew nearer and nearer, and as it reached the land some twenty men jumped on shore, and disappeared up a dark passage which divided the prison from the custom-house. Almost immediately after, Bertram could hear a tumult in the outer yard of the bridewell, and, being unable to guess what its meaning was, he awoke Dinmont.

The smell of fire now commenced to reach the room, and, on Dinmont looking out of the window, he exclaimed: "Lord's sake, captain! come here; they have broken in the custom-house!"

Looking from the prison window they could see the gang of smugglers hurrying here and there, some with lighted torches, others carrying barrels towards the shore. It was plain, too, from the thick clouds of smoke that rolled past the window that the prison was itself on fire.

Dinmont roared loudly for Mac-Guffog to let them out, but all was silent in the gaol. Outside, the shouts of the smugglers and the mob resounded far and wide, and it seemed as if the keeper had himself escaped, and left his prisoners to perish in the flames.

But now a new and fierce attack was heard at the outer gate. It was soon forced in with sledgehammers and crows, and, before long, some three or four of the principal smugglers hurried to the apartment of Bertram with lighted torches, and armed with cutlasses and pistols. Two of them seized on Bertram, but one of them whispered in his ear, "Make no resistance till you are outside." They dragged him roughly to the gate, but amid the riot and confusion which prevailed, the sound as of a body of horse advancing was heard. A few moments after, the dragoons were engaged with the rioters. Shots were fired, and the glittering broadswords of the soldiers began to flash in the air. "Now," whispered the man at Bertram's left, "shake off that fellow and follow me."

Bertram, with a violent and sudden effort, burst away from the man on his right, and closely following his mysterious friend, attended by the faithful Dinmont, who never left him, ran quickly down a narrow lane which led from the main street.

No pursuit took place, as the smugglers had enough to do to defend themselves against the dragoons. At the end of the lane there was a post-chaise and horses waiting.

"Are you here in God's name?" said the guide to the driver.

"Ay, troth I am," said he.

"Open the carriage, then. You, gentlemen, get into it; in a short time you'll be in a place of safety, and remember your promise to the gipsy wife."

Bertram and Dinmont got in at once, followed by little Wasp, and in a moment found themselves travelling at a breakneck pace, neither of them knowing where on earth they were going to.

They were, in fact, on the way to Woodbourne, for the carriage had been sent by Colonel Mannering, after he had read the letter which the dominie brought him from Meg Merrilies. The note had given him no intimation, however, of the persons who were to be conveyed in the chaise to Woodbourne, merely telling him that it should bring the folk that should ask if it were there in God's name.

As the colonel's clock was striking one that night the sound of carriage wheels was heard in the distance, and in no long space after, Bertram and Dinmont found themselves at Woodbourne. Bewilderment and astonishment were depicted on the faces of all as Bertram stepped into the parlour. The colonel saw before him the man whom he supposed he had killed in India; Julia beheld her lover; and Lucy Bertram at once recognised the person who had fired upon young Hazlewood. Each one remained silent, not knowing what to say, when the absent-minded dominie, looking up from a book he had been studying in a corner, exclaimed:

"If the grave can give up the dead, that is my dear and honoured master!"

A lawyer friend of the colonel's, a Mr. Pleydall, was staying at Woodbourne that night, and he at once set about endeavouring to solve the mystery. He questioned Bertram as to his recollections of childhood, and elicited from him some of the incidents of his early life, with which the reader is already acquainted. Amongst the persons whom Bertram recalled, "there was," he said, "a tall, thin, kind-tempered man, who used to teach me my letters and walk with me."

On hearing this, the poor dominie could contain his feelings no longer, and rising hastily from his chair, with clasped hands, trembling limbs and streaming eyes, he called out aloud:

"Harry Bertram, look at me! Was I not the man?"

"Yes," said Bertram, starting from his seat as if a sudden light had burst in upon his mind. "Yes, that was my very name, and that is the voice and the figure of my kind old master!"

The following day Colonel Mannering and Mr. Pleydall succeeded in getting Sir Robert Hazlewood to accept bail for Bertram. While they were so engaged, Bertram, with his newly-found sister and Miss Mannering, went walking to the castle of Ellangowan.

Close by the ruin they were suddenly confronted by Meg Merrilies, who addressed Bertram, saying:

"Remember your promise, and follow me."

It was in vain that his sister and her companion urged him not to go with the gipsy. He told them he must obey. Then, bidding them good-bye, he started to follow Meg Merrilies, accompanied by Dinmont, who had come up a few minutes before.

With quick, long strides the gipsy proceeded straight across the wintry heath. She turned neither to the left nor the right, and moved more like a ghost than a human being. On reaching the wood, she plunged into it, moving still rapidly in the direction of Derncleugh. After travelling thus for some time, she came at length to the ruined tower where Bertram had previously spent the night in concealment from the smugglers. Producing a key from her pocket, the gipsy opened the door and led the way in. She offered Bertram and Dinmont food and drink, and fearing to offend her, they took a little.

"And now," she said, "ye must have arms; but use them not rashly; take captive, but save life; let the law have its own—he must speak ere he die."

She then supplied the two with loaded pistols, and started afresh through the wood in the direction of Warroch Point. She led them by a long and winding passage almost overgrown with brushwood, until they suddenly found themselves by the seashore. They were soon outside the secret cave.

"Follow me as I creep in," she said. "I have placed the firewood so as to screen you. Bide behind it for a space, till I say— *The hour and the man are both come*. Then run in on him, take his arms and bind him tight."

And having said so, she crept in upon her hands and knees, followed by Bertram and his friend.

As they were creeping in, Dinmont, who was last of the party, felt his leg caught by someone from behind. He with difficulty suppressed a shout, and was much relieved when he heard a voice behind him say: "Be still, I am a friend—Charles Hazlewood."

He had been sent after the others by Lucy Bertram and Miss Mannering, and had only overtaken them as they were making their way into the cavern.

Meg Merrilies, on reaching the interior, was greeted by Dirck Hatteraick with a curse in his old fashion—the smuggler had been expecting her, and was waiting with anxiety for news of his band. The only light within the cave was from a charcoal fire, the dark-red glow from which gave a dismal and unearthly appearance to the smuggler's hiding place.

Bertram and his friends had advanced far enough to enable them to stand upright, and concealed from the view of Hatteraick, they listened to his conversation with the gipsy.

"Have you seen Glossin?" he said to her.

"No," replied Meg Merrilies; "you've missed your blow, ye blood-spiller! and ye have nothing to expect from the tempter."

"What am I to do, then?" said the smuggler, with a Dutch oath.

"Do?" answered the gipsy. "Die like a man, or be hanged like a dog. Didn't I tell ye, when ye took away the boy Harry Bertram, in spite of my prayers, that he would come back again in his twenty-first year? You'll never need to leave this."

"What makes you say that?" asked Hatteraick.

And Meg, who now threw some flax upon the fire, which rose in a bright flame, answered: "*Because the hour and the man are both come.*"

At the appointed signal, Bertram and his companions rushed upon Hatteraick. The ruffian, who instantly saw he was betrayed, turned his first vengeance on Meg Merrilies, at whom he discharged a pistol.

She fell, with a piercing shriek, muttering, "I knew it would be this way."

A terrific struggle ensued between the smuggler and his assailants, in which Hatteraick contrived to discharge a second bullet at Bertram, which only missed its mark by a lucky accident. Strong, however, as the ruffian was, he was not equal to the joint efforts of the three men, and at length he was fairly mastered, disarmed, and tightly bound.

Hazlewood, whose horse was outside the cave, then rode off for assistance, and after some time returned with several others. The prisoner was carried out, still firmly bound, and also Meg Merrilies, who was still living, though desperately wounded in the chest.

They wished to take her to the nearest cottage, but she refused to be moved anywhere but to the Kaim of Derncleugh. Accordingly they bore her to the vault in the ruined tower.

The alarm had now spread through the countryside that Kennedy's murderer had been taken on the very spot where the murder had been committed years before; and a crowd of people, with a clergyman and a surgeon, had flocked to the place where the dying gipsy lay. She, however, refused all offers of assistance, and called for Harry Bertram.

When Bertram approached the wretched bed on which she lay, she took his hand.

"Look at him," she said to those about her, "the image of his dead father. And hear me now — let that man," pointing to Hatteraick, "deny what I say if he can." And then she told the story of how the young boy had been carried off from Warroch Wood; how she saved his life from smugglers who would have murdered him; and how she swore an oath to keep the secret till he was one-and-twenty, and vowed that if she lived to see the day of his return she would set him again in his father's seat, though every step was on a dead man. "Dirck Hatteraick," she said, "you and I will never meet again until we are before the Judgment-seat — will ye dare deny it?"

And as Hatteraick refused to open his lips, she added: "Farewell! and God forgive you! your hand has sealed my evidence."

And shortly after, as she heard the crowd about her greet Bertram with enthusiastic cheers as the true Laird of Ellangowan, her troubled spirit passed peacefully away.

The following day, Hatteraick was brought before the magistrates at Kippletringan. The dying declaration of Meg Merrilies was proved by the surgeon and the clergyman who had heard it. Bertram again told his recollections of early childhood. Gabriel, the gipsy, the same man who had avoided meeting Bertram's eye when out hunting with Dandie Dinmont, told the whole story of Kennedy's murder, as he was at Warroch Point on the day of its occurrence. He stated that Glossin was present and accepted a bribe to keep the matter a secret. This witness also stated that it was he that had told his aunt, Meg Merrilies, that Bertram had returned to the country; and that it was by her orders that three or four of the gipsies had mingled in the crowd when the custom-house was attacked, for the purpose of helping Bertram to escape. He also added that Meg Merrilies had often said that Harry Bertram carried the proof of his birth hung round his neck.

Bertram here produced the velvet bag which had been worked by his mother, and which he said he had always continued to wear. On its being opened, Colonel Mannering instantly recognised his own writing on the paper it enclosed, proving to everyone's satisfaction that the wearer was the real heir of Ellangowan.

The investigation was concluded by both Hatteraick and Glossin being sent to gaol.

The smuggler, whose violence and strength were well known, was secured in what was called the condemned ward. In this apartment, which was near the top of the prison, his feet were chained to an iron bar firmly fixed at the height of about six inches from the floor. The chain enabled him to move a distance of about four feet from the bar, and when thus secured his handcuffs were removed.

Glossin was confined in another room, his mind still teeming with schemes of future deceit to cover his former villainies. As he reflected on his position, he came to a determination to see Hatteraick, if possible, and to induce him by a tempting bribe to give evidence in his favour when his trial came on.

Accordingly, when Mac-Guffog, the keeper, appeared at night time, he gave him some gold pieces, and so obtained his consent to an interview with his fellow prisoner.

The keeper, however, told him that as the prison rules were now much stricter than before, his seeing Hatteraick would be only on condition that he should spend the whole night with him.

As the prison clock tolled ten, Glossin slipped off his shoes, and silently followed Mac-Guffog to the smuggler's room. As he entered, the door was locked on the outside; and he found himself alone with the former partner of his guilt. The cell was so dark that it was some time before he could detect the form of the smuggler, who was lying on a pallet-bed beside the bar.

"Dirck Hatteraick," he whispered. And the smuggler, recognising his voice, told him with a curse to begone.

"Speak to me no more. I'm dangerous."

"Then," said Glossin, losing his temper, "at least get up, for an obstinate Dutch brute!" But he had barely uttered the words when Hatteraick sprang from where he lay and grappled with him. So sudden and irresistible was the attack, that Glossin fell, the back part of his neck coming full upon the iron bar with stunning violence. Nor did the ruffian release the deadly grip upon his throat until the last remnant of life had left his victim's miserable corpse.

On the day following the death of Glossin, Dirck Hatteraick was himself found dead in the cell, having hanged himself by means of a cord taken from his bed, which he had cunningly contrived to attach to the prison wall.

Little more remains to be told. Bertram was before long restored to the possession of his father's house and property, and Julia Mannering became his wife.

His sister Lucy found a husband in her old lover Charles Hazlewood, and the dominie was raised once again to a condition of ecstatic happiness, seeing "his little Harry" — as he still continued to call him — now Laird of Ellangowan, and himself librarian in the house to which he had been so long a stranger.

THE STARTLING ADVENTURES OF BARON MUNCHAUSEN

_Although the short book from which these stories are taken was written in 1785 by Rudolf Erich Raspe, a German of many talents who took up his residence in England, there really was a Baron Munchausen who served the author as a model. His whole name was Hieronymus Karl Friedrich von Munchausen, a German, of course, but serving in the Russian army. After several campaigns against the Turks, he retired from the army and amused himself by telling awful whoppers about his bravery as a soldier and huntsman.

A German editor who visited the baron two years before he died was told by the baron's neighbors that he really did tell wonderful stories in his younger days._

AN ADVENTURE WITH A LION
AND A CROCODILE

By R. E. Raspe

Some years before my beard announced approaching manhood, or, in other words, when I was neither man nor boy, but between both, I expressed in repeated conversations a strong desire of seeing the world, from which I was discouraged by my parents, though my father had been no inconsiderable traveller himself. A cousin by my mother's side took a liking to me, often said I was a fine forward youth, and was much inclined to gratify my curiosity. His eloquence had more effect than mine, for my father consented to my accompanying him in a voyage to the island of Ceylon, where his uncle had resided as governor many years.

We sailed from Amsterdam with despatches from their High Mightinesses the States of Holland, and in about six weeks we arrived at Ceylon, where we were received with great marks of friendship and true politeness.

After we had resided at Ceylon about a fortnight I accompanied one of the governor's brothers upon a shooting party.

Near the banks of a large piece of water, which had engaged my attention, I thought I heard a rustling noise behind; on turning about I was almost petrified (as who would not be?) at the sight of a lion, which was evidently approaching with the intention of satisfying his appetite with my poor carcass, and that without asking my consent.

What was to be done in this horrible dilemma? I had not even a moment for reflection; my piece was only charged with swan-shot, and I had no other about me. However, though I could have no idea of killing such an animal with that weak kind of ammunition, yet I had some hopes of frightening him by the report, and perhaps of wounding him also. I immediately let fly, without waiting till he was within reach; and the report did but enrage him, for he now quickened his pace and seemed to approach me full speed. I attempted to escape, but that only added (if an addition could be made) to my distress; for the moment I turned about I found a large crocodile, with his mouth extended almost ready to receive me. On my right hand was the piece of water before mentioned, and on my left a deep precipice, said to have, as I have since learned, a receptacle at the bottom for venomous creatures; in short, I gave myself up as lost, for the lion was now upon his hind legs, just in the act of seizing me. I fell involuntarily to the ground with fear, and, as it afterward appeared, he sprang over me. I lay some time in a situation which no language can describe, expecting to feel his teeth or talons in some part of me every moment. After waiting in this prostrate situation a few seconds, I heard a violent but unusual noise, differing from any sound that had ever before assailed my ears; nor is it at all to be wondered at, when I inform you from whence it proceeded. After listening for some time, I ventured to raise my head and look round, when, to my unspeakable joy, I perceived the lion had, by the eagerness with which he sprang at me, jumped forward, as I fell, into the crocodile's mouth! which, as before observed, was wide open; the head of the one stuck in the throat of the other, and they were struggling to extricate themselves. I fortunately recollected my hunting knife which was by my side; with this instrument I severed the lion's head at one blow, and the body fell at my feet! I then, with the butt-end of my fowling-piece, rammed the head farther into the throat of the crocodile, and destroyed him, by suffocation, for he could neither gorge nor eject it.

Soon after I had thus gained a complete victory over my two powerful adversaries, my companion arrived in search of me; for finding I did not follow him into the wood, he returned, apprehending I had lost my way or met with some accident.

After mutual congratulations we measured the crocodile, which was just forty feet in length.

CROSSING THE THAMES WITHOUT THE AID OF BRIDGE, BOAT OR BALLOON

By R. E. Raspe

My first visit to England was about the beginning of George the Third's reign. I had occasion to go down to Wapping to see some goods shipped, which I was sending to some friends at Hamburgh: after that business was over, I took the Tower Wharf in my way back. Here I found the sun very powerful, and I was so much fatigued that I stepped into one of the cannon to compose me, where I fell fast asleep.

This was about noon; it was the fourth of June, the king's birthday. Exactly at one o'clock these cannon were all discharged in memory of the day they had been all charged that morning, and having no suspicion of my situation, I was shot over the houses on the opposite side of the river, into a farmer's yard, between Bermondsey and Deptford, where I fell upon a large haystack without waking, and continued there in a sound sleep till hay became so extravagantly dear (which was about three months after), that the farmer found it to his interest to send his whole stock to market. The stack I was reposing on was the largest in the yard, containing about five hundred load; they began to cut that first. I waked (with the voices of the people who had ascended the ladders to begin at the top) and got up, totally ignorant of my situation. In attempting to run away, I fell upon the farmer to whom the hay belonged, and broke his neck, yet received no injury myself! I afterwards found, to my great consolation, that this fellow was a most detestable character, always keeping the produce of his grounds for extravagant markets.

TWO STRANGE ADVENTURES IN RUSSIA

By R. E. Raspe

I set off from Rome on a journey to Russia, in the midst of winter, from a just notion that frost and snow must, of course, mend the roads, which every traveller had described as uncommonly bad through the northern parts of Germany, Poland, Courland, and Livonia. I went on horseback as the most convenient manner of travelling; I was but lightly clothed, and of this I felt the inconvenience the more I advanced northeast. What must not a poor old man have suffered in that severe weather and climate, whom I saw on a bleak common in Poland, lying on the road, helpless, shivering and hardly having wherewithal to cover his nakedness? I pitied the poor soul; though I felt the severity of the air myself, I threw my mantle over him, and immediately I heard a voice from the heavens, blessing me for that piece of charity, saying: "You will be rewarded, my son, in time."

I went on: night and darkness overtook me. No village was to be seen. The country was covered with snow and I was unacquainted with the road.

Tired, I alighted and fastened my horse to something, like a pointed stump of a tree, which appeared above the snow. For the sake of safety, I placed my pistols under my arm and lay down on the snow, where I slept so soundly that I did not open my eyes till full daylight. It is not easy to conceive my astonishment to find myself in the midst of a village, lying in a church-yard, nor was my horse to be seen, but I heard him soon after neigh somewhere above me. On looking upwards, I beheld him hanging by his bridle to the weathercock of the steeple. Matters were now very plain to me: the village had been covered with snow overnight; a sudden change of weather had taken place; I had sunk down to the church-yard whilst asleep, gently, and in the same proportion as the snow had melted away; and what in the dark I had taken to be a stump of a little tree appearing above the snow, to which I had tied my horse, proved to have been the cross or weathercock of the steeple!

Without long consideration I took one of my pistols, shot the bridle in two, brought down the horse, and proceeded on my journey. He carried me well. Advancing into the interior parts of Russia, I found travelling on horseback rather unfashionable in winter, so I submitted, as I always do, to the custom of the country, took a single horse sledge, and drove towards St. Petersburg.

I do not exactly recollect whether it was Eastland or Jugemanland, but I remember that in the midst of a dreary forest I spied a terrible wolf making after me with all the speed of ravenous winter hunger. He soon overtook me; there was no possibility of escape. Mechanically I laid myself down flat in the sledge, and let my horse run for our safety. What I wished, but hardly hoped or expected, happened immediately after. The wolf did not mind me in the least, but took a leap over me, and falling furiously on the horse, began instantly to tear and devour the hind part of the poor animal, which ran the faster for his pain and terror. Thus unnoticed and safe myself, I lifted my head slyly up, and with horror I beheld that the wolf had ate his way into the horse's body. It was not long before he had fairly forced himself into it, when I took my advantage and fell upon him with the butt-end of my whip. This unexpected attack in his rear frightened him so much that he leapt forward with all his might, the horse's carcass dropped on the ground, but in his place the wolf was in the harness, and I on my part whipping him continually, we both arrived in full career safe at St. Petersburg, contrary to our respective expectations, and very much to the astonishment of the spectators.

SHOOTING A STAG WITH CHERRY-STONES

By R. E. Raspe

You have heard, I dare say, of the hunter and sportsman's saint and protector, St. Hubert, and of the noble stag which appeared to him in the forest with the holy cross between his antlers. I have paid my homage to that saint every year in good fellowship, and seen this stag a thousand times, either painted in churches or embroidered in the stars of his knights; so that, upon the honor and conscience of a good sportsman, I hardly know whether there may not have been formerly, or whether there are not such crossed stags even at this present day. But let me now relate that which happened to myself some little time ago.

I had been out shooting all day, and had quite expended my powder and shot, when I found myself unexpectedly in presence of a stately stag, looking at me as unconcernedly as if he had known of my empty pouches. I charged immediately with powder, and upon it a good handful of cherrystones, for I had sucked the fruit as far as the hurry would permit. Thus I let fly at him, and hit him just on the middle of the forehead, between his antlers; it stunned him— he staggered—yet he made off, and I lost sight of him, to my chagrin.

This happened to me in France. Afterwards I visited Russia, and remained there for about a year.

At length, there being no immediate prospect of war with Turkey, I returned to France on leave for a few months, and was staying in the same chateau as I had been when I had fired off this remarkable charge.

We hunted again in the fine forest I had then traversed, with a gay party of French nobles and sportsmen. I had separated myself somewhat from my companions, when, in the opening of a beautiful glade, I beheld a noble stag, with a fine full-grown cherry-tree above ten feet high between his antlers.

I immediately recollected my former adventure, looked upon him as my property, and brought him to the ground by one shot, which at once gave me the haunch and cherry sauce, for the tree was covered with the richest fruit, the like of which I had never tasted before.

THE BARON'S WONDERFUL DOG

By R. E. Raspe

I had married a lady of great beauty, who, having heard of my sporting exploits, desired, a short time after our marriage, to go out with me on a shooting expedition. I went on in front to start something, and I soon saw my dog stop before several hundred coveys of partridges. I waited for my wife, who was following me with my lieutenant and a servant. I waited a long time; nobody came.

At length, very uneasy, I went back, and, when I was half-way to the place where I had left my wife, I heard lamentable groans. They seemed quite near, and yet I could see no trace of a human being. I jumped off my horse; I put my ear to the ground, and not only heard the groans distinctly rising from beneath, but my wife's voice and those of my lieutenant and servant.

I remarked at the same time, not far from the spot, the shaft of a coal-pit, and I had no doubt that my wife and her unfortunate companions had been swallowed up in it. I rode full speed to the nearest village to fetch the miners, who after great efforts succeeded in drawing the unfortunate individuals buried in the pit—which measured ninety feet—to the surface.

They first drew up the man-servant; then his horse; next the lieutenant; next his horse; and at length my wife on her little palfrey. The most curious part of this affair was that, in spite of the awful depth to which they had fallen, no one was hurt, not even the horses, if we except a few slight contusions. But they had had a terrible fright, and were quite unable to pursue our intended sport.

In all this confusion I quite forgot my setter, as no doubt you also have.

The next day I was obliged to go away on duty, and did not return home for a fortnight. On my return I asked for Diana, my setter. No one knew anything about her. My servants thought she had followed me. She was certainly lost, and I never hoped to see her again! At length a bright idea occurred to me:

"She is perhaps still watching the partridges."

I hastened, full of hope and joy, to the spot, and actually there she was! — my noble Diana — on the very place where I had left her a fortnight before.

"Hi, Diana!" I cried. "Seize them!"

She instantly sprang the partridges; they rose, and I killed twenty-five at one shot. But the poor beast had scarcely strength enough to follow me, she was so thin and famished. I was obliged to carry her back to the house on my horse, where rest, feeding, and great care soon restored her to health.

I was thoroughly glad to get her back again.